Caroline Chanter

From Colour to Form

A Glimpse into Gerard Wagner's Approach to Rudolf Steiner's Indications for Painting

Caroline Chanter

FROM COLOUR TO FORM

A Glimpse into Gerard Wagner's Approach to Rudolf Steiner's Indications for Painting

SteinerBooks | Anthroposophic Press
834 Main Street, Box 358 Spencertown, New York 12165

steinerbooks.org

Published by SteinerBooks 2024

Typesetting and Cover Design: Sven Baumann, Rickenbach
Print: Jelgavas Tipogrāfija, Jelgava, Latvia
ISBN 978-1-62148-371-7

CONTENTS

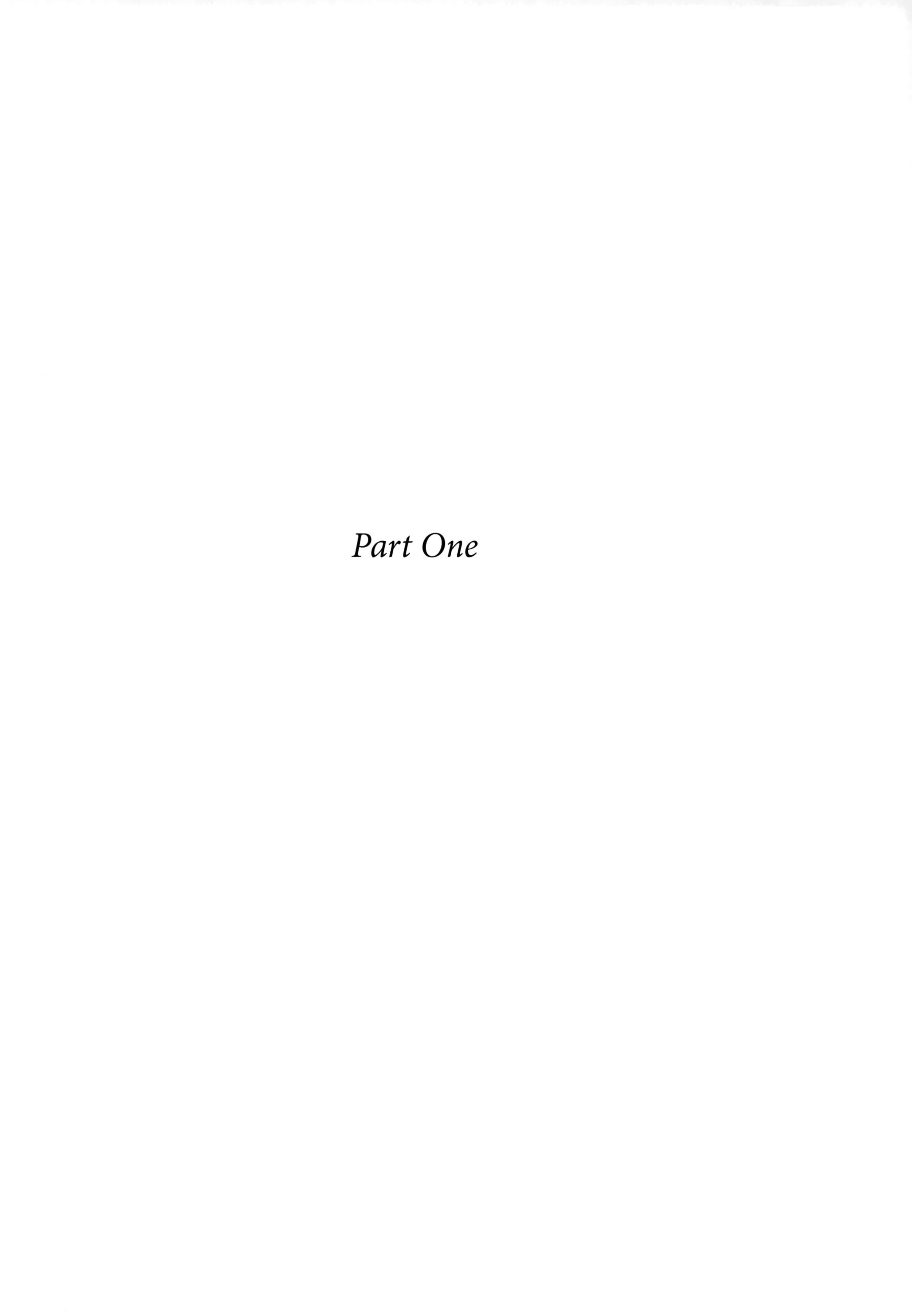

Part One

INTRODUCTON

More than 100 years ago – along with other new beginnings emerging from the art world – Rudolf Steiner[1] spoke about the need for painters to find the form, the motif of their paintings, 'out of the colour'. He spoke of this and of a new painting impulse in lectures he gave on the art of the first Goetheanum, in Dornach, Switzerland;[2] in München, Germany, at the time new art movements were developing there,[3] and in other contexts. This new attitude to painting was also given prominence through the painter Johannes Thomasius, one of the chief characters in Rudolf Steiner's Mystery Plays.[4]

What does painting out of the colour mean and how is it achieved? These were questions that gripped the talented young painter Gerard Wagner when he began his life in Dornach in 1926 and became part of a thriving anthroposophical community that shared high ideals in their artistic work. He became a seeker who went through considerable inner and outer struggles in his quest to find an answer. His work developed slowly – over years – in the seclusion of his studio, and it was not until the early 1940s that he began exhibiting his work regularly in the modest Carpenters workshop (the 'Schreinerei') at the Goetheanum.

Rudolf Steiner's indications were the starting point of Gerard Wagner's chosen path. He familiarized himself with all Rudolf Steiner's paintings and drawings with the understanding they would give direction for the unravelling of the mystery of how form arises out of colour. Wagner's methodical way of experimenting with the order in which he painted the colours when composing a painting became a hallmark of his approach. He discovered that this played a decisive role in how a motif comes about and therefore could give insight into how colour creates form.

In an excerpt from the monograph *Gerard Wagner–Die Kunst der Farbe* (The Art of Colour)[5] we learn of the influences that surrounded the young painter as he began his search, and how colour experimentation became for him a path of knowledge. He wrote:

> 'To have the artistic work of Rudolf Steiner constantly present, as well as the intensive experience of the spiritual life in Dornach, the eurythmy and the stagework, the influence of such personalities as Marie Steiner,[6] Albert Steffen[7] and many others, was the precondition for following this path. It is self evident that this had the strongest influence on my work. It would have been unthinkable without it. In this context the 'merely personal' became meaningless.

> Gradually the colour experiments which were carried out ever more consequently over years and decades took on clearer form. They led to metamorphosis which shows an attempt to arrive at knowledge of colour through a methodical way of working. Basically speaking all my pictures can be seen as belonging to this practise for they were painted above all to establish the relation between colour and form. Painting pictures that could possibly be exhibited or sold was not my intention. The process of painting – the mysterious activity of balancing the colours in a weightless equilibrium – is what interested me. The motifs arose only gradually through the ever more developing insights into the lawfulness of the colour build up: the order of colours through which the painting is created and in which the origin of the motif-formation lies.

Rudolf Steiner was not a trained artist yet the scope and versatility of the work he produced in many areas of art including painting, sculpture and architecture were an inspiration to those working with him, particularly during the building of the first Goetheanum in Dornach, Switzerland which began in 1913. As regards colour, Steiner was thoroughly familiar with Goethe's colour theory from which his own teaching can be seen to be a continuation. His insights into colour and painting have been an inspiration to artists for over a hundred years. Well known painters such as Piet Mondrian, Wassily Kandinsky, Hilma af Klint, and more lately the artist Josef Beuys, have been influenced by Rudolf Steiner's work.

The relatively unknown painter Gerard Wagner was not only inspired by Rudolf Steiner's work but developed a way of painting that grew directly out of Steiner's indications. This gives his work a significant place within the history of painting. The difference between Wagner's relation to the impulses given by Steiner and that of other artists was characterised by Michael Piotrovsky, the director of the Hermitage Museum, St Petersburg, Russia in the catalogue of Gerard Wagner's exhibition there in 1997:[8]

> 'Many artists have been inspired by Rudolf Steiner's ideas: Kandinsky, Mondrian, Klee…But by creating new worlds themselves and developing very different artistic languages, they wandered far from Steiner's ideas about the being of the arts. […] The painter Gerard Wagner has not only kept his life long enthusiasm but has remained true to Rudolf Steiner's ideas. His work is a consequential realisation of the principle of how form arises out of colour.'

What Gerard Wagner left for posterity by way of his paintings encompasses a wide diversity of motifs in which soul and spirit life in relation to the kingdoms of nature, the human being and higher worlds are revealed. The majority of the over 5000 paintings in his archive still wait to be appreciated by a larger public. They are painted in an artistic language that speaks of higher realms of existence and is not easily accessible to people today. Yet alongside this mysterious and more hidden aspect of his work, Gerard Wagner wished to show in a basic and understandable way the process involved in building up a painting. Indications in this direction can be found in the workbook *The Individuality of Colour*.[9]

In the 1970s two folders with images and text on the subject of metamorphosis: *A Glance into Nature's Workshop* and *Animal Metamorphosis* were published. Both are artistic-scientific studies that give a glimpse into his working method. In 1980 a monograph was published which gives an overview of his paintings from the 1950s and a study of the development of his work can be found in the biography *A Life with Colour, Gerard Wagner 1906–1999*.

The intention of this present volume *From Colour to Form* is to give further insight into Gerard Wagner's working method by showing some of the basic colour experiments and exercises he developed, initially as a learning tool for himself but which later formed the basis of what he taught pupils in his painting school and in the many courses he gave over the years. Another aim of the book is to inform others of the training sketches Rudolf Steiner gave to help artists connect more deeply with the being of colour. These sketches were the foundation for Gerard Wagner's research and knowledge of colour.[10]

BEGINNINGS – RUDOLF STEINER'S INDICATIONS

Gerard Wagner's studies in painting began in the spring of 1924 at the art colony of St Ives in Cornwall, England and continued from the autumn of 1925 at the Royal College of Art in London. At St Ives he was taught by the well-known landscape and portrait painter John Anthony Park.[11]

Once in Dornach Gerard Wagner took up a quite different artistic path. His interest was Rudolf Steiner's anthroposophy (spiritual science) and the various arts that were evolving out of it. He took lessons at the Goetheanum in eurythmy, speech and drama, and sculpture but most decisive for his future life were the months he spent at the Goetheanum Painting School in 1928–1929 as a pupil of Henni Geck.[12] She was the painter for whom Rudolf Steiner had sketched a number of motifs specifically for teaching purposes, at her request. These motifs from Rudolf Steiner's hand, – drawings and paintings known as the 'Training Sketches', awoke a tremendous interest in the young painter Gerard Wagner and they became the stimulus for his further artistic work. They comprise essentially two groups of pictures: the Nature Moods Sketches and the Motif-Sketches. Years later Wagner referred to these sketches, putting them into historical context, in the introduction to the folder *Animal Metamorphosis*,[13] as follows:

> 'How does form arise out of colour? In this way Rudolf Steiner, at the beginning of our century [20th century], formulated the question which is the decisive one for painters of today and of the next future. He showed the painter how to gain a deeper and objective feeling for colour and, through this, come to an experience of the world of formative forces. In his sketches and paintings he gave examples of how colour can lead to form. For this reason, these works can be regarded as the beginning of a new art of painting which is in accordance with the development of modern consciousness.'

Very little is known as to what Rudolf Steiner said to Henni Geck when he created these works in her presence, but one can be sure that the artistic language was meant to speak for itself and verbal instructions were few. Later she wrote briefly about the Training Sketches and how they were meant to be approached; she emphasised the fact that they were not to be looked upon as works of art but as picture seeds out of which something further could develop.

In addition to the Training Sketches, which can be understood as indications given in picture form, Rudolf Steiner gave lectures on art and painting that included various aspects of colour phenomena, the two-dimensional picture plane, colour perspective, weightless colour and other subjects. In May 1922, in Dornach, he gave what are known as the 'colour lectures' in which he introduced a new theory of colour.[14] Albert Steffen, who heard the lectures, wrote valuable reviews which appear in English for the first time in this publication. They have been found to be helpful for understanding the original lectures.[15]

The Training Sketches

THE NATURE MOOD SKETCHES 1922

The Nature Moods which consist of nine pastel drawings were the first sketches given to Henni Geck for her painting school. They comprise four pairs of motifs and a single motif:

Sunrise – Sunset
Shining Moon
Summer Trees – Fruiting and Blossoming Trees
Moonrise – Moonset
Sunrise – Sunset

The pairs stand in dynamic relation to each other most visibly in the sun and moon motifs of rising and setting. These images are not naturalistic although it is clear they are motifs of nature. Gerard Wagner's work with the sketches reveals that the motifs are interwoven and that transformative impulses live within and between them.

THE MOTIF SKETCHES 1922–1924

Nineteen Motif Sketches followed the nine Nature Moods. This series of images begins with various motifs of the human being. The first sketch *Group Souls–the Human Being* is a striking image showing the human being of primeval times, not yet individualised and still part of a group soul, united with the prototypes of eagle, lion and bull or cow. Further motifs of the human being include:

The Threefold Human Being
The Human Being in the Spirit
The Spirit in the Human Being
The Human Being in Relation to the Planets

Adam Kadmon in Early Lemuria

More elaborate compositions include a motif of the elemental beings active in nature; druid priests conducting a ceremony beside dolmen, (an image inspired by Rudolf Steiner's visit to Ilkley and Penmaenmawr in Britain); an imagination of midsummer showing the interwoven realms of nature between the forces of sun and moon, and other motifs. The four watercolours of *Mother and Child, Easter, The Archetypal Plant and The Archetypal Animal/Archetypal Human Being* conclude the series.[16]

The motif sketches in particular gave rise to some lengthy and intricate metamorphic sequences painted by Gerard Wagner.

THE FRIEDWART SKETCHES 1923–1924

Although these motifs were not given to Henni Geck for teaching purposes, the so-called 'Friedwart Sketches' are also working material for painters. They consist of a series of pastel sketches executed by Rudolf Steiner for teachers of a school situated in the Goetheanum grounds (later at Haus Friedwart). Steiner visited the classes regularly and at the request of the teachers gave instruction for painting exercises. He felt that the pupils, who were aged between 13 and 17, should be given concrete themes to paint. The first four motifs, also given as pairs, were:

Sunrise – Sunset
Trees in Sunny Air – Trees in Storm

These nature moods were concluded with the motif *Sunlit Tree by a Waterfall.*

The group of seven sketches, which Rudolf Steiner painted in the classroom before the teachers and pupils, culminated in two motifs of the human being: a *Head Study* and *Mother and Child.*

Gerard Wagner researched all three groups of 'Training Sketches': the Nature Moods, the Motif-Sketches and the Friedwart Sketches. He made countless painting experiments based on them with the intention of learning about colour and its relation to form.

EXPERIMENTING WITH COLOUR

Little of Gerard Wagner's early colour experiments have survived yet there are some characteristic examples from the 1950s onwards which give an indication of how he worked. One example is a series of small paintings, painted in rows of three, that shows images of trees in which the colour of the trunk and branches changes from one picture to the next. The trees stand on an undulating green ground; in the first picture the tree colour is yellow-brown, in the second picture red-brown and in the third picture violet. The sequences start at the top of the page: the yellow-brown in the first column, the red- brown in the second and the violet in the third. The colours are painted first on a white background, then on a blue background (the paper is toned blue), then on a yellow background, on an orange background, on a red background and finally on a violet background. (A background colour gives a mood but also a creative force which influences the way the colour painted onto it forms itself.) One can observe the subtle changes in the gestures of the trees caused by the different background colours. (See plate 1)

The green ground, the brown, and the violet are then painted on the same background colours as before but with green painted again as 'foliage', which also varies its shape in each painting. The variations are caused by the colour of the trunk and branches and by the background colour. (See plate 2)

The colours are painted in the following order:

1 Green
2 Brown or violet
3 Green

Subtle differences in the background colours stimulate awareness and help the painter to be more sensitive to the feeling of the colour. With this in mind, the experiment continues with the background colours changing in more gradual steps as follows:

1 cool yellow, yellow, warm yellow,
2 orange, warm-red, red,
3 cool red, red-violet, violet,
4 blue-violet, indigo, blue,
5 blue-green, green, yellow-green.

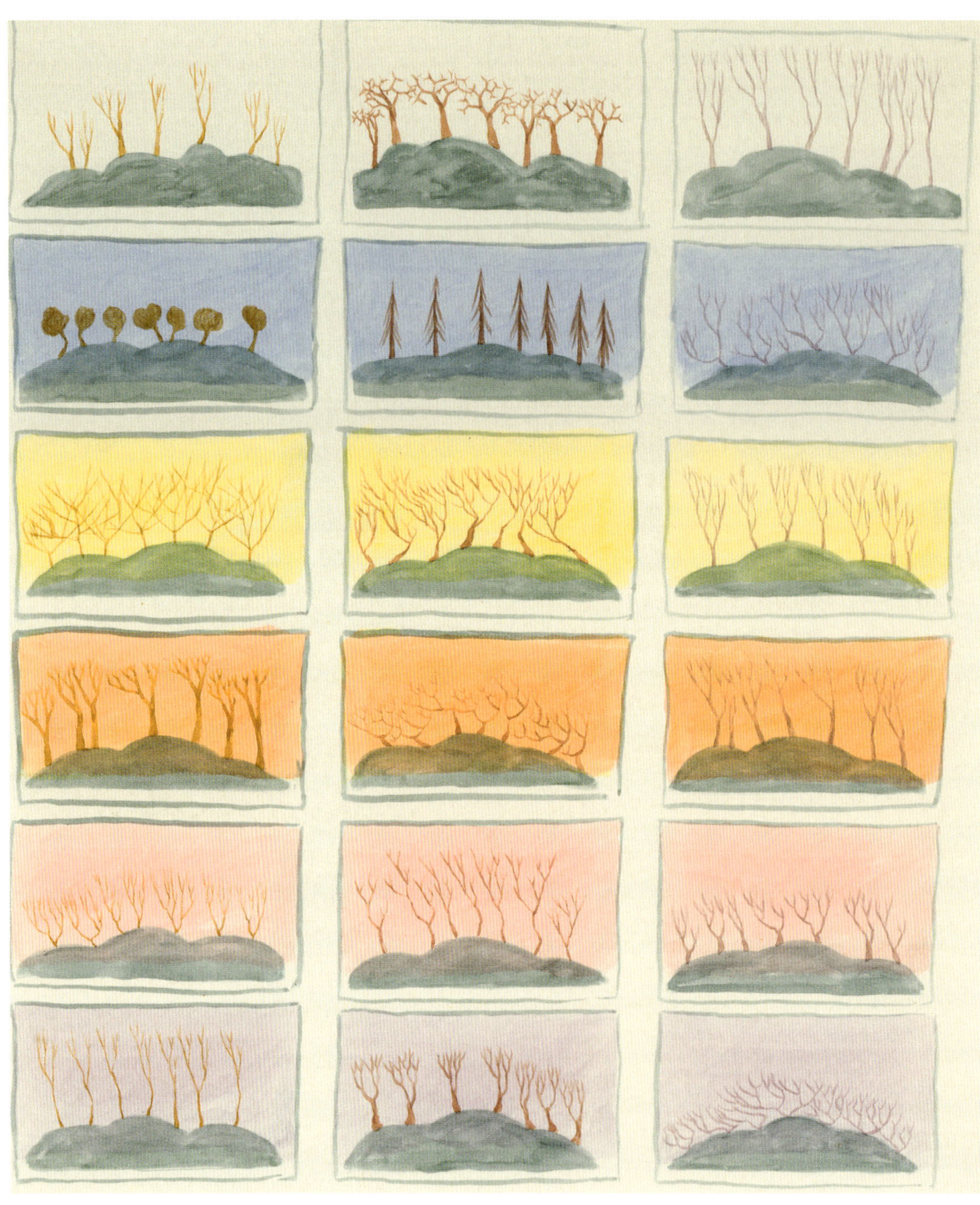

1 2 3

Plate 1: Yellow-brown, red-brown, and violet on: white, blue, yellow, warm red, cool red and violet backgrounds.

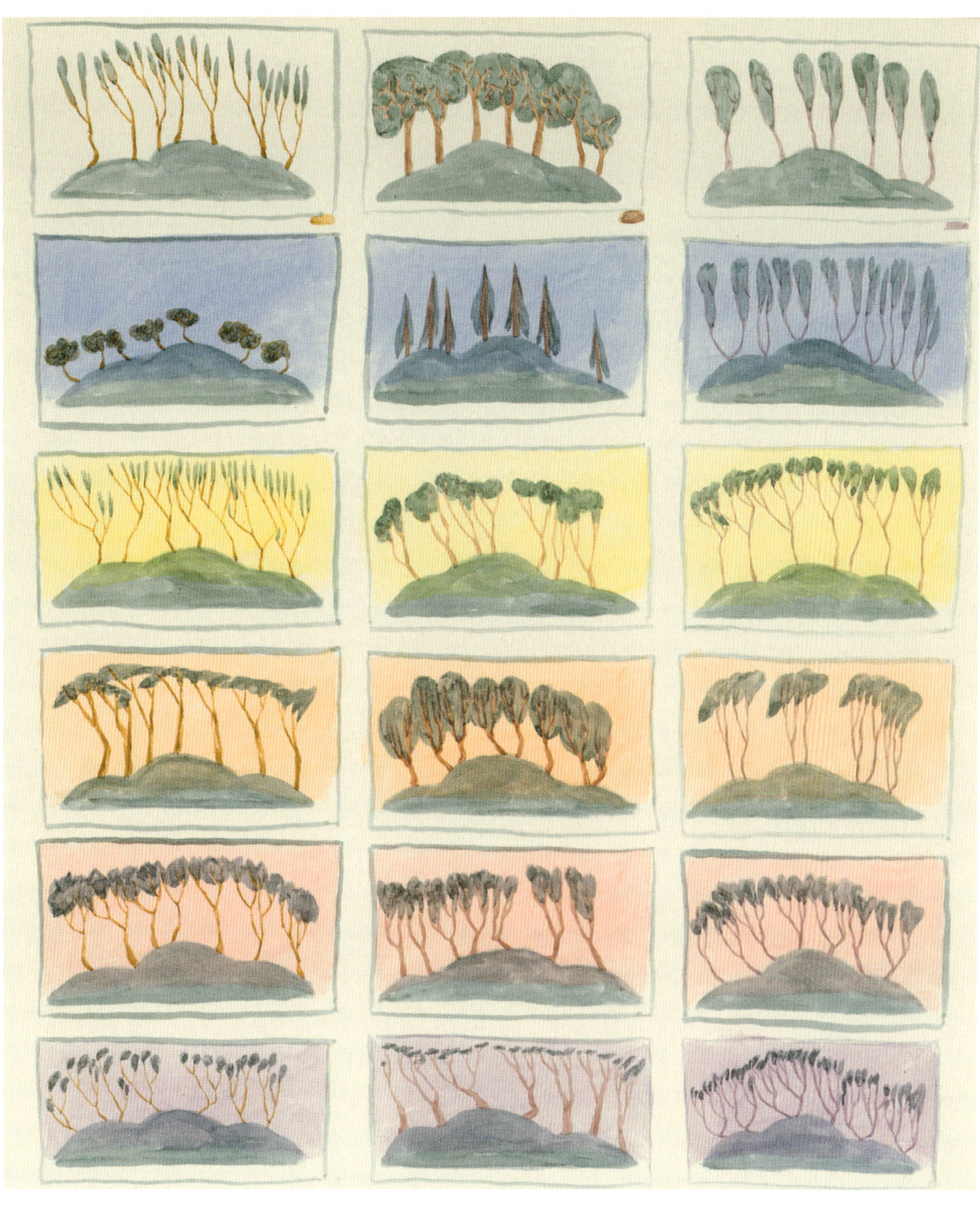

Plate 2: Green is added as third colour.

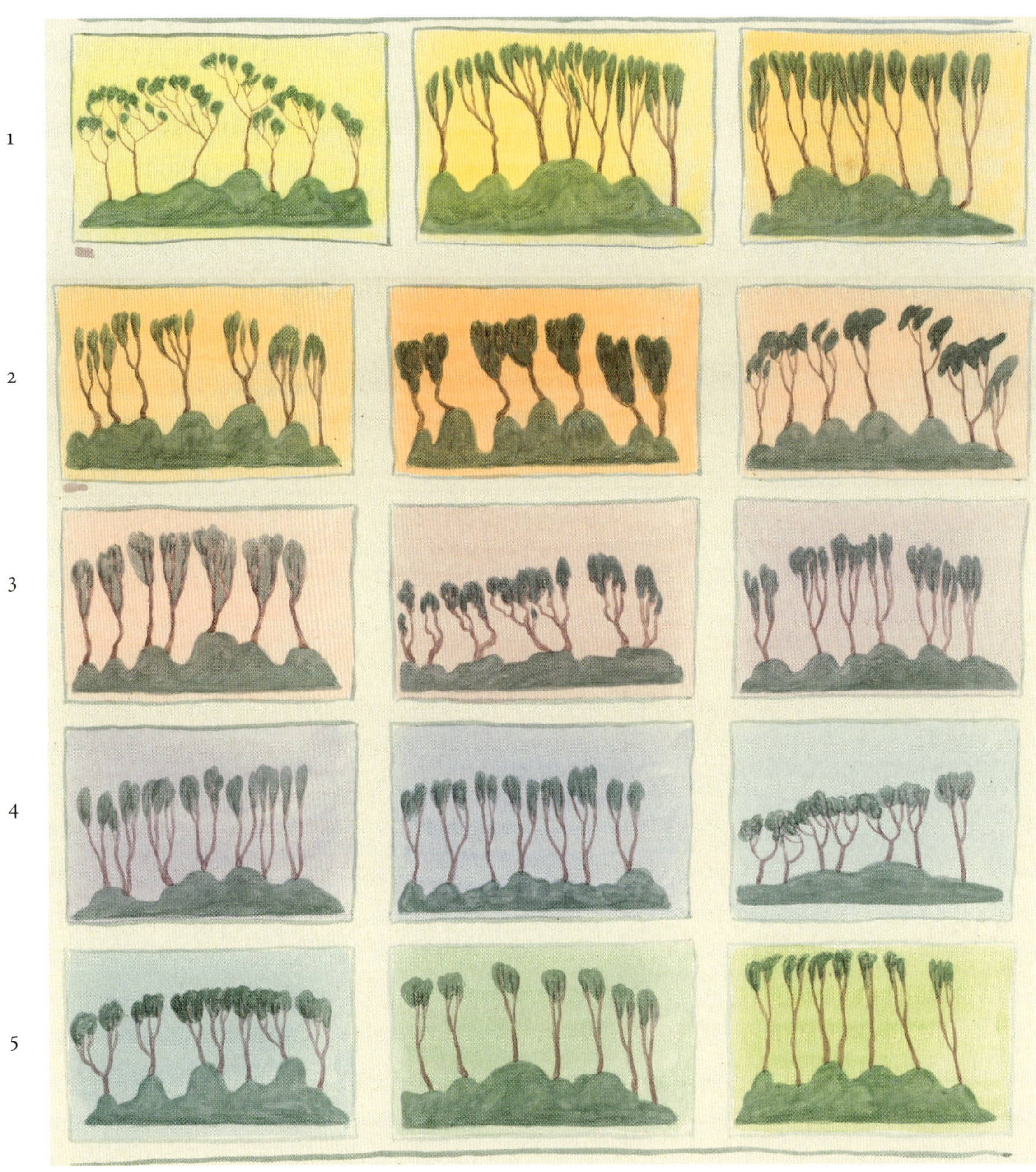

Plate 3: Violet and green on different coloured backgrounds.

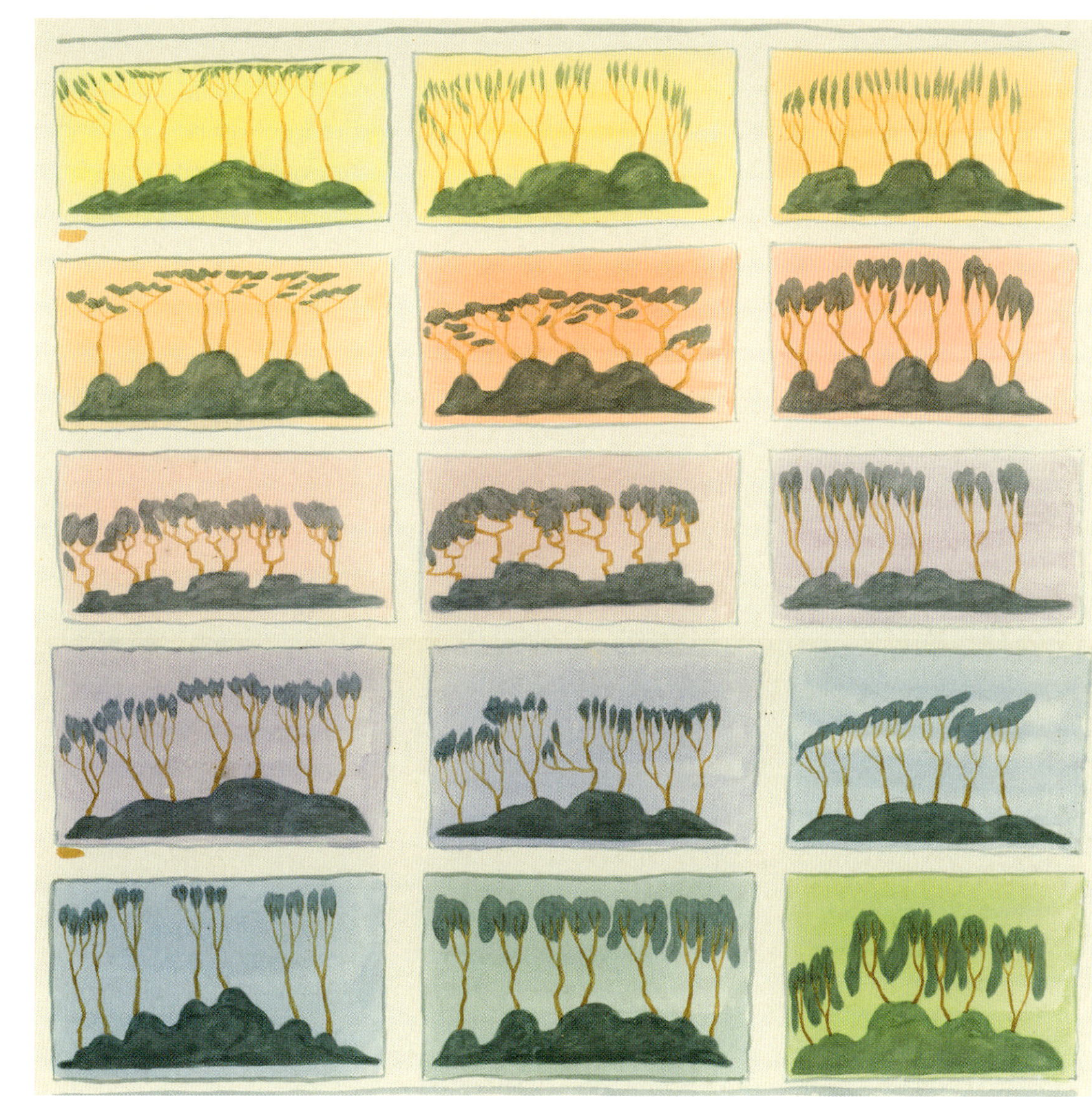

Plate 4: Yellow-brown and green on different coloured backgrounds.

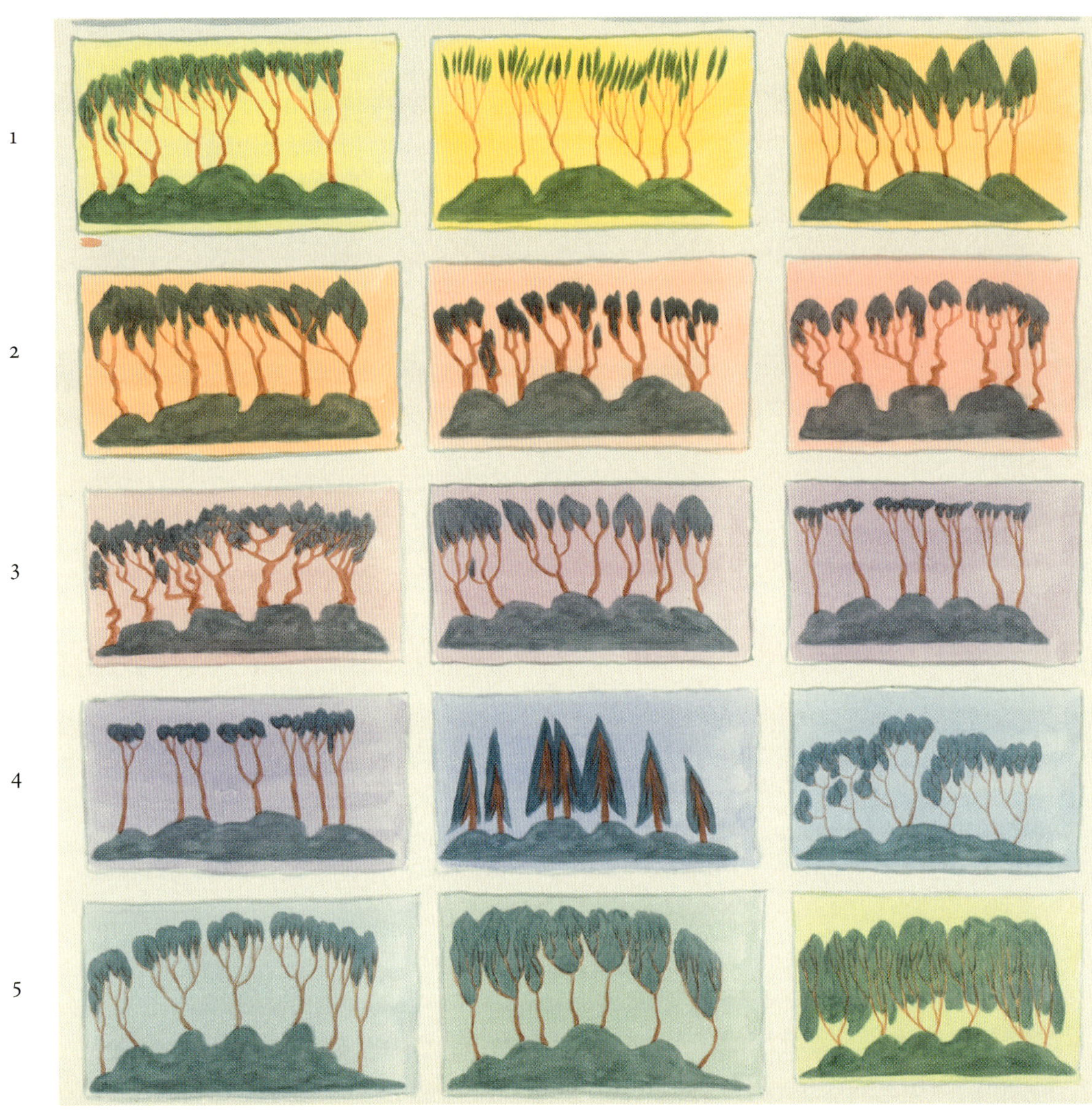

Plate 5: Red-brown and green on different coloured backgrounds.

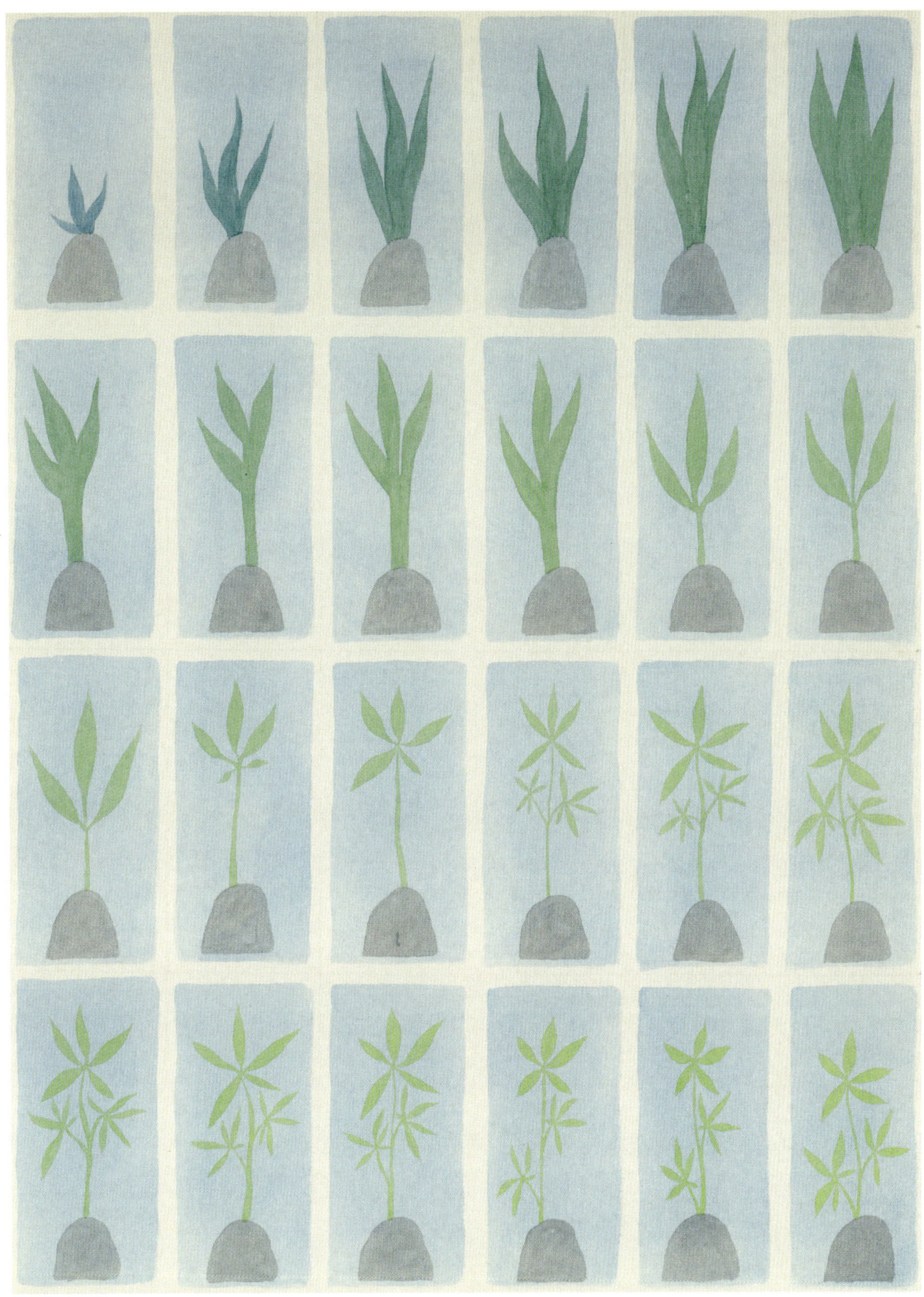

Plate 6: The green changes from blue-green to yellow-green in small steps.

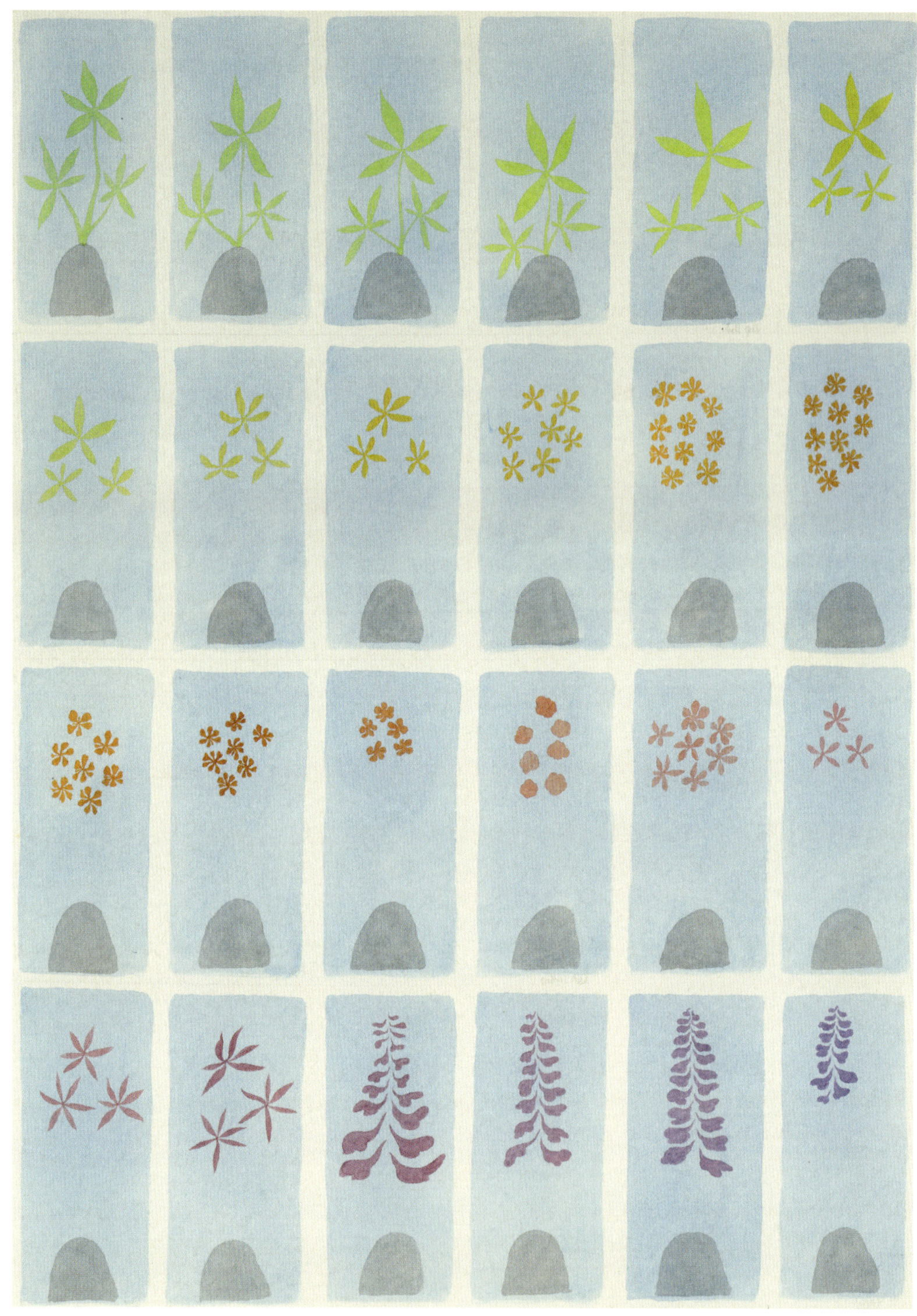

Plate 7: Blossoms take on clearer form when the greenish-yellow changes to yellow, orange, red, violet and blue.

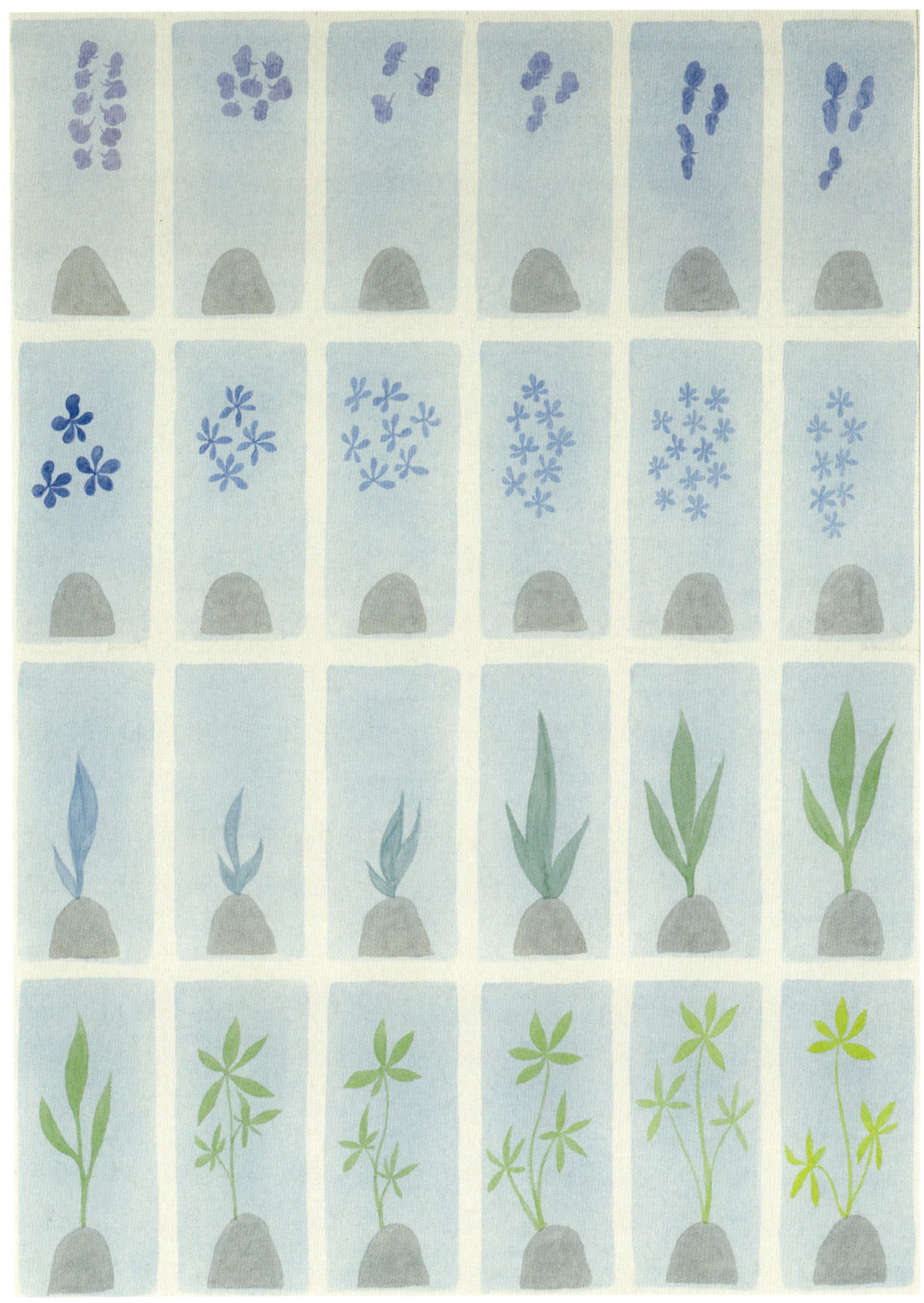

Plate 8: Then, like a repetition of a basic theme in a musical composition, the first sequence begins again with green as second colour.

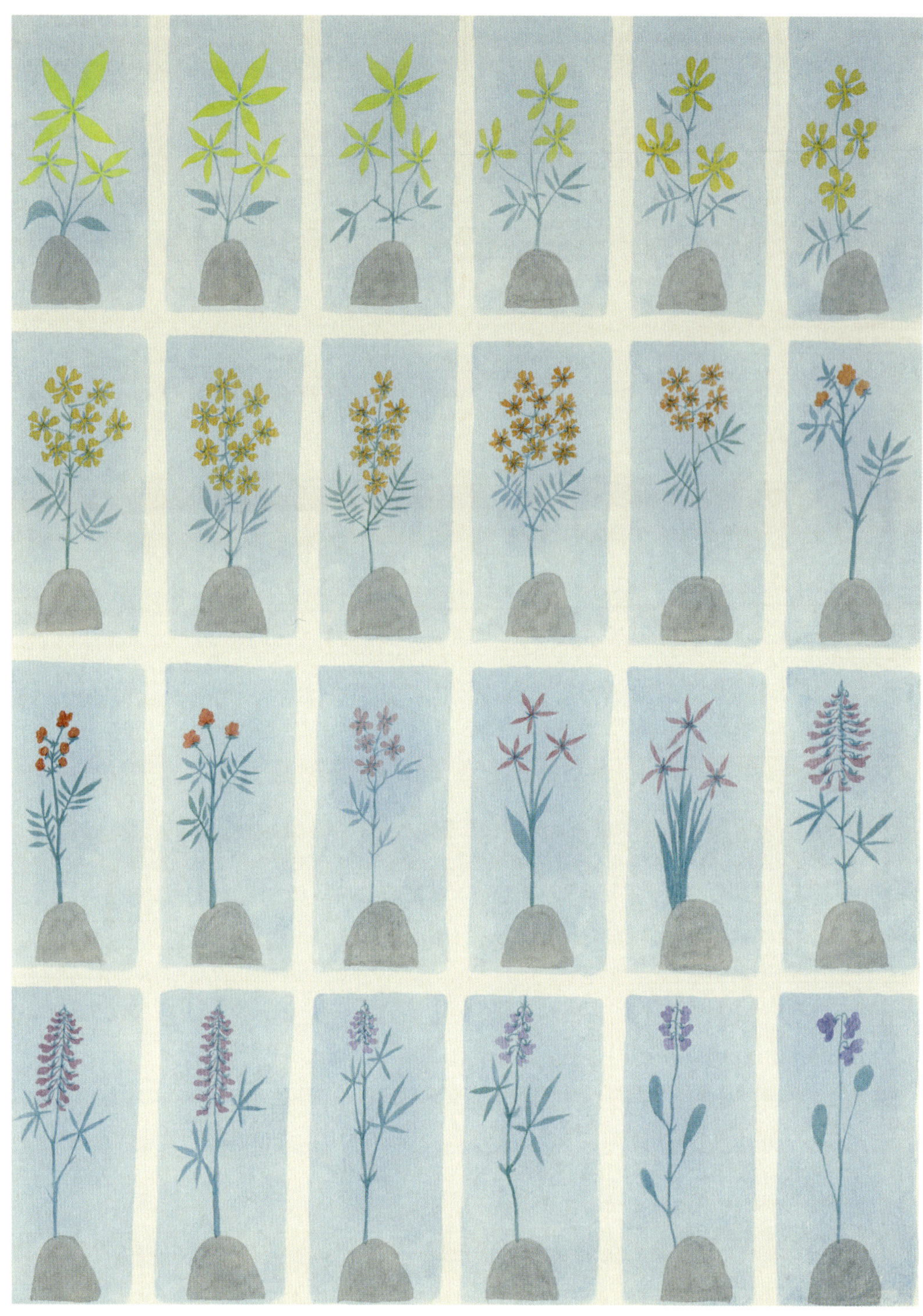

Plate 9: Green is taken as third colour to all the blossom colours and forms itself in relation to the colour of the blossoms.

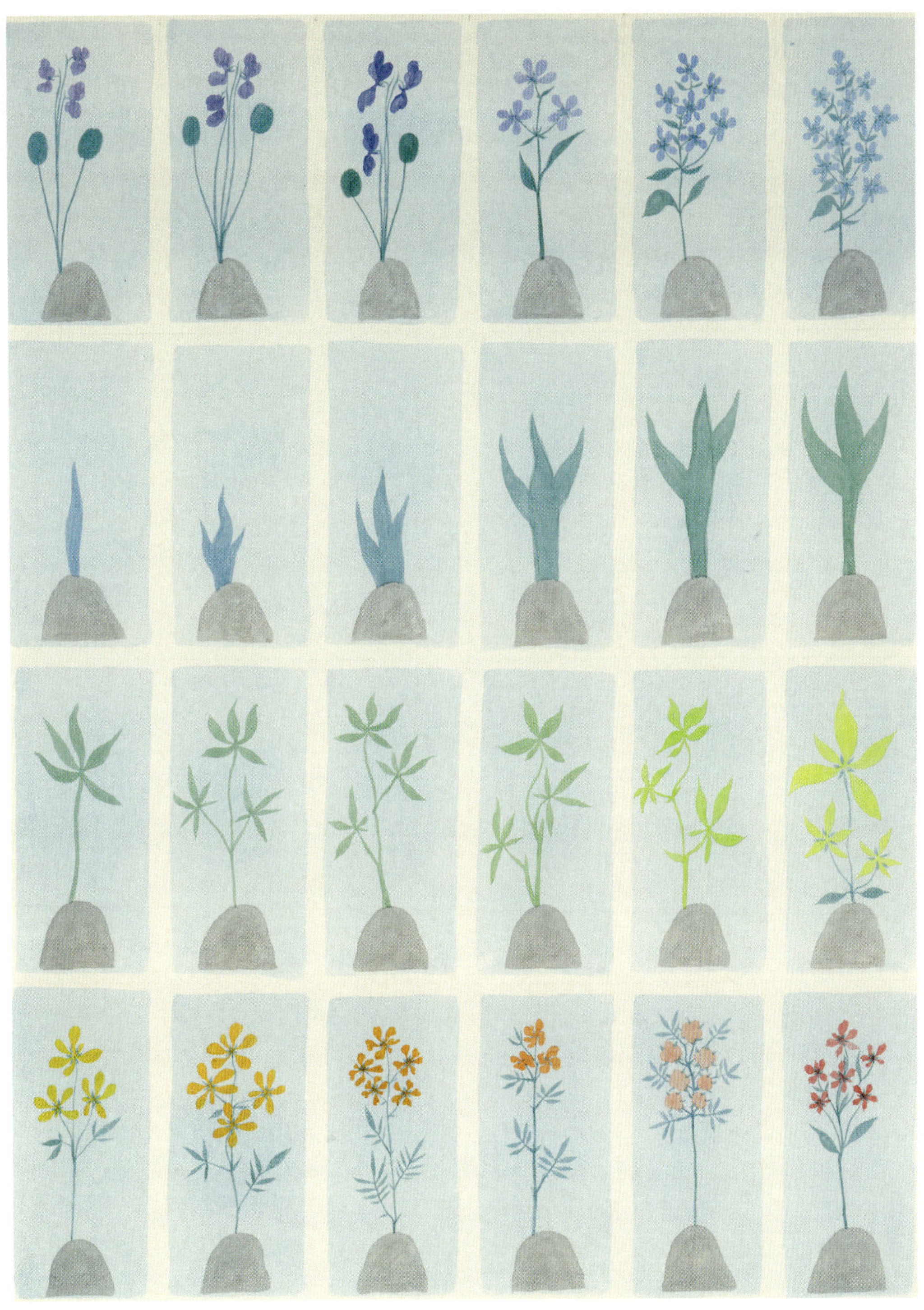

Plate 10: Green is taken as third colour to all the blossom colours.
Then a new sequence begins again with green as second colour.

First the violet and green are painted on all these background colours; then the yellow-brown and green; and lastly the red-brown and green. (See plates 3 to 5)

These experiments, which relate pictorially to the tree motif but more essentially to the interaction of brown, violet and green, are just a few examples of many similar colour research questions created by Gerard Wagner. For the sake of clarity a methodical approach was applied: basically speaking, if in a sequence the background colours changed, the colours painted onto it, and the order in which they were painted, did not change; if the background colour stayed the same, the first or second colour changed. Wagner found such an artistic-scientific approach helpful for evaluating the results of his experiments.

The second experimental series shown here has the plant motif as its focus and shows a similar way of testing the action of colour. The sequences are in rows of six, each sheet of paper showing 24 small pictures. They are painted on an elongated upright format on a background colour of blue. As first colour, a black/grey mound is painted at the bottom of each picture. The second colour is green, which changes in each picture from blue-green to yellow-green in multiple small steps. As the green colour changes, different plant-like forms emerge. (See plate 6)

When the second colour changes from green to yellow, orange, warm red, red, cool red, red-violet, violet, blue-violet, indigo, warm blue and cool blue, blossoms appear. (See plates 7 to 8) In the next sequence green is taken as third colour and forms the stem and leaves of the plant. (See plates 9 to 10) Here the colours are painted in the following order:

1 Black/grey
2 Blossom colours of yellow, orange, warm red, red, cool red, red-violet, violet, blue-violet, indigo, blue
3 Green

As in the previous tree experiments the method is clear and simple. Only two or three colours are tested at the same time, in a particular order and in a particular situation, i.e. on a white background or on a coloured background. Gerard Wagner may have been inspired by Rudolf Steiner's suggestion to follow the dialogue between two colours rather than to focus on a single colour. Steiner spoke of this in a lecture he gave about the painting of the First Goetheanum cupolas[17] as follows:

> '[...] If you can experience the world of colour rightly, you find in the colours something world-creating. Whoever can immerse themselves in the world of colour will be able to rise up to the feeling that in this mysterious world of colour there

> sprouts forth a world of being. Colour itself, through the forces that lie within it, wants to develop itself into a world of being. [...]
>
> Nevertheless, it is not a question of simply having a feeling for a single colour. As a rule, a single colour will only establish a relation between the person and the colour as such. Seeing blue means to experience the longing to accompany the colour into the space in which it shows itself, to follow the colour. Seeing red calls up a feeling of being attacked, and needing to defend oneself against something. The other colours too should be considered in this way. [...] But what I mean here has much less to do with a single colour than what the colours have to say to each another: what red has to say to blue, green to blue, green to red, orange to lilac, and so forth. In this conversation and reciprocal working of the forces of colour a whole world expresses itself. [...]'

Colour experiments, such as those just described, were not created by Gerard Wagner simply to achieve more variety in the figurative aspect of his paintings, nor was the research character of these experiments essentially an expression of his enquiring mind. At the core of Wagner's investigations was his drive to learn how colour creates form. Rudolf Steiner had spoken on more occasions about the task of painters to 'paint out of colour'. For instance in the lecture quoted above on the subject of the painting of the Goetheanum cupolas, he said:[18]

> 'To let the form manifest as the creation of colour is what was wanted to be carried out here; when one follows the history of painting, it will be found that this principle of bringing all painting out of the colour can only now stand at the beginning of its realisation.'

It is generally assumed that the idea of 'painting out of the colour' was not new and there were artists who were already carrying it out independently of any connection to Rudolf Steiner and to anthroposophy. Indeed it was a time when colour as an independent phenomenon was being celebrated and explored by painters in budding new art movements. But Gerard Wagner was convinced that painting out of the colour, in the way Rudolf Steiner meant it, was something that had not yet been achieved or even approached with the right understanding. For him this concept was founded on an understanding of colour that transcended what was already known, and was not easily accessible. He saw it as a challenge which he enthusiastically took up.

In the monograph *Gerard Wagner – The Art of Colour*,[19] Wagner describes how he began experimenting and what arose out of it. He begins by referring to his time as a student at the Goetheanum Painting School:

> 'The teaching had left me a great riddle. Rudolf Steiner always said that form should arise out of colour – be the deed of the colour. One can assume that this happened in his own pictures. With Henni Geck we had begun the first three sketches by

painting vermilion red, first in the form of a rising sun, then in the form of a setting sun, and in the third sketch as three crescent moons. And the question arose in me: when beginning three very different motifs with the same colour (as first colour on white paper), how could these differences in form be reconciled with the requirement to find the form out of the colour?

I began to look for answers. I asked myself: if, when building up a Training Sketch (the first ones were painted with only three to four colours), I were to change one colour just a little, how would the form change? In addition I followed a suggestion of Rudolf Steiner's to colour the paper, or to imagine the paper already coloured before painting the motif.

On single sheets of paper of the same format, experimental series were begun with one colour or with two colours, one of which changed in very small steps from one painting to the next (e.g. from blue-green to yellow-green, from cool red to warm red and so on), and with each change of colour the question arose as to the corresponding change in form. One attempted to participate in the life of colour through one's own experience. Thus the goal was set: to find the life of colour, that universal life-element which permeates the whole process of painting; to discover how the individual colours behave differently within this life element; to find how living form arises out of colour. These crucial ever-present questions are what one grapples with a whole life long. One never knows the answers – one tests their accuracy constantly. A large part of the work that I finally produced consisted of this.

The practice was a way of schooling one's own colour feeling. For the sketches of Rudolf Steiner had taught one relatively soon that the life in which his colours are always steeped, and which is brought to form and made visible by means of these colours, can only be grasped by a feeling capacity that has stripped off the 'merely subjective'. One sought entry into the sphere of the living, into the world of formative forces. This could only be done, and indeed be permitted, when working out of a higher principle.

And so one stood at that time at the beginning of a long journey. Many years passed by in apparent groundless practising. To know how long one would need to arrive at the 'beginning of painting' so as to be able to paint a picture in the sense striven for was naturally impossible – perhaps twelve to fourteen years.

The question of how form arises out of colour and to what extent it can be answered depends on how far one is able to have an objective colour experience strong enough to supplant the mental image. Not until much later does one know why it is so difficult and what it means. One is not spared the many hours of applying colour after colour and experiencing nothing. Only in isolated instances – as in a flash – does it seem to one that a real experience penetrates. One tries to seize it hoping for it to repeat itself. This continues for years until the experiences increase. Some day it must be possible that they become a continuous stream.

But even if one should never reach the goal of finding form out of colour – of lifting the 'Veil of Isis' – the schooling as such shows itself to be a path towards becoming truly human, and whoever notices it cannot help but continue on the path. Learning became the single motivation for painting.'

One aspect that stands out in the description Gerard Wagner gives of his path is the long time – at least a decade – he invested in the process of learning to experience colour. In time, through strenuous meditative work, his feeling for colour became deepened enough for him to be able to begin painting pictures 'in the sense striven for'.

Something of his path is echoed in the following words of Rudolf Steiner as he spoke of a new kind of preparation for artistic activity that 'will be experienced much more intensely in the human soul'. The following quotes from the lecture *Moral Experience of Colour and Tone as Preparation for Artistic Creation*[20] are also relevant for getting a glimpse into the kind of world a deepened feeling for colour can lead:

'[...] We can see a time coming when we shall be able to enter fully into the feelings that can arise from the spiritual-scientific world conception – a time when the way to artistic creation will in many respects be different from the past. It will be much more alive, and the medium of artistic creation will be experienced much more intensely in the human soul; the soul will be capable of experiencing colour and sound far more inwardly, in a kind of moral-spiritual way, and in artists' creations we shall meet, as it were, traces of the artists' experiences in the cosmos. Essentially the attitude of artistic creation and artistic appreciation in this past epoch was a kind of external observation, an appeal to something that affects the artist from outside. The need to refer to nature and to a model for external observation has become greater and greater. Not that in the art of the future there is to be any one-sided rejection of nature and outer reality. Far from it, for there will be a much more intimate union with the external world – so strong a union that it will cover not merely the external impression of colour and sound and form, but that which one can experience behind the sound and the colour and the form, what is revealed through it.

Human beings will make important discoveries in the future in this respect. They will actually unite their moral-spiritual nature with the results of sense perception. An infinite deepening of the human soul can be foreseen in this domain.

Let us pick a particular example to start from. We will simply imagine that we are looking at a surface shining all over with the same shade of strong vermilion, and let us assume we succeed in forgetting everything else around us and concentrate entirely on experiencing this colour, so much so that we feel ourselves within it, totally united with it. You will then be able to feel as though the whole of you has become colour, the whole of your innermost soul, and wherever your soul goes in the world you will be a soul filled with red, – living in, with and out of red. Yet you will not be able to experience this intensely in the soul unless the corresponding feeling is transformed into moral experience, real moral experience.'

Rudolf Steiner then guides his audience through a sequence of colours – from red to blue – revealing aspects of colours' essential being, and giving an example of how form can arise out of a deepened experience, in this instance, of red. What follows is a continuation of the quotation above:

'If we swim through the world as though we were red, had identified ourselves with red, and our very soul and the whole world were entirely red, we shall not be able to help feeling that this whole red world is filling us with the substance of divine wrath, coming towards us from all sides in response to all the possibilities of evil and sin in us. In this infinite red space we shall be able to feel as though we were before the judgment of God, and our moral feeling will become the kind of moral experience our souls can have in infinite space. And when the reaction comes, when something emerges in our soul as we are having this experience in infinite red [...] – I can only describe it by saying one learns to pray. If you can experience the raying and glowing of divine wrath, together with all the possibilities of evil in the human soul, and if you can experience in the red how one learns to pray, the experience of red is enormously deepened. One can also experience the form red takes on when it enters space.

We can then understand how we can experience a being that radiates goodness and is full of divine kindness and mercy, a being that we want to feel in the realm of space. Then we shall feel the need to express this divine mercy and goodness in a form which arises out of the colour itself. We shall feel the need to let space be pushed aside so that goodness and mercy may shine forth. Before space was there it was all concentrated at the centre, and now goodness and mercy enter space and, just as clouds are driven apart, space is rent asunder and recedes to make way for mercy, and we have the feeling that what is being scattered must be drawn in red. Here in the centre we shall have to indicate faintly a kind of rose-violet shining into the scattering red.'

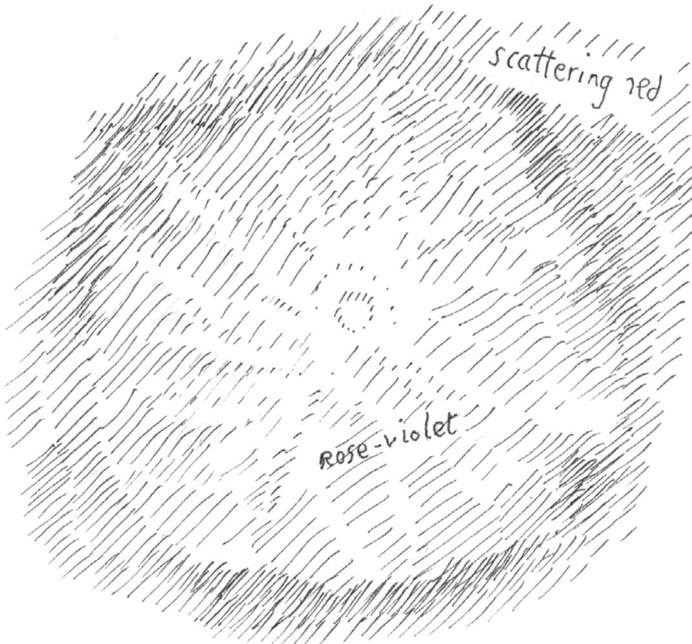

'We shall then be present with our whole soul as the colour takes on form. And we shall feel an echo of how the beings who belong especially to our Earth process felt, when they had ascended to the Elohim stage and learnt to fashion the world of forms out of colours. We shall learn to experience something of the creative activity of the Spirits of Form who are the Elohim, and we shall then understand how colour can create forms, as indicated in our first Mystery Play. [...]

Orange

Let us take another example. Let us imagine we do the same thing with a more orange coloured surface. We shall experience something quite different this time. If we submerge ourselves in it and unite with it, then instead of feeling divine wrath bearing down on us, we shall have the feeling that what comes to meet us has much less of the severe aspect of wrath about it and does not only want to punish us, but wants to impart itself to us and arm us with inner strength.

When we enter the world and unite with the orange surface we move in such a way that with every step we take, we feel that by experiencing orange, by living in the forces of orange, we are becoming stronger and stronger, and that what comes to us out of orange does not come merely to punish us and break us with its judgment, but is a source of strength. This is how we go into the world in orange. We then feel the longing to understand the inner nature of things and to unite it with ourselves. By living in red we learn to pray, by living in orange we experience the desire for knowledge of the inner nature of things.

Yellow

If we do the same thing with a yellow surface we feel as though we were transported back to the beginning of our cycle of time. We feel that we are then living in the forces out of which we were created when we entered upon our first earthly incarnation. We feel an affinity between what we are throughout the whole of earth existence, and what comes to meet us from the world into which we take the yellow with which we are united.

Green

And if you identify yourself with green and accompany green into the world – which can be done very easily by gazing at a green meadow, shutting out everything else and concentrating completely on it, and then trying to immerse yourself in the green meadow as if the green were the surface of a coloured sea – you experience an inner increase in strength in what you are in this particular incarnation. You feel yourself becoming inwardly healthy, yet at the same time becoming inwardly more egoistic, you feel a stimulus of the egoistic forces within you.

Blue

If you did the same with a blue surface, you would go through the world with the desire to accompany the blue forever and to overcome your egoism, become macrocosmic, as it were, and develop devotion. And you would find it a blessing if you could remain like this for your meeting with divine mercy. You would feel blessed by divine mercy if you could go through the world like this.

Thus we learn to know the inner nature of colour and, as I said before, we can foresee a time when an artist's preparation will mean a moral experience in colour of this kind, when the experience preparatory to artistic creation will be much more inward and intuitive than it ever was in past ages. These are only a few indications I am giving you, and they will be developed much further in the future. They will take hold of human souls and enliven them with a tremendous sense for artistic creativity, whereas the materialistic culture that has entered our modern age has dried up the soul and made it passive. Souls must be stimulated again by a power from within; they must be taken hold of by the inner forces of things. As a specific example I have taken the colours that flood the world.'

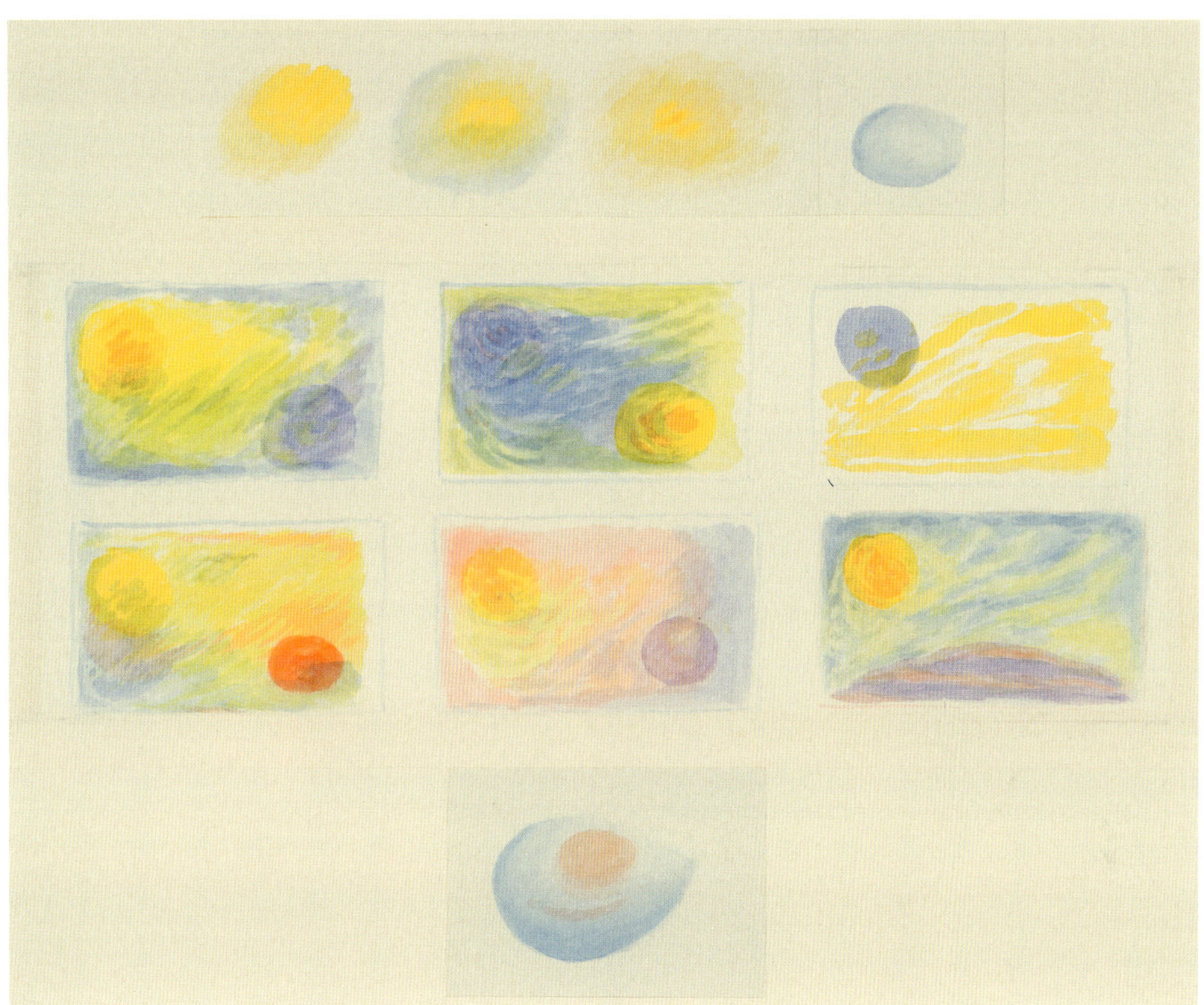

Plate 11: Colour Exercise

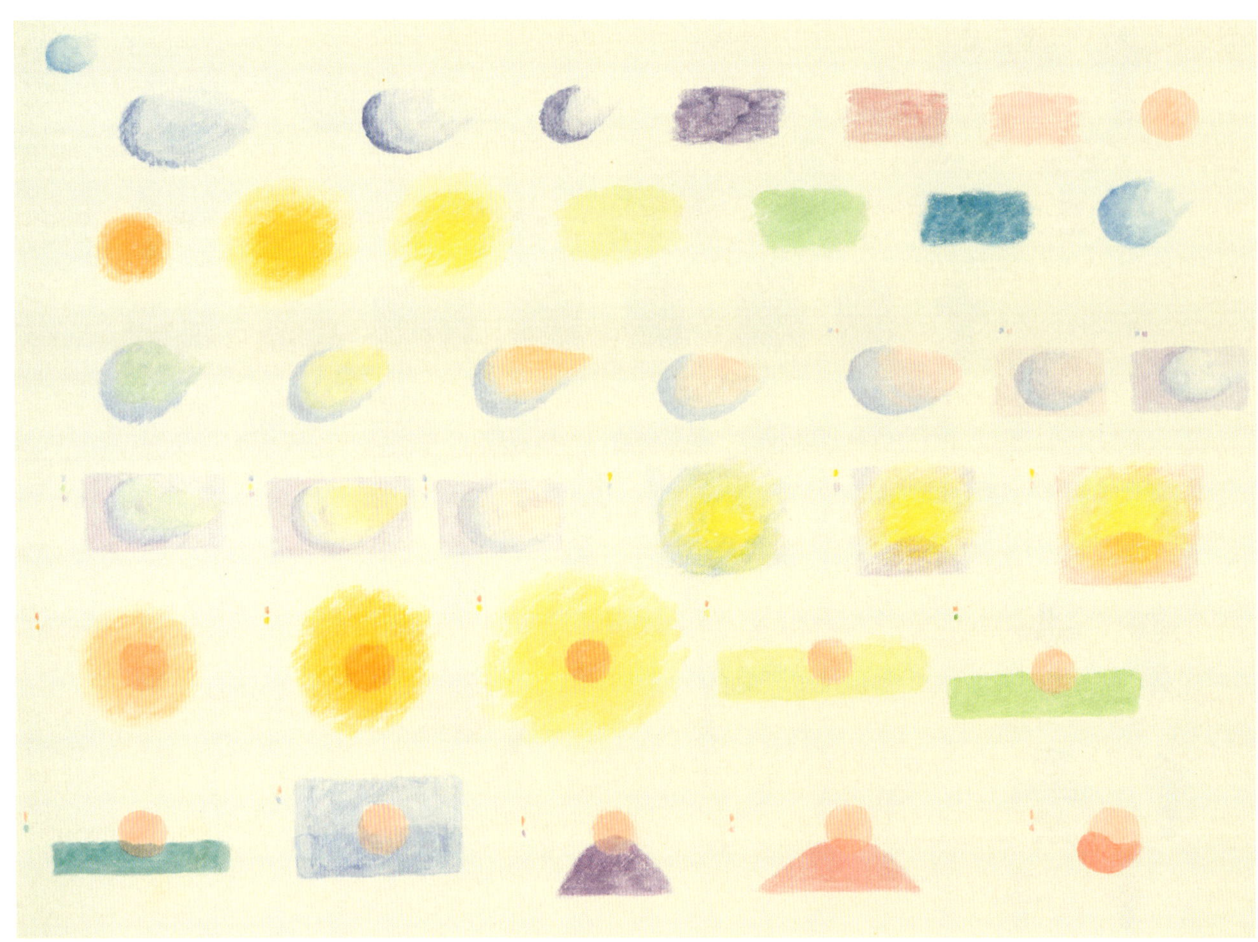

Plate 12: Experiments after Rudolf Steiner's description of the colours and their gestures from lectures given in May 1921 in Dornach. The lustre colours of yellow, blue and red show an inner dynamic through their individual gesture or form. The image colours of green, violet and cool red are painted simply as undifferentiated surfaces.

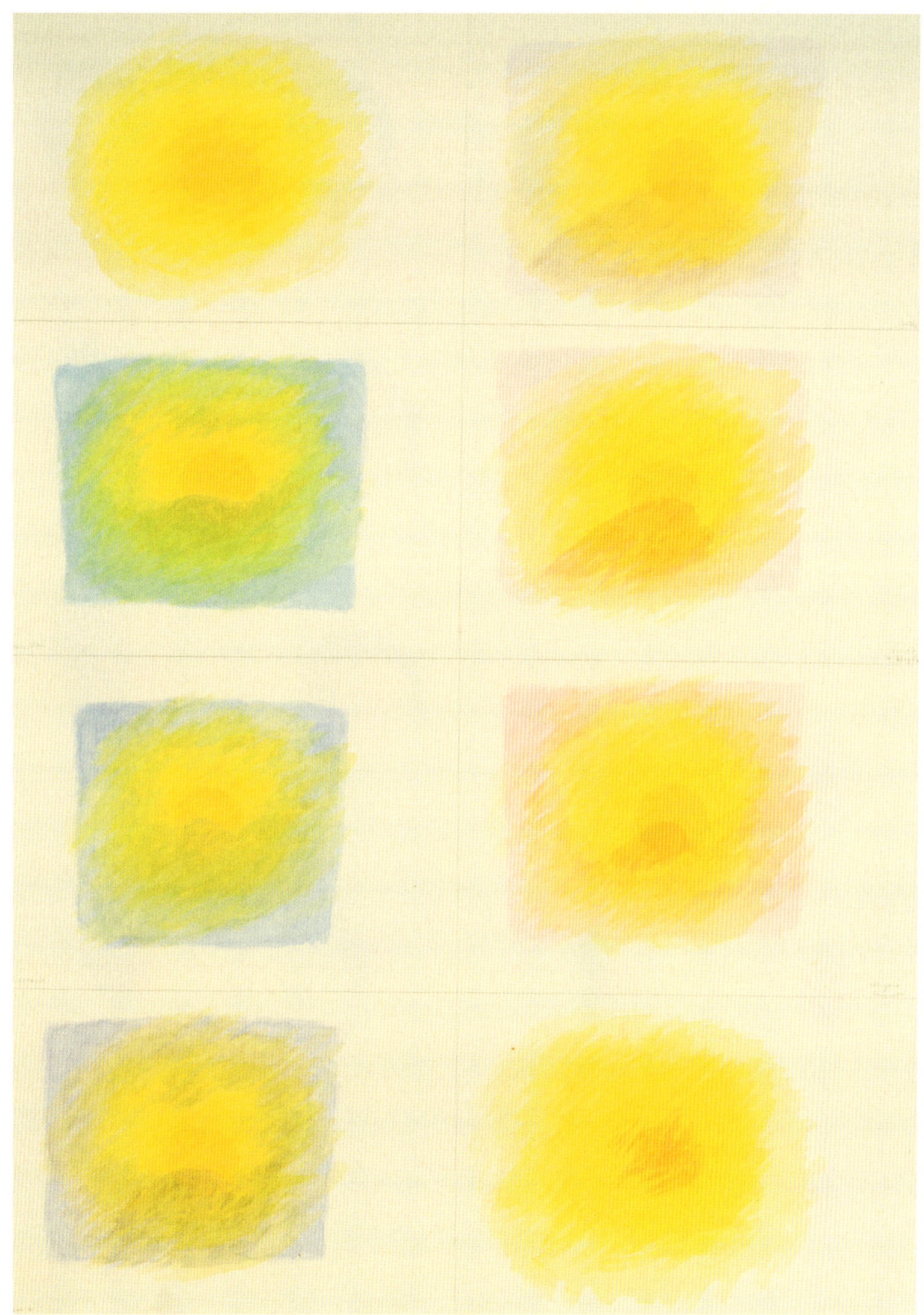

Plate 13: Yellow, in its archetypal gesture, is painted eight times. In the first picture no second colour is added. In the second picture cool blue is added; in the third: warm blue; in the fourth: blue violet; in the fifth: violet; in the sixth: red violet; in the seventh: cool red; in the eight: warm red. The aim of the second colour is to create a harmonious balance with the yellow.

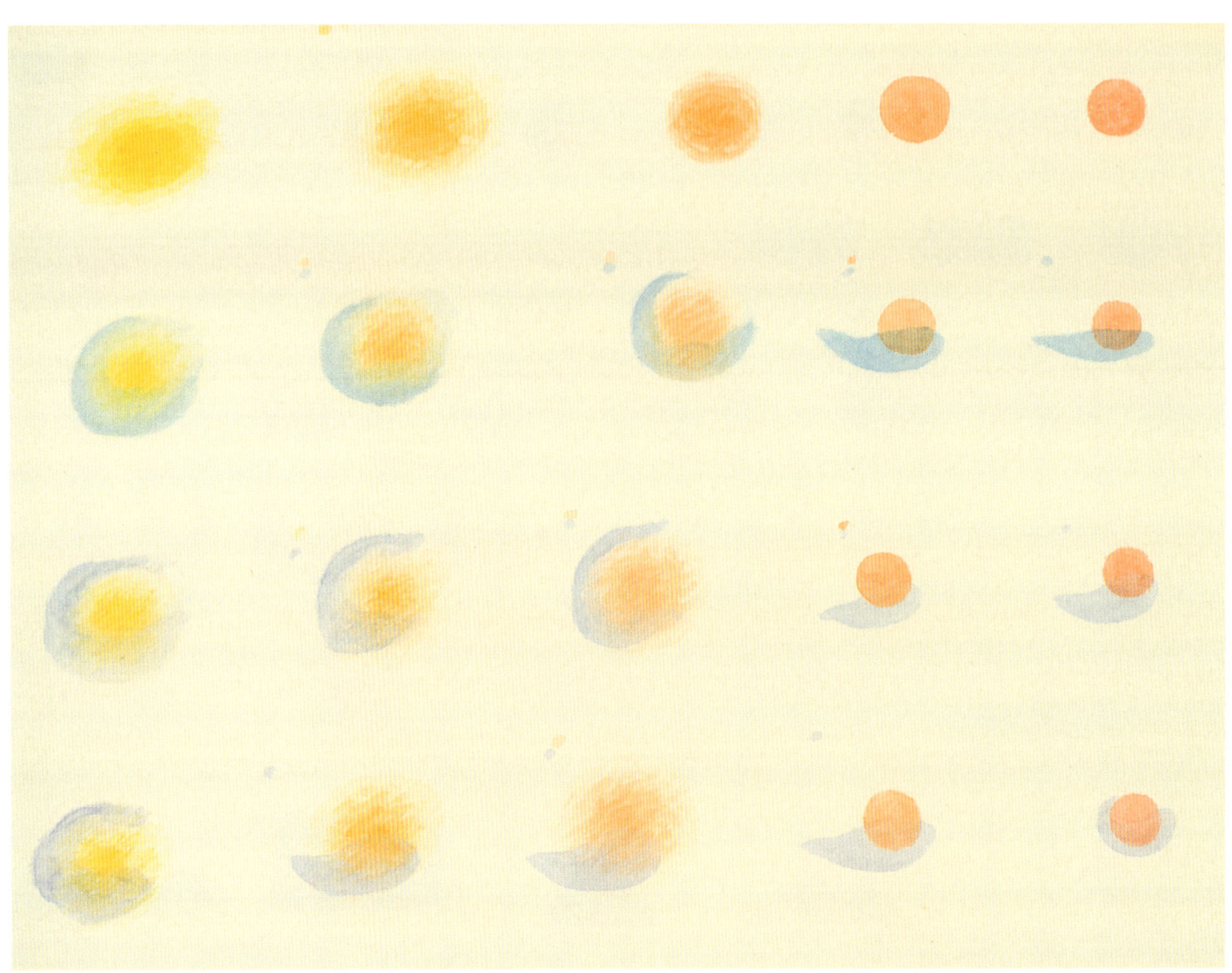

Plate 14: An experimental sequence from yellow through orange to red. In each row the yellow intensifies step by step to orange, warm red and red. In the second row cool blue is added; in the third row, warm blue; in the fourth row, violet blue.

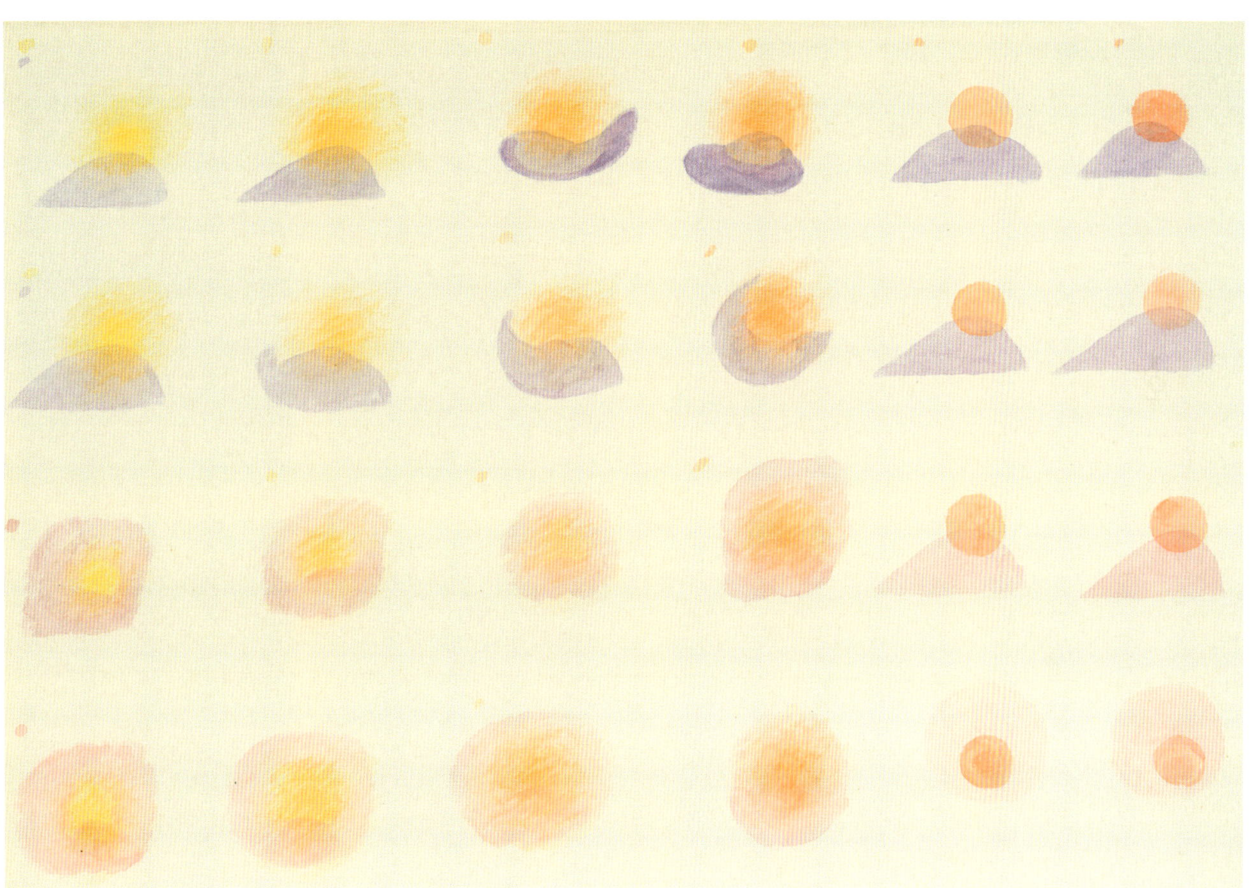

Plate 15: A continuation of the exercise seen on the opposite page. Here the second colours are blue violet, violet, red violet and cool red. Research questions arise in regard to the meeting of the two colours: How can the second colour bring about the most positive reaction in the first colour? What is the lawful gesture for the second colour to adopt when seeking harmony with the first colour yet retaining its individual character?

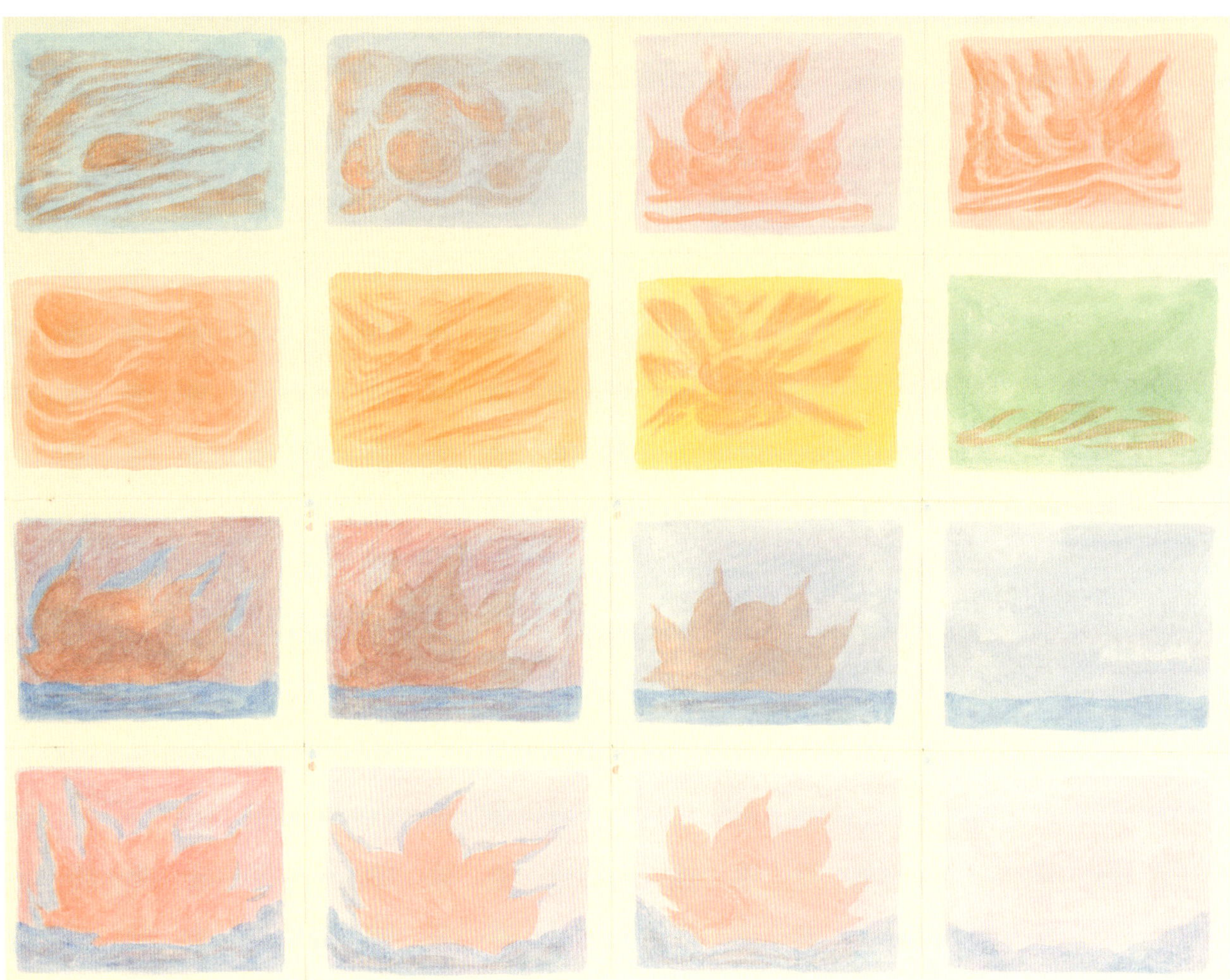

Plate 16: Red on different coloured backgrounds. In the bottom two rows, blue is the first colour followed by red. When researching the Nature Mood sketches, red was painted on different background colours. The change in the form of the red is influenced by the different background colours. On a yellow background the red opens in accordance with the character of yellow; on a blue background the red takes on a more passive form in accordance with the inward nature of blue.

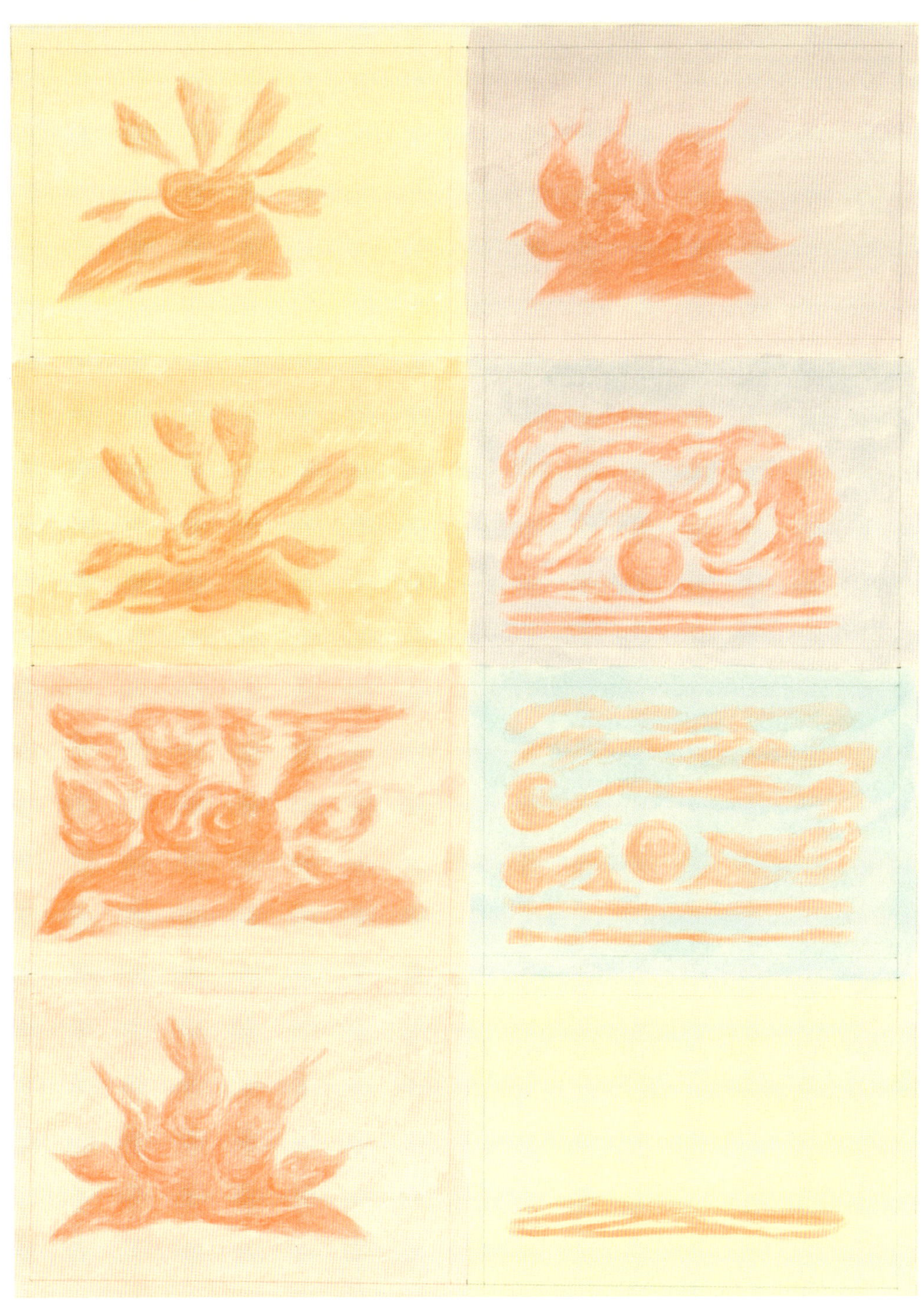

Plate 17: The Nature Mood motifs take on clearer form.
Red is painted on various background colours
from yellow through the rainbow colours to green.

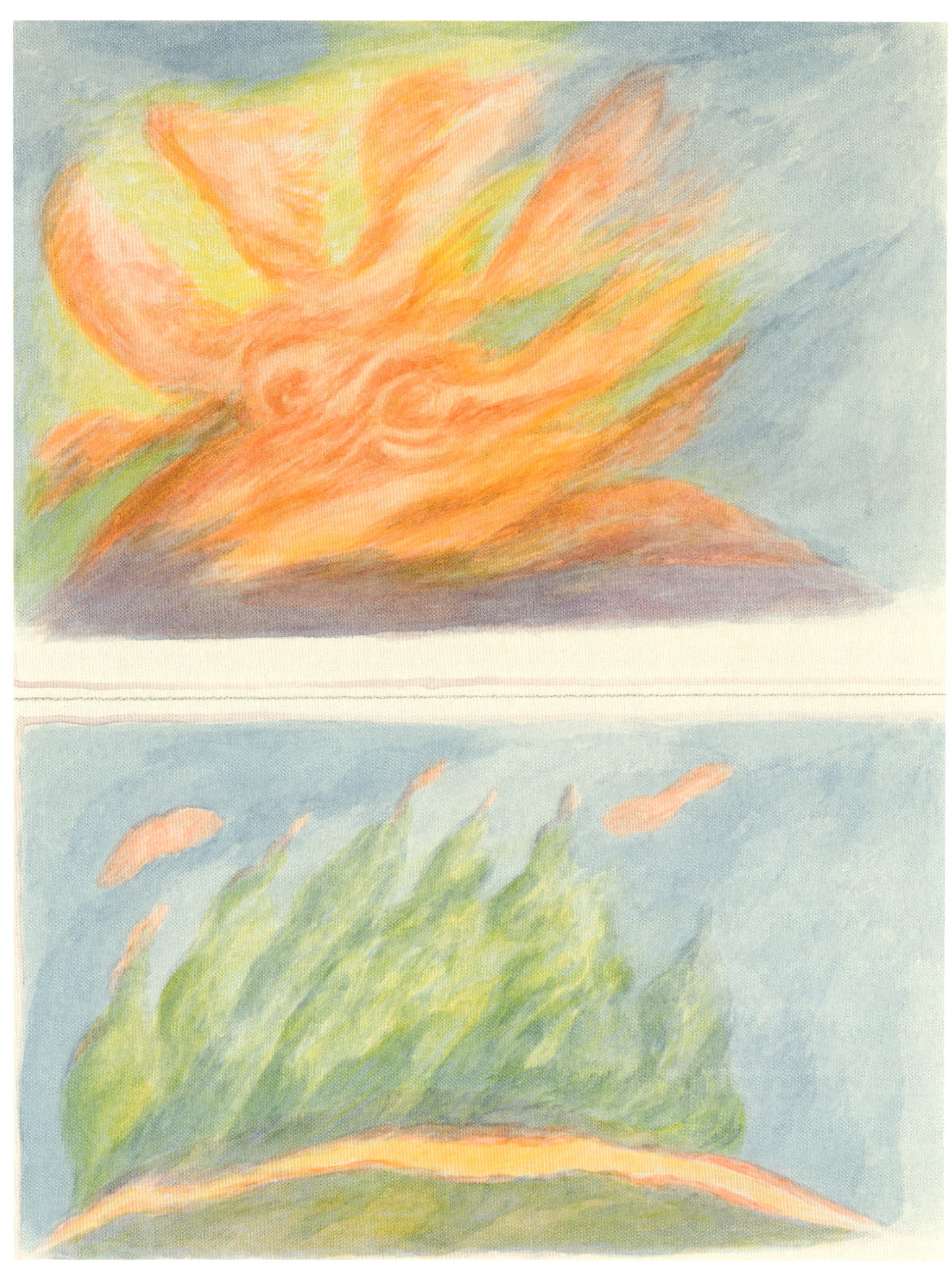

Plate 18: *Sunrise* on a yellow background; *Summer Trees* on a green background

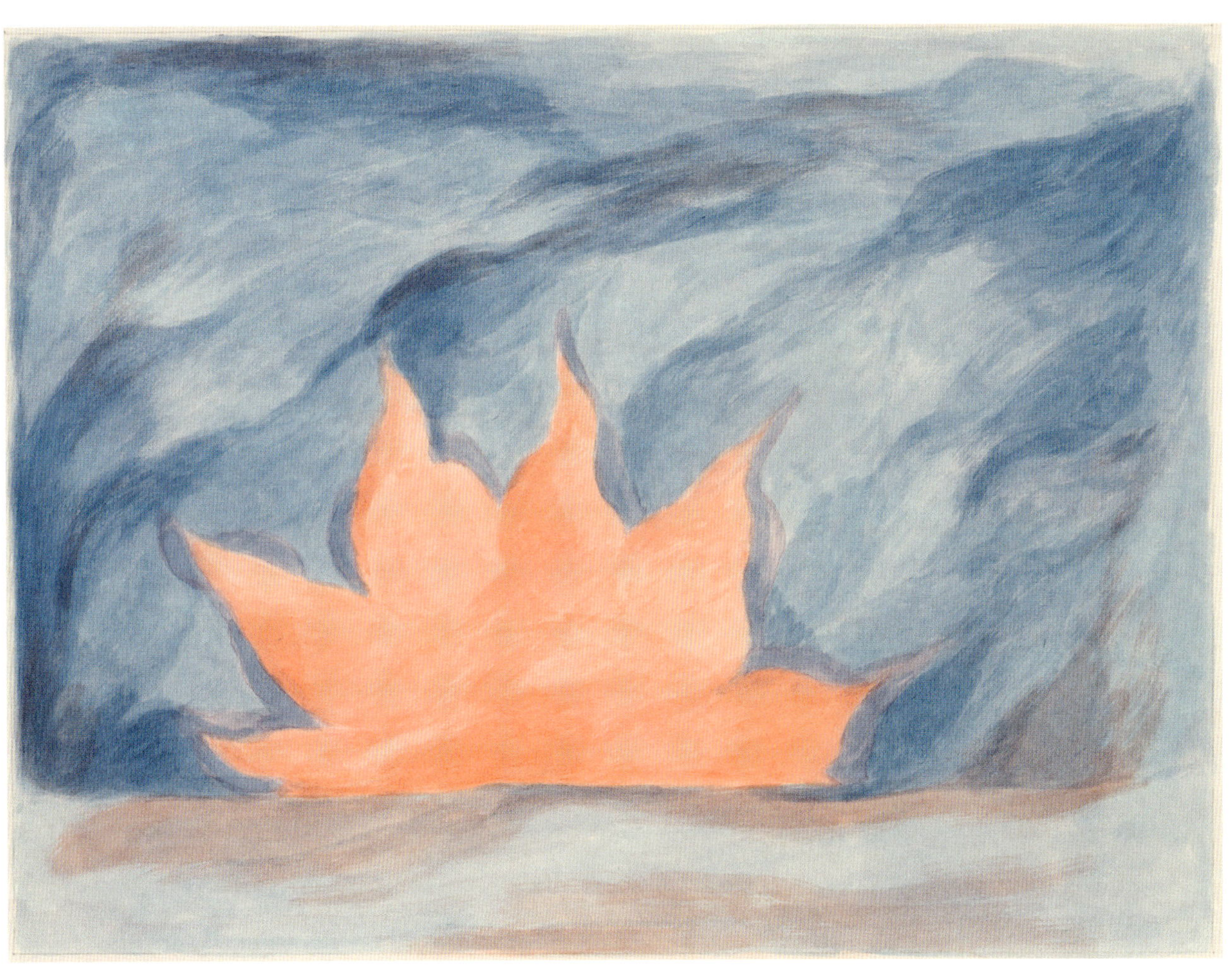

Plate 19: *Sunset* on a violet background

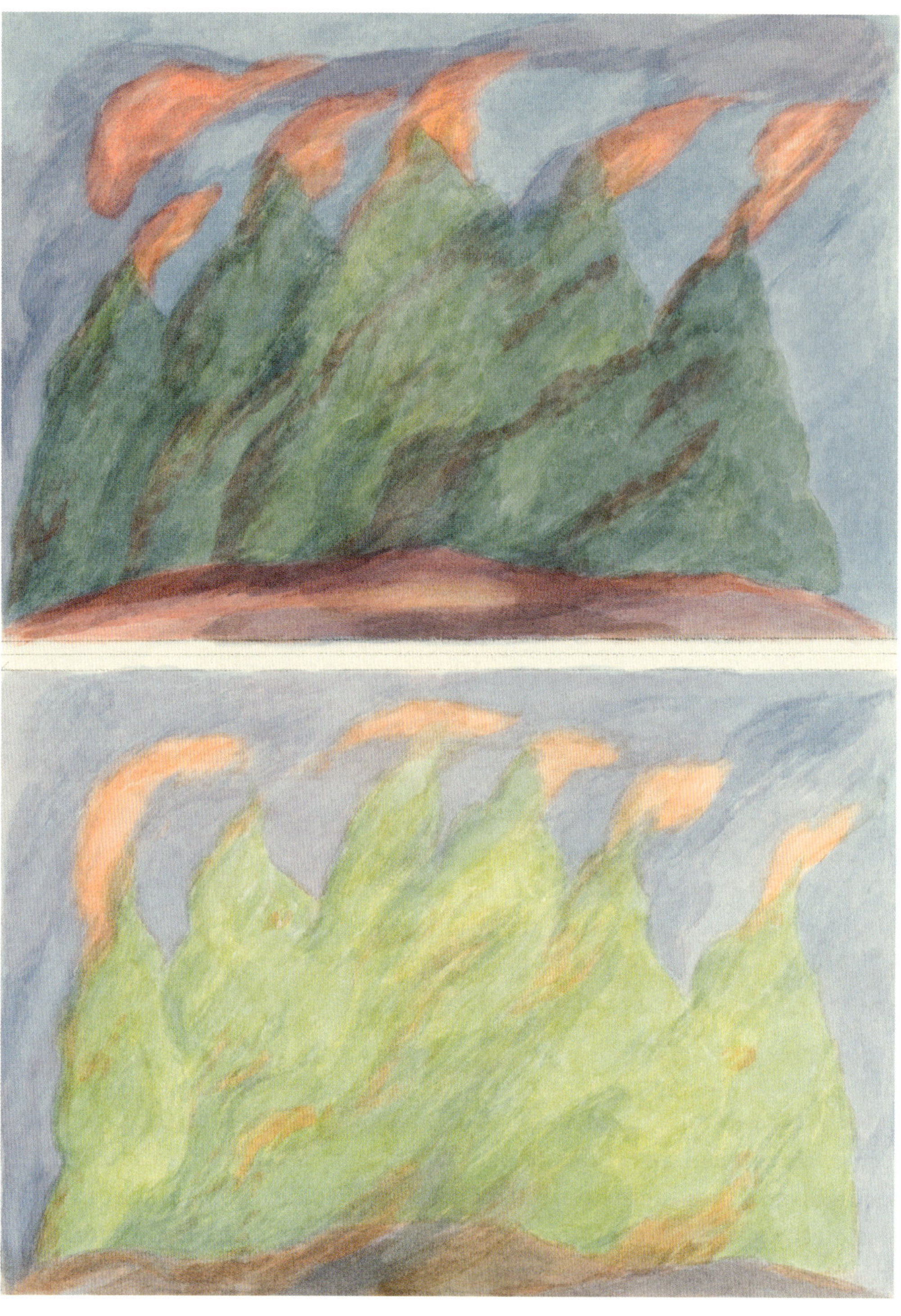

Plate 20: *Fruiting and Blossoming Trees* on a white background: the picture at the top is painted with a blue-green, the picture below with yellow-green.

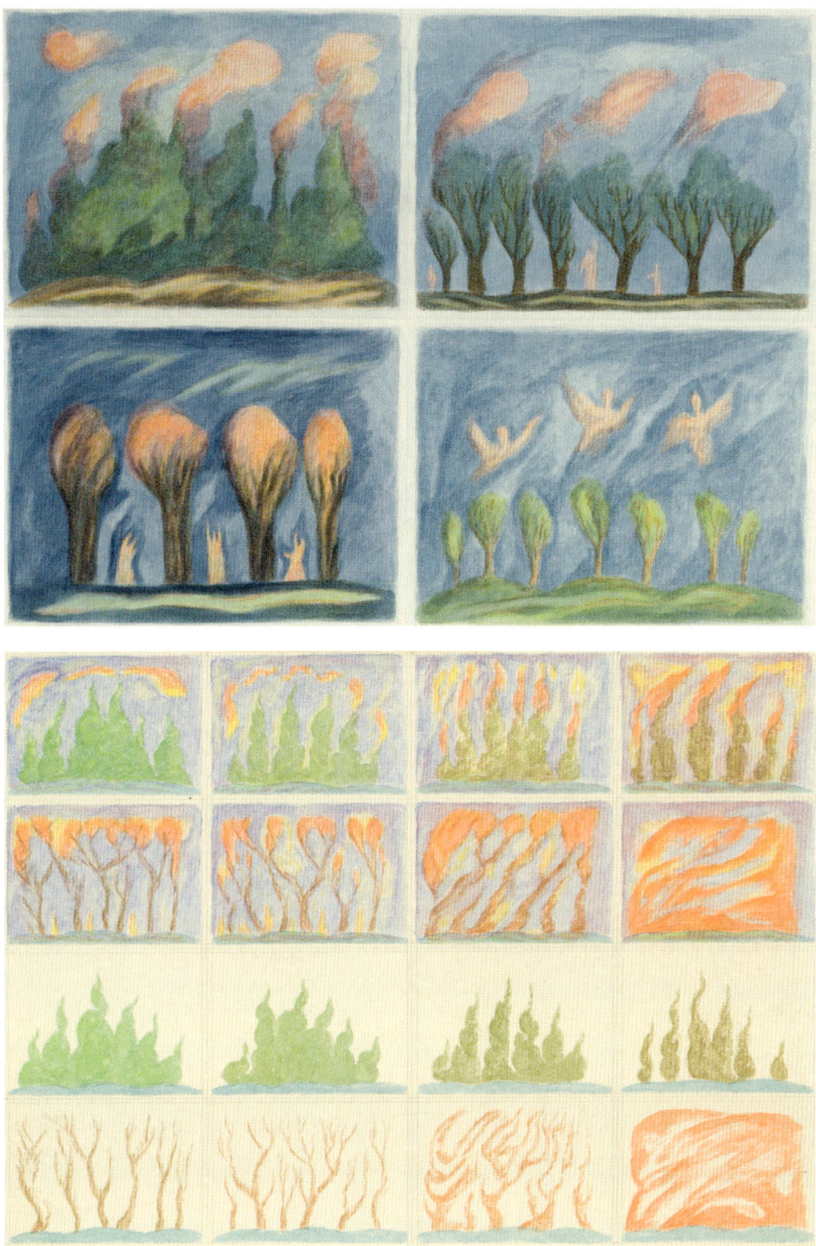

Plate 21a: A change in the order of the first two colours causes the change of motif. In the first picture, brown in the first colour and green the second; in the other pictures, green is the first colour and brown the second. The different form tendencies of green and brown are visible.

Plate 21b: This series shows a motif-transformation beginning with *Fruiting and Blossoming Trees* and ending with *Sunrise.* The two lower rows show the build-up of the motif. The first colour painted at the bottom of the page was a blue-green. The second colour changes from green to red in gradual steps.

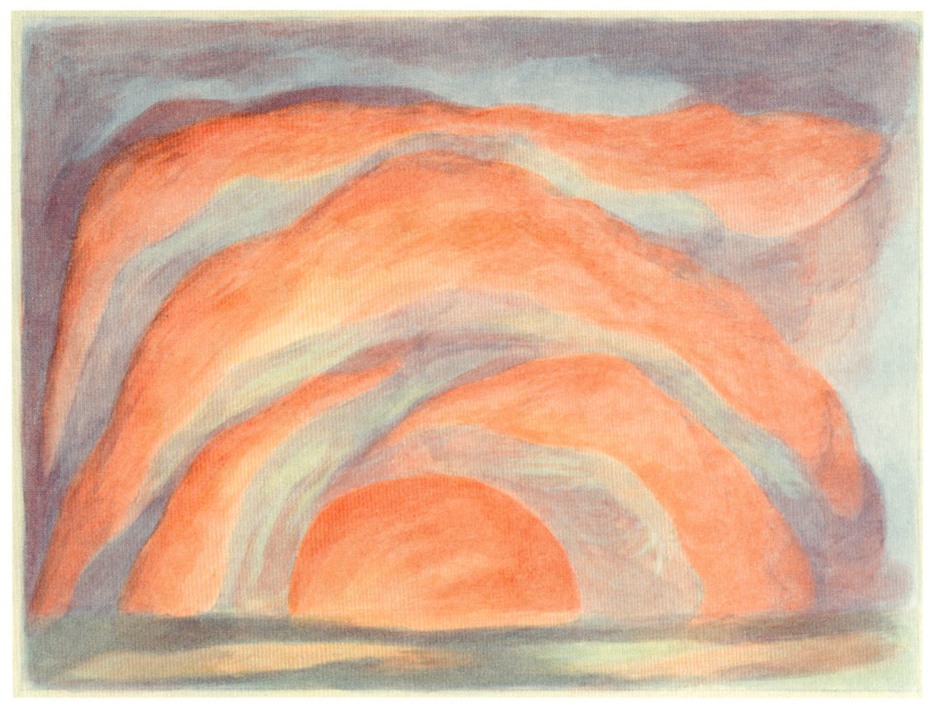

1

Plates 22–24: A motif-transformation beginning with *Sunrise* and ending with *Fruiting and Blossoming Trees.*

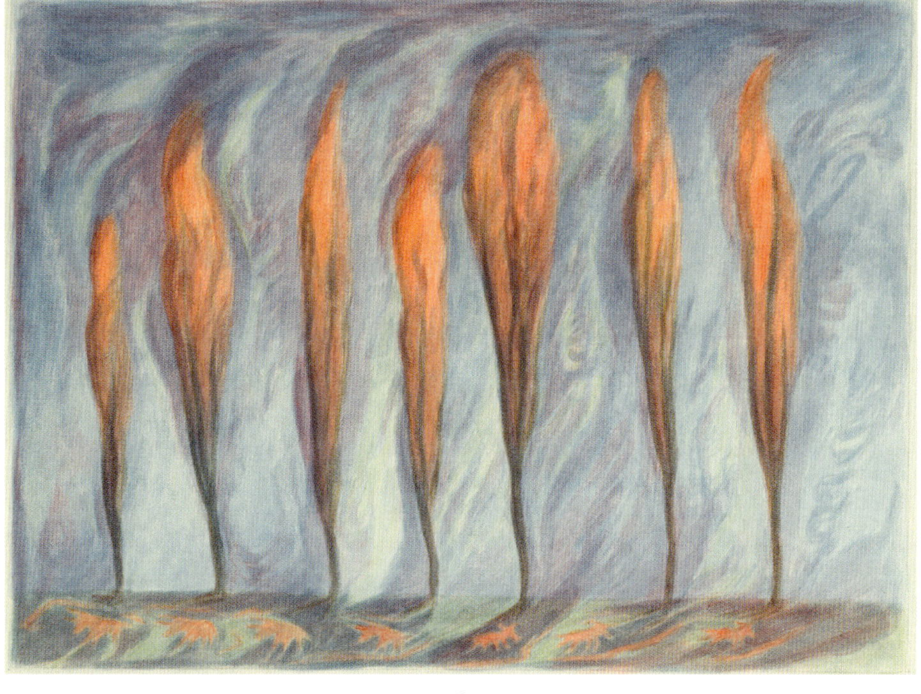

3

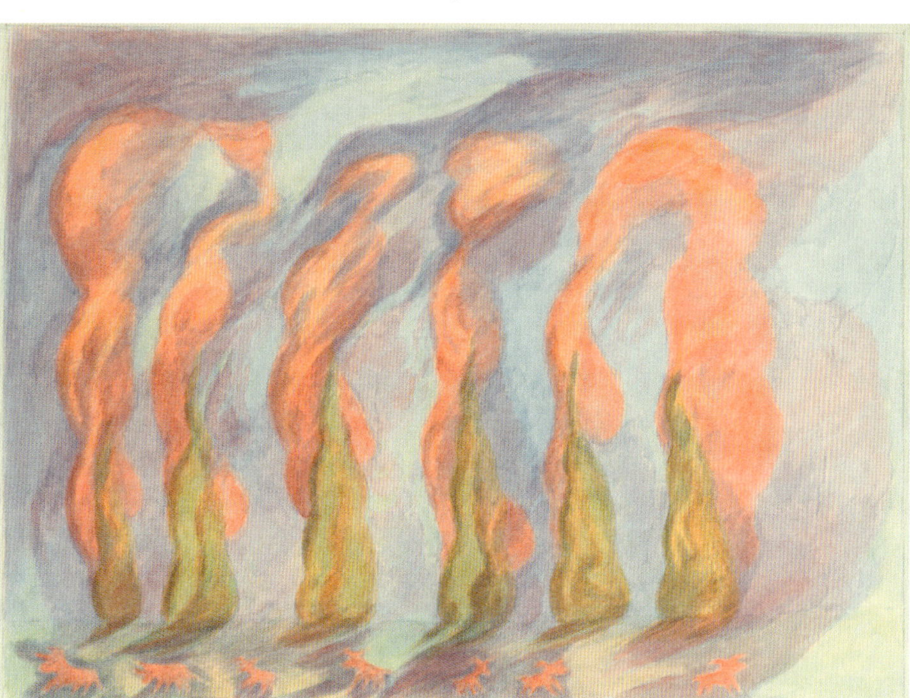

Plates 22–24: A motif-transformation beginning with *Sunrise* and ending with *Fruiting and Blossoming Trees.*

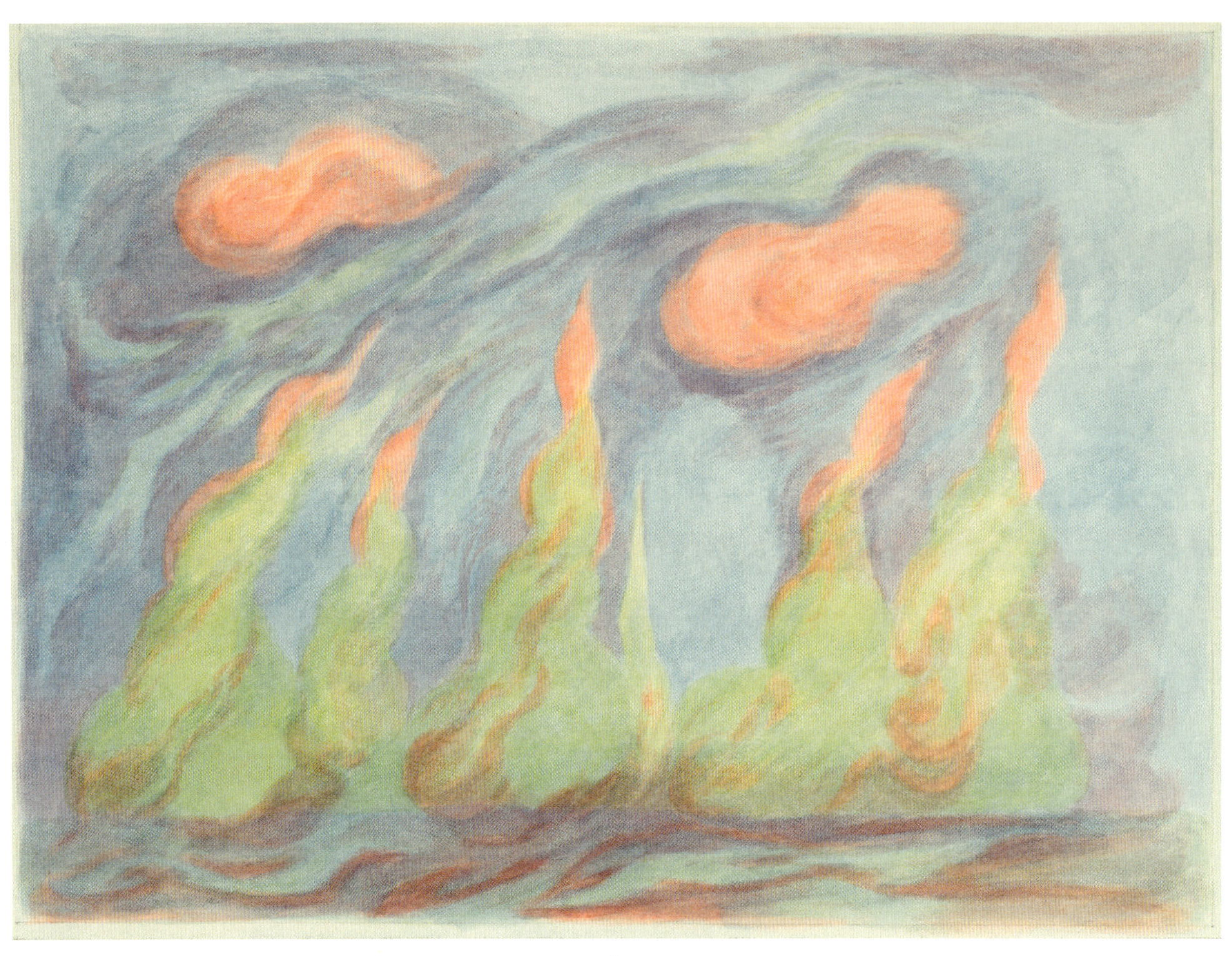

5

Plates 22–24: A motif-transformation beginning with *Sunrise* and ending with *Fruiting and Blossoming Trees.*

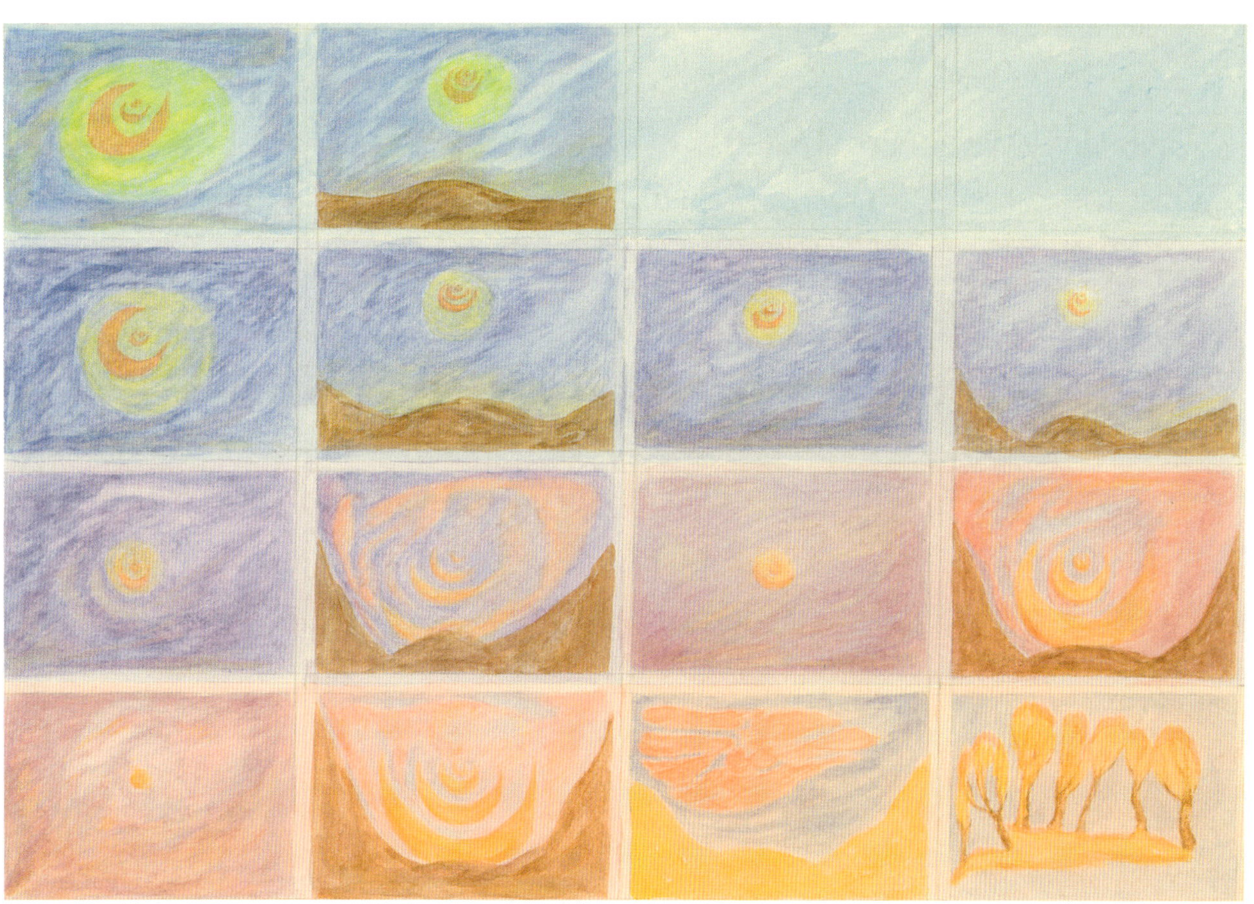

Plate 25: *Shining Moon* and *Moonrise* are painted on a blue background; *Moonset* on a violet background. The first colour in *Moonrise* and *Moonset* is brown.

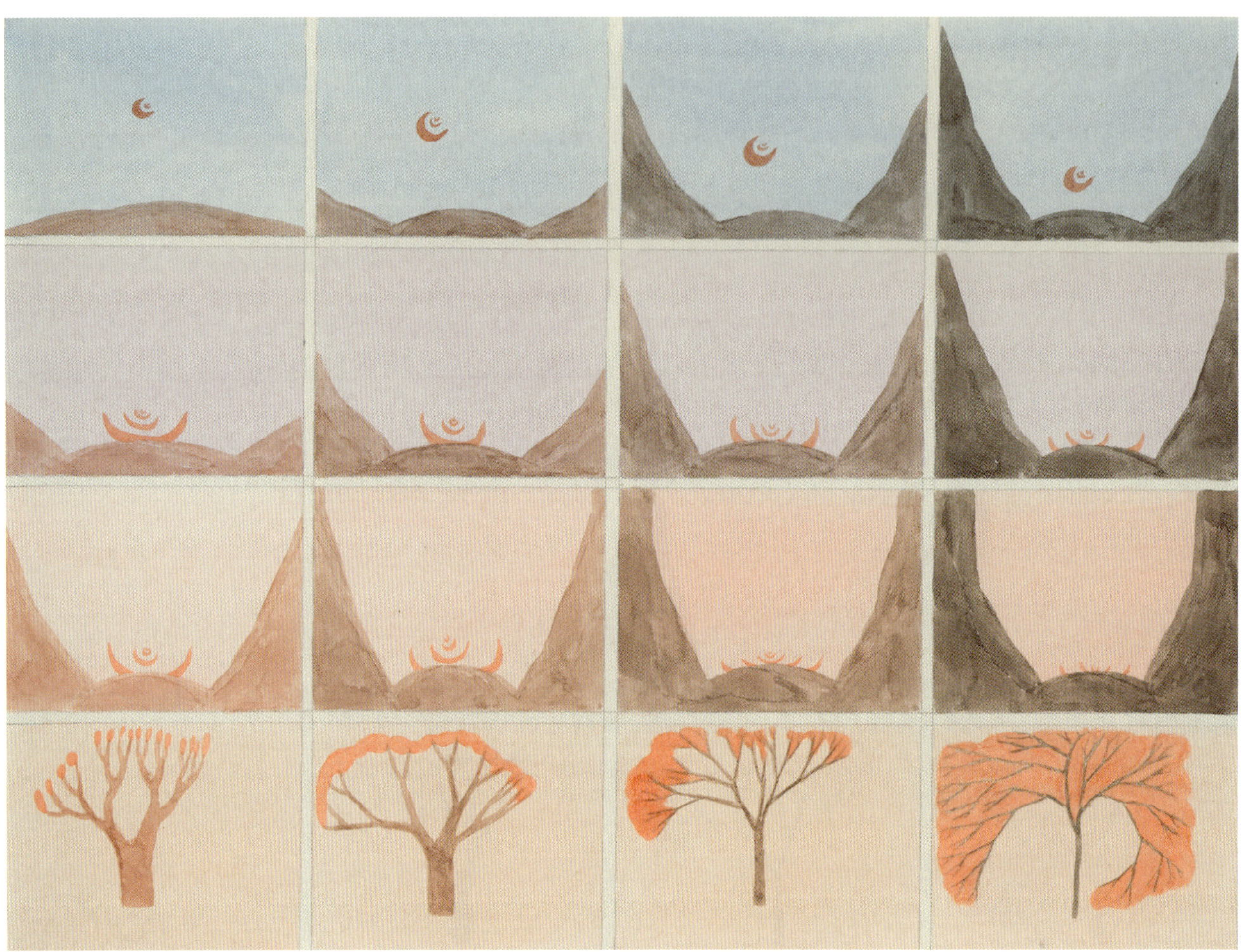

Plate 26: This series shows a transformation from *Moonrise* to *Moonset,* and further to a tree motif. Warm brown changes in four steps to dark brown. The second colour is red. The first row is painted on a blue background; the second row on a violet background; the third row on a cool red background; the fourth row on a warm red background. (In Gerard Wagner's colour experiments the change from a cool red background to a warm red background is often, as seen here, the reason for a marked change of form.)

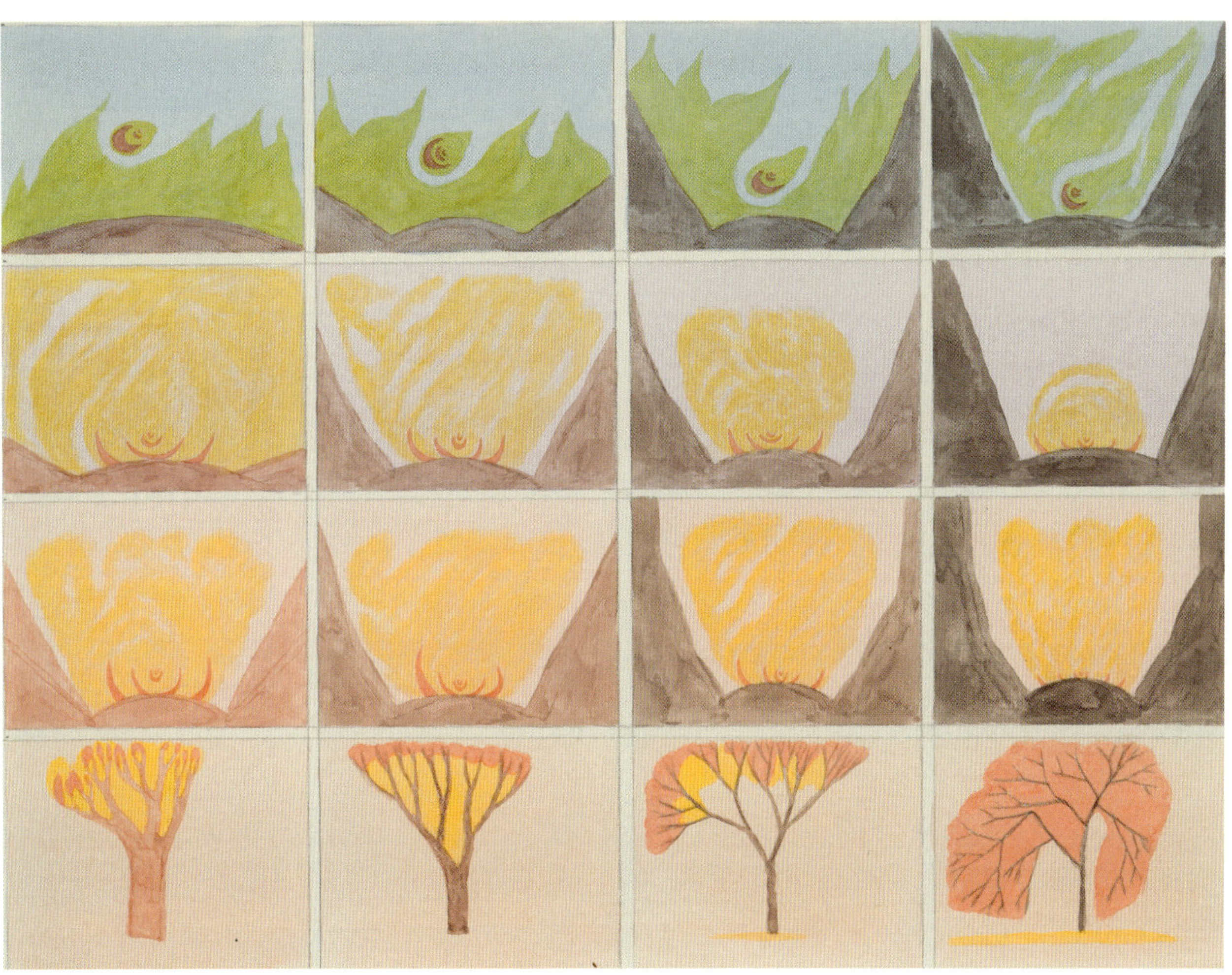

Plate 27: The series continues with the addition of warm yellow.

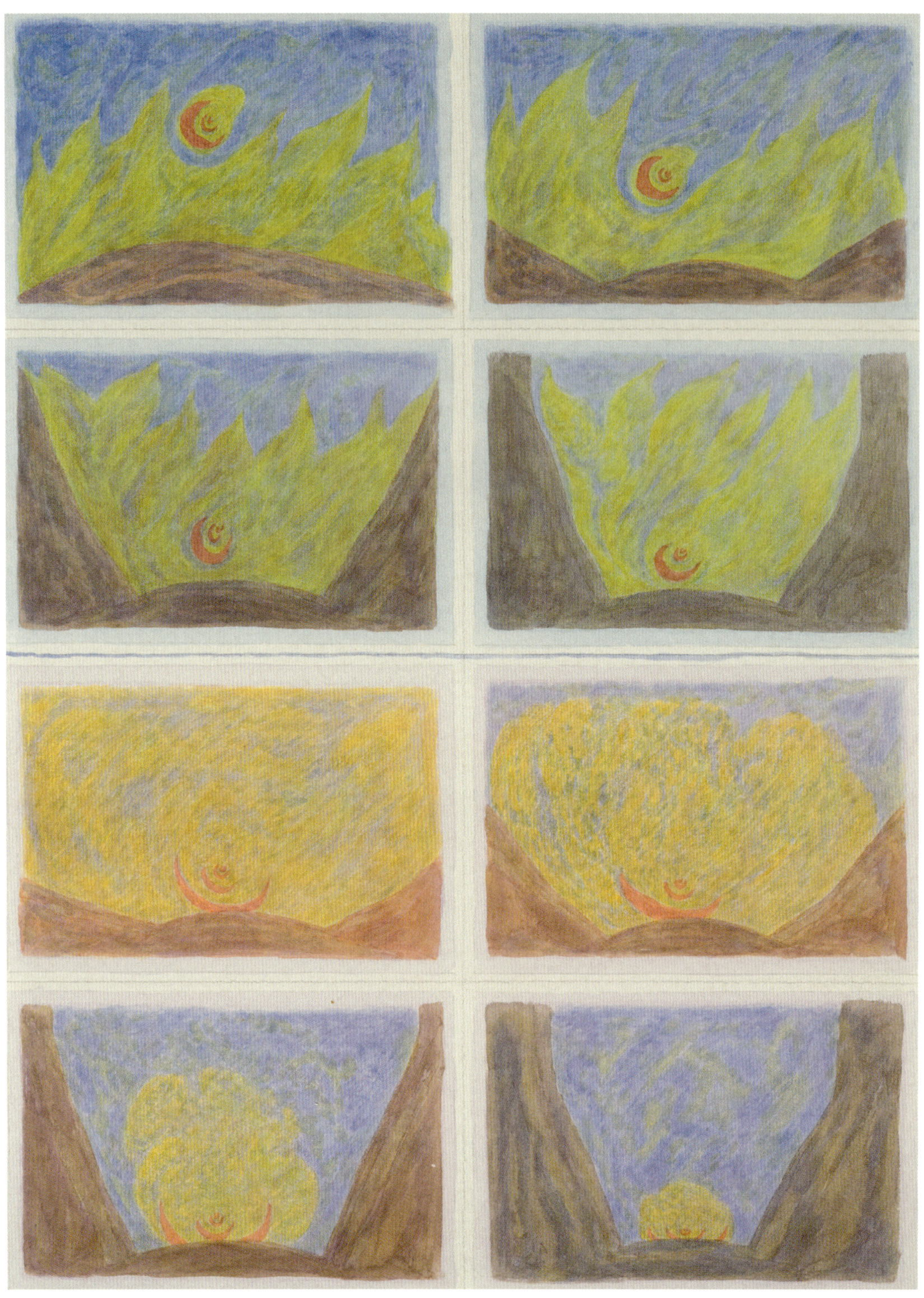

Plate 28: The series continues with the addition of blue and violet.

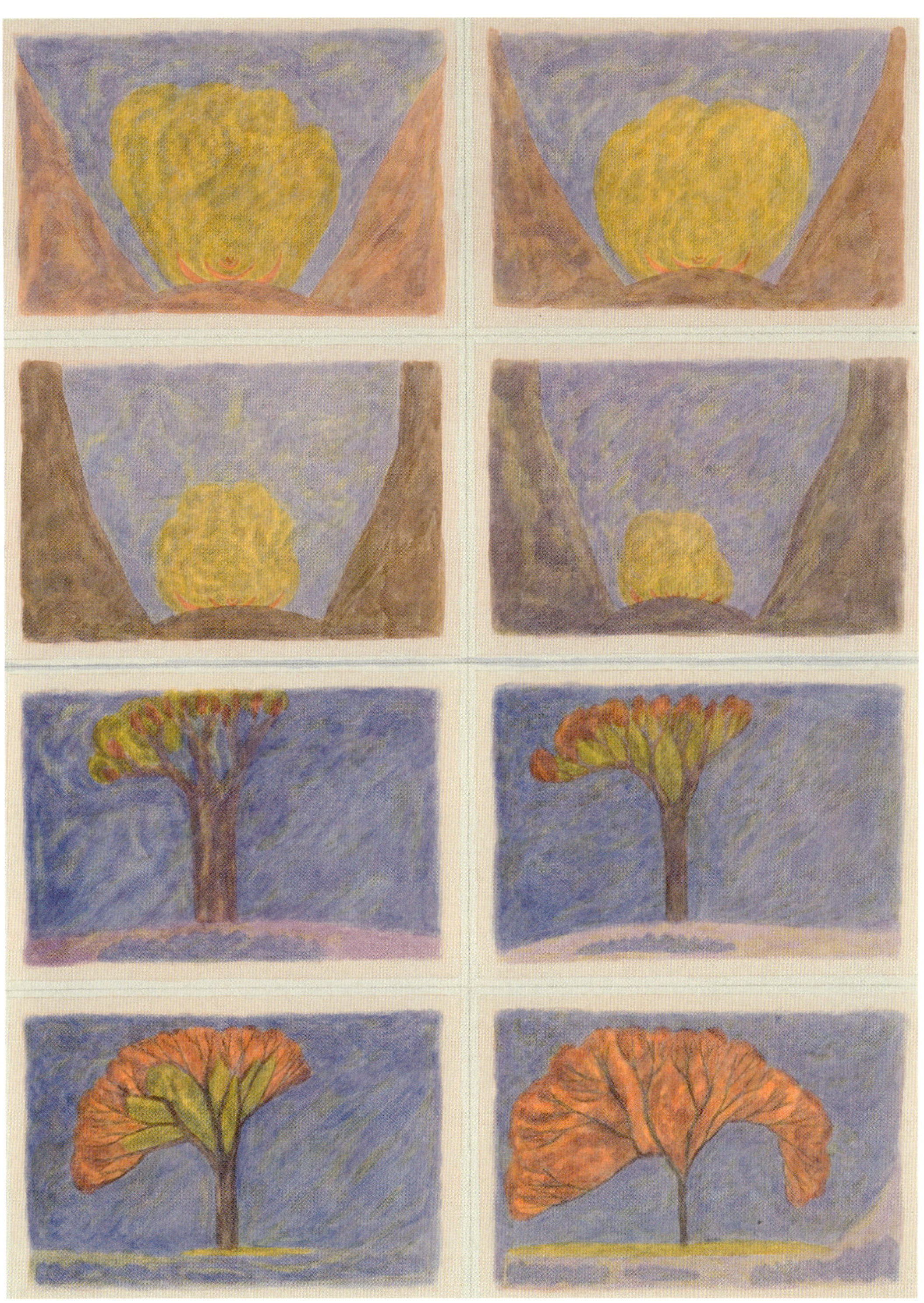

Plate 29: The series continues with the addition of blue and violet.

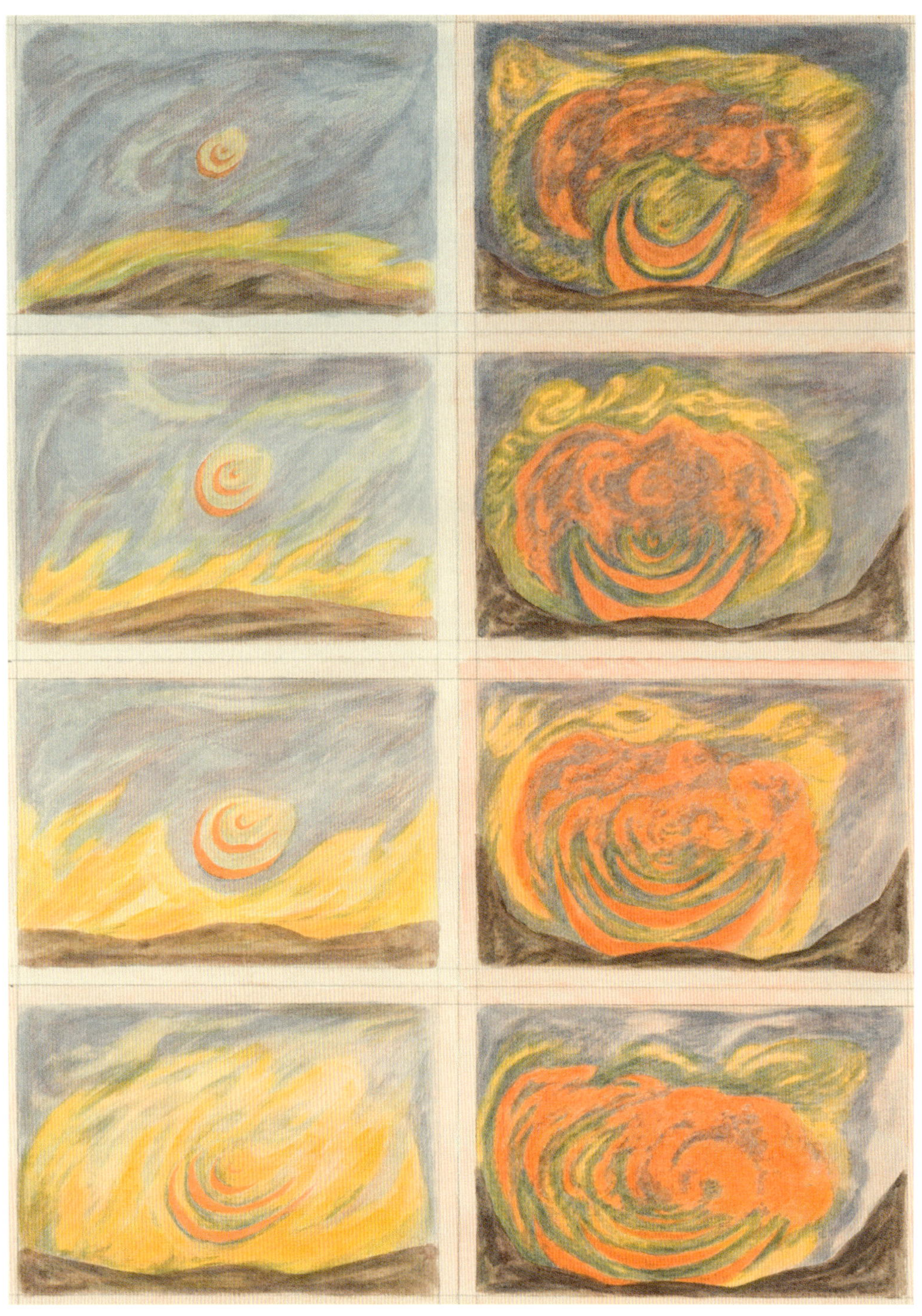

Plate 30: *Moonrise* changes to *Moonset* as the background colour changes from cool blue to warm violet in eight steps. The colours are the same in each picture and are painted in the same order: brown, red, yellow, blue, violet.

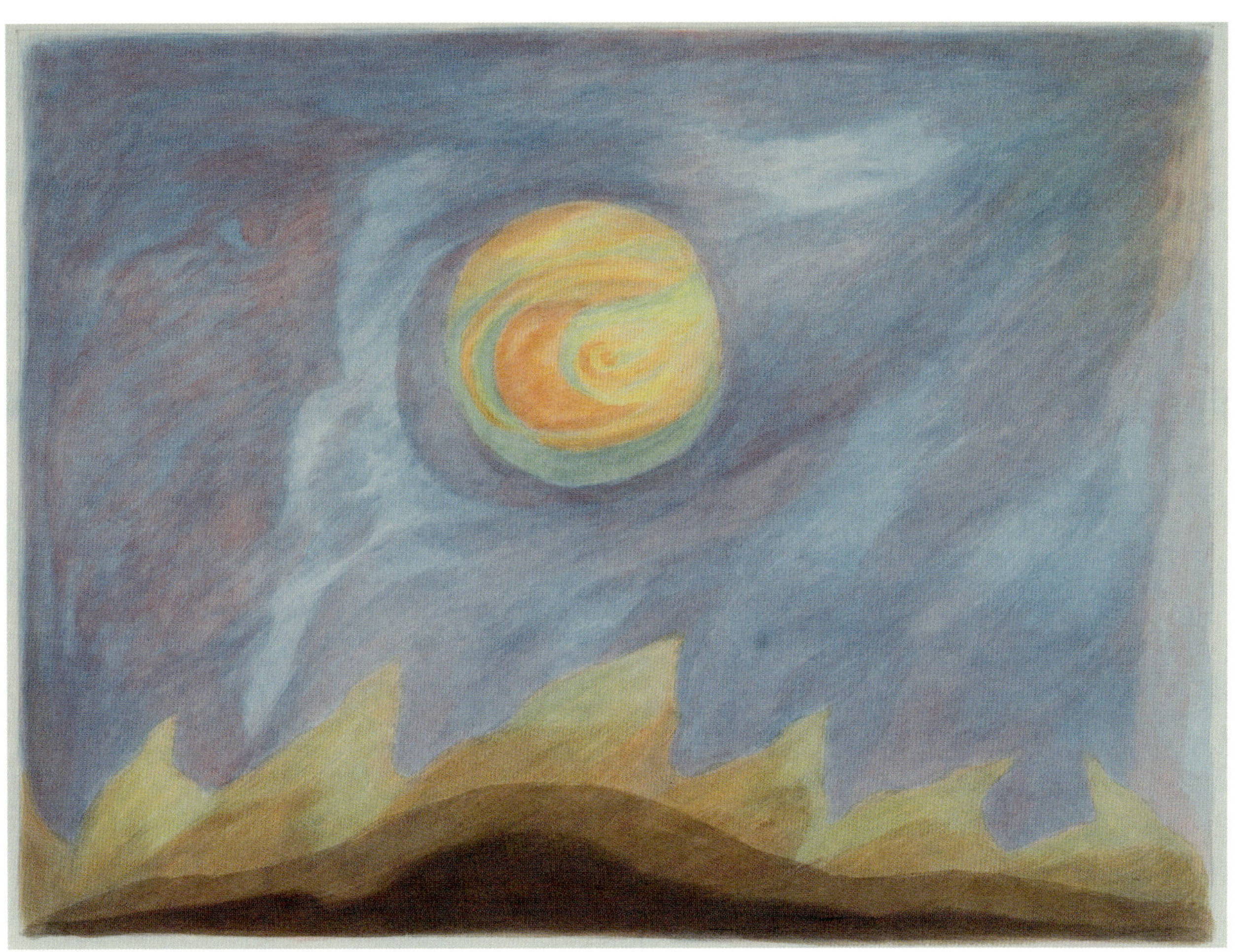

Plate 31: *Moonrise* painted on a blue background.

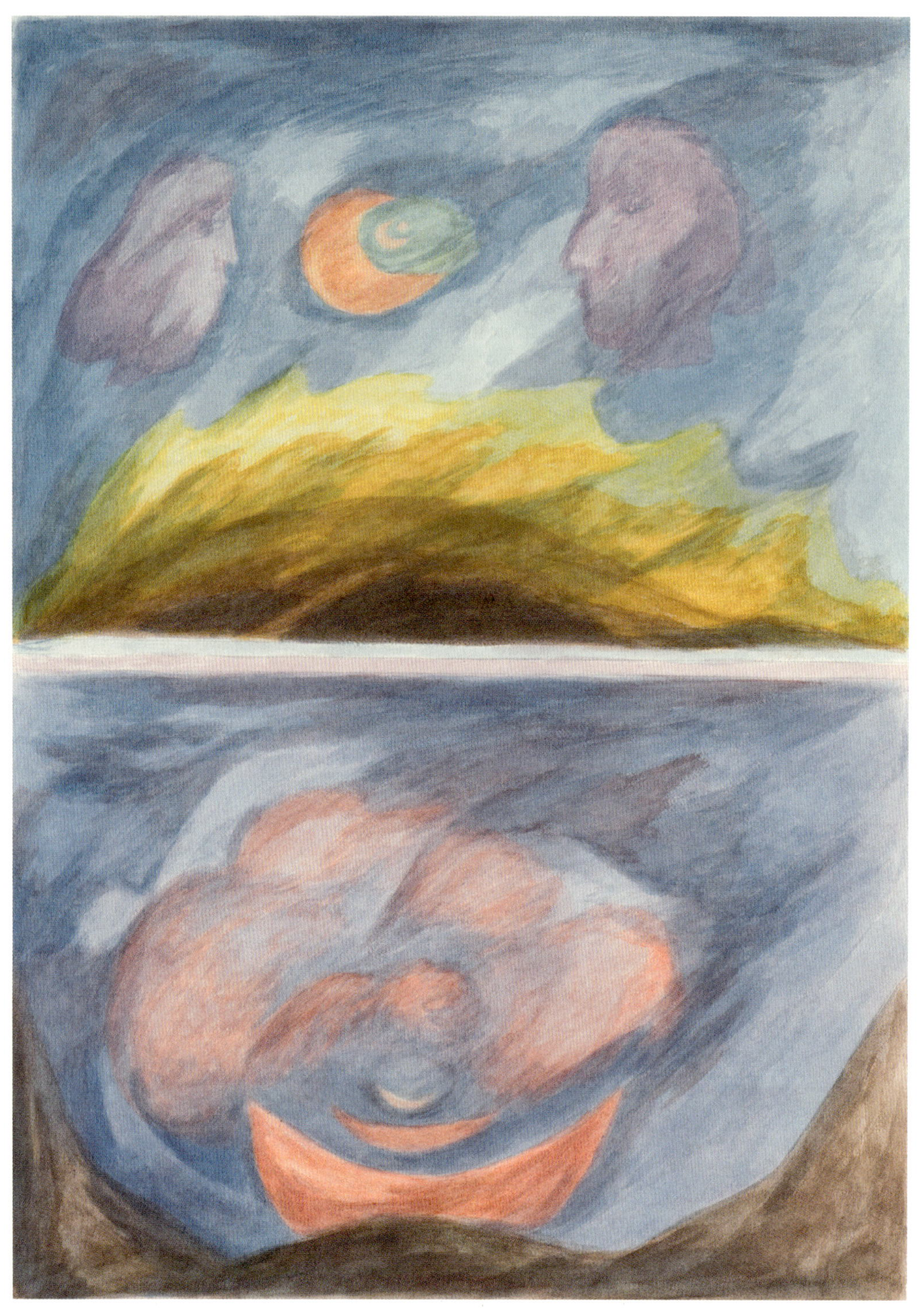

Plate 32: *Moonrise* is painted on a blue background; *Moonset* painted on a violet background.

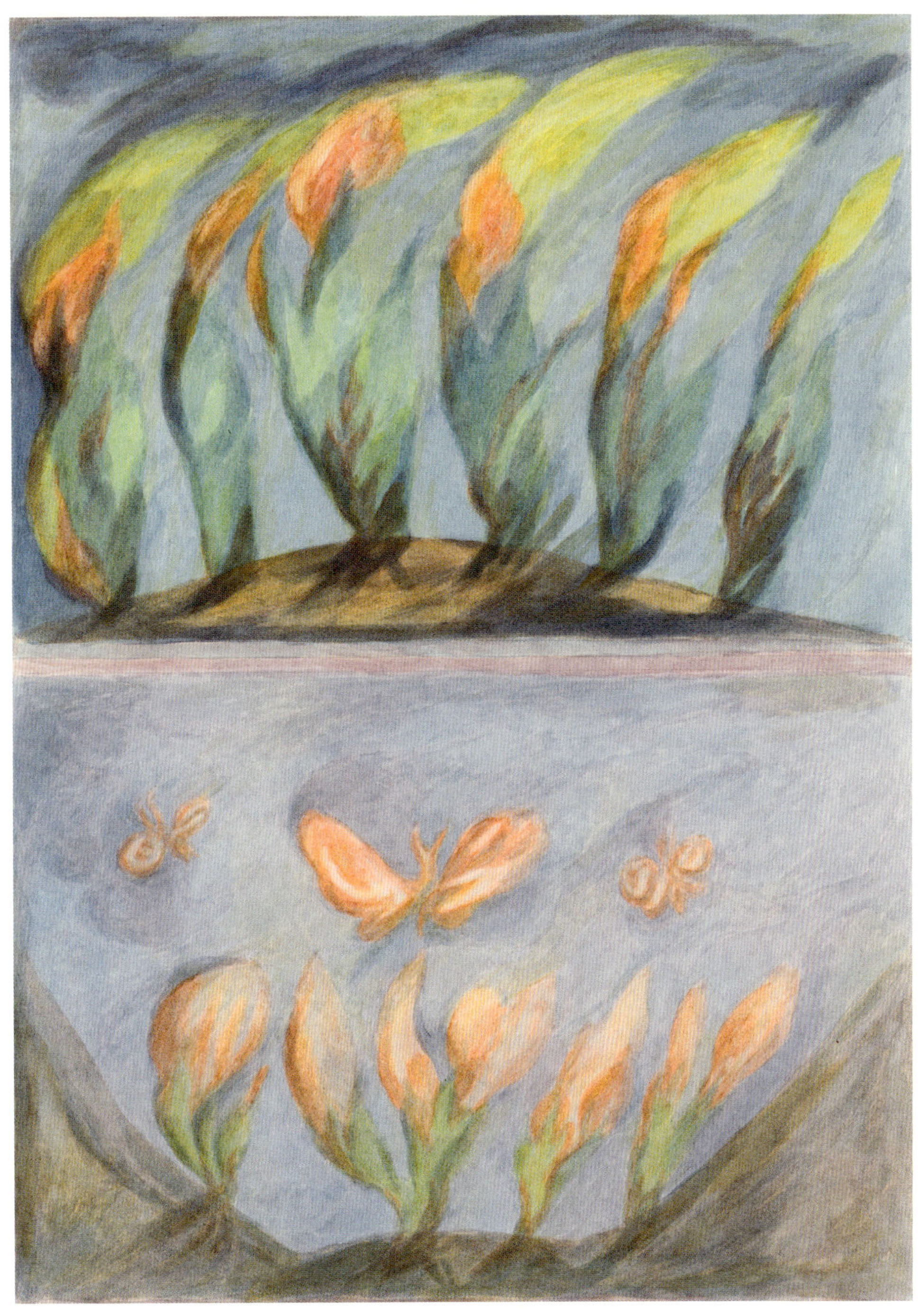

Plate 33: *Fruiting and Blossoming Trees.* This is a companion picture to *Moonrise* and *Moonset* on the opposite page, painted at the same time and with the same background colours. Red is the second colour after brown in the moon motifs; green is the second colour after brown in the tree/plant motifs.

LIFE IN COLOUR

Artists of the early 20th century were searching for life in colour; one could mention Wassily Kandinsky, or Franz Marc with his paintings of animals. Earlier, landscapes of William Turner and John Constable were inspired by elemental life in light, water and clouds. The Impressionists explored pure colour phenomena in the landscape but remained attached to the outer visual impression. Even Paul Cézanne's 'colour landscapes' are never altogether free of the place where they were painted.

Gerard Wagner's teacher at St Ives, John Anthony Park, was a Post Impressionist who had studied at the Académie Colarossi in Paris. He taught his young pupil how to create colour compositions out of what he saw in the landscape. But Gerard Wagner was obviously searching for something more. If not, how could he have been so moved when he first saw the paintings of Henni Geck (large watercolours painted after the Motif Sketches of Rudolf Steiner) shortly after arriving in Dornach. He described the effect these paintings had on him in the monograph *The Art of Colour.*[21] He refers to himself here in the third person:

> '[...] These pictures made a mighty impression on the young painter: a saturation of colour, a quality of light and a certainty of form which he had never seen before in watercolour painting. The motifs were not taken from the world he had known up until then. He found them unique with captivating effect, complete in their formation and without a trace of naturalism – a totally new art of painting.'

He also described the impression the Nature Mood Sketches made on him when he was a pupil at Henni Geck's school and first became aware of what distinguished them from other art works. The students had to transpose the pastel sketches into watercolour which meant observing them closely in the process:[22]

> '[...] Through careful observation and inner participation of the colours, lines and forms of these images a strong interest was awakened. I was aware of something that could be expressed more or less in the following words: "Why, they are organisms, they are exact without arbitrariness or chance. They are not naturalistic yet the details of their forms and gestures are so harmoniously integrated with one another as only in a living organism in which every detail is a necessary part of the whole: they do not portray, they *live.*" This was an impression which gradually became more conscious as the years went on.'

And many years later towards the end of his life Gerard Wagner spoke during an interview in his usual modest way about creative life in the colours themselves:

> 'It is the colour's own life that we are trying to discover, how form arises through colour. Not that one takes a form from nature but rather one notices when experiencing colour that nature is in the colours themselves, and that they are really creative forces [...]. Following Rudolf Steiner one would say the colours have created the whole of nature: mineral, plant, animal, human being – and if one could work out of these forces, a new art of painting could come about. This in the long run is what we want to search for. We can, of course, only achieve the very first step.'[23]

He was convinced that Rudolf Steiner's drawings and paintings were a revelation of elemental life, of the life forces existing behind the physical world. In the monograph *The Art of Colour* he wrote the following:[24]

> 'Whoever attempts to tread this path can come to the conviction that the indications of Rudolf Steiner, if they are sufficiently penetrated and experienced, can lead one to grasp the creative formative forces of colour and to create within this life element without harming it. By giving us such pictures of life shaped by colour, Rudolf Steiner has set goals for a far future of painting.'

Rudolf Steiner spoke of the connection between art and elemental life as a task for the future in the lecture *The Creative World of Colour* as follows:[25]

> '[...] We are really already living in a time when we must begin to immerse ourselves in the spiritual activity at work in natural forces, that is to say, in the spiritual forces behind nature, if we are not to lose all contact with the world. [...] Art must endeavour to penetrate again into elemental life. Art has spent long enough merely observing and studying nature, and trying to solve nature's riddles [...]. Art will arise anew when one learns how to enter into elemental life with one's innermost soul. People may argue that this ought not to be done, but this argument is only prompted by laziness. Human beings will either live their way with full humanity into the forces of the elements and accept the soul and spirit in the creations around them, or art will become more and more the product of individual hermits; in which case we might come across things of considerable interest with regard to the psychology of individuals, but it will never be able to attain to what can come about solely through art. [...]'

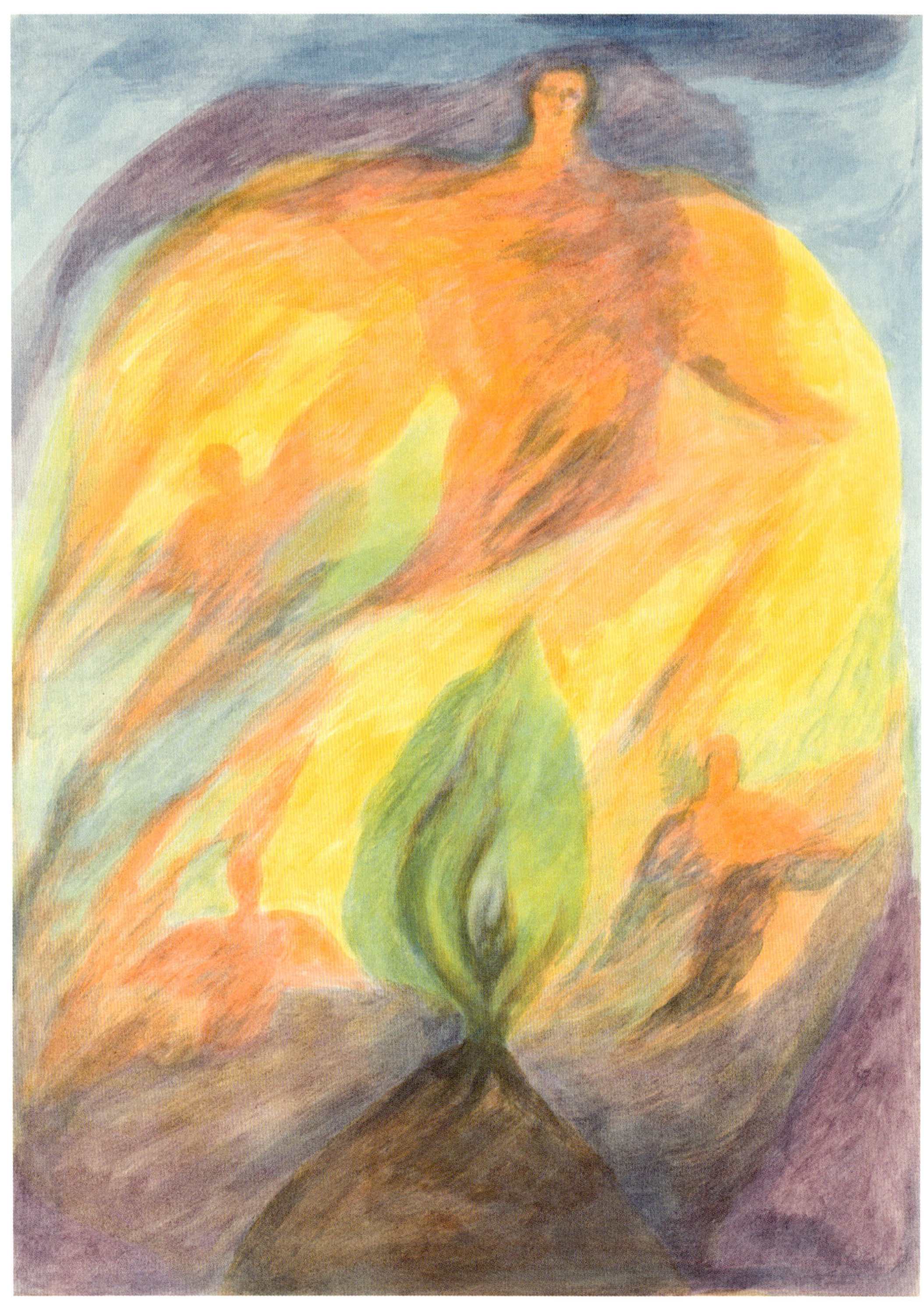

Plate 34: New Life

MOTIFS ARISING FROM THE TRAINING SKETCHES

Plant Life

The theme of the plant appears again and again in the various epochs of Gerard Wagner's work. Not surprising perhaps as he had a great love of plants, and events recounted from his early childhood show his deep interest in nature and in the colours he saw in nature. And, as a highly perceptive young child, he was already noticing the effect the colour of cherry blossom or of the mysterious little violet was having on his feelings.

Working with the nine Nature Mood Sketches gave Wagner insight into the connection between colour and nature processes. The polarities of sunrise and sunset, moonrise and moonset, and the processes of growing and fading led him into the living dynamics of colour. He found, for example, that the Nature Mood sketch of the *Fruiting and Blossoming Trees* with its predominant colours of black, green and red was a key to exploring how the motif of the plant comes about. The motif sketch of the *Archetypal Plant* was an invaluable guide which led Gerard Wagner to further research, as he explained in the introduction to the folder *A Glance into Nature's Workshop*:[26]

> 'Through a number of years the writer of this introduction gave a holiday painting course for teachers of a Waldorf school. The request of a teacher, that in the following year we should busy ourselves with the painting of plants, led to a closer study of the question: how in the plants do form and colour hang together, and how can the latter cause the former?
>
> How also does the colour of the 'ground' and of the 'surroundings' influence the form of the plant, how does the form of the flower change as its colour changes, and how in turn does this influence the form of the leaf? This and other questions led to numerous rows of experimental paintings.
>
> What gave the details of this work their unity, was the attempt to understand and build up artistically – (as well as this at present was possible) –the 'Archetypal Plant', as Rudolf Steiner has painted it, and then to follow its development into the single forms. Watching how these changed through the gradual changing or concentration of one colour, or through changing the colour of the background; carrying the 'Archetypal Plant' through all kinds of colour moods as a colour problem – such were the steps.

The realisation, which grew out of these experiments, that with colour one really is dealing with nature-forces, was the impulse which led during nearly twenty years to some hundreds of colour experiments. [...]'

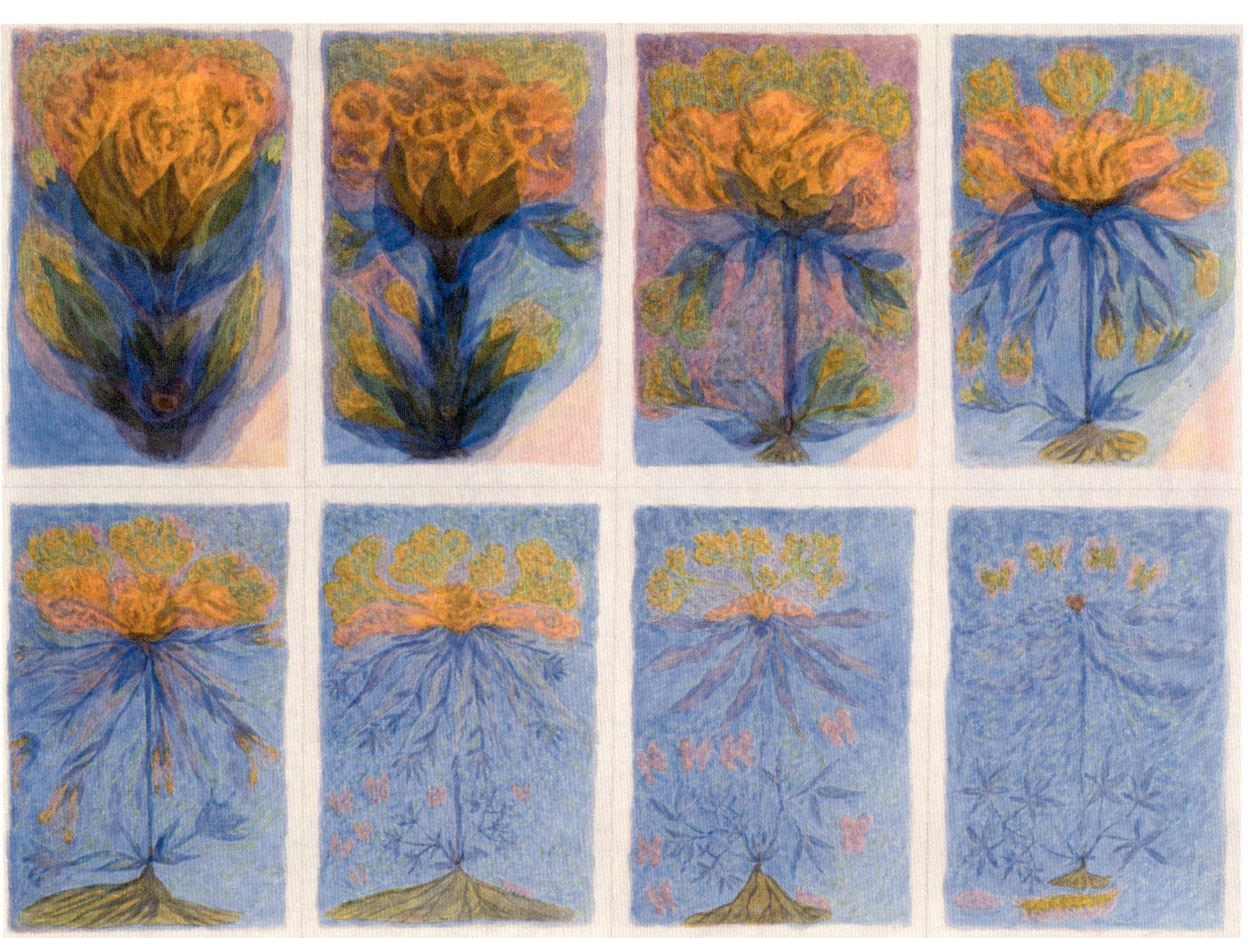

Plate 35: Archetypal Plant Metamorphosis

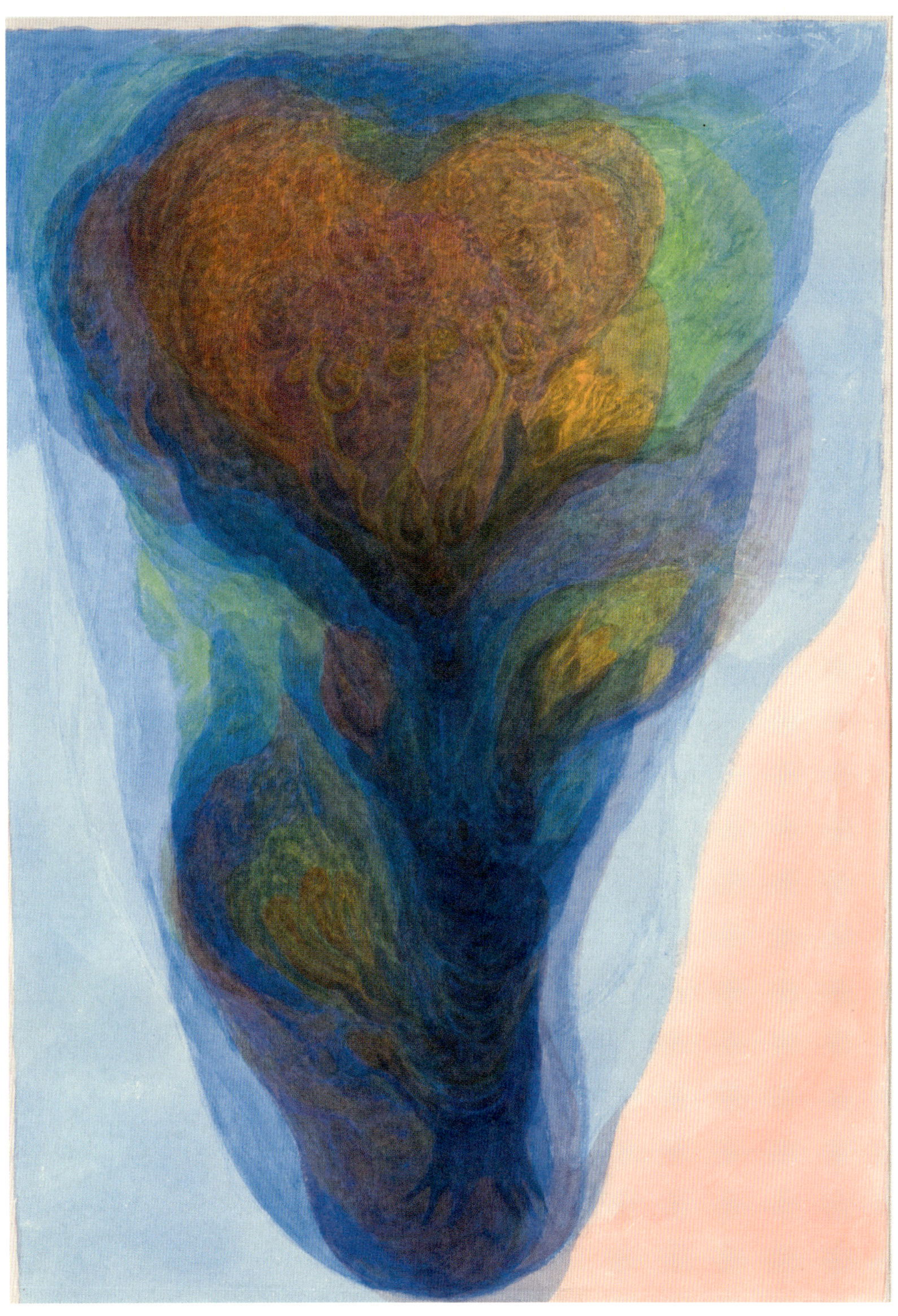

Plate 36: *Archetypal Plant*

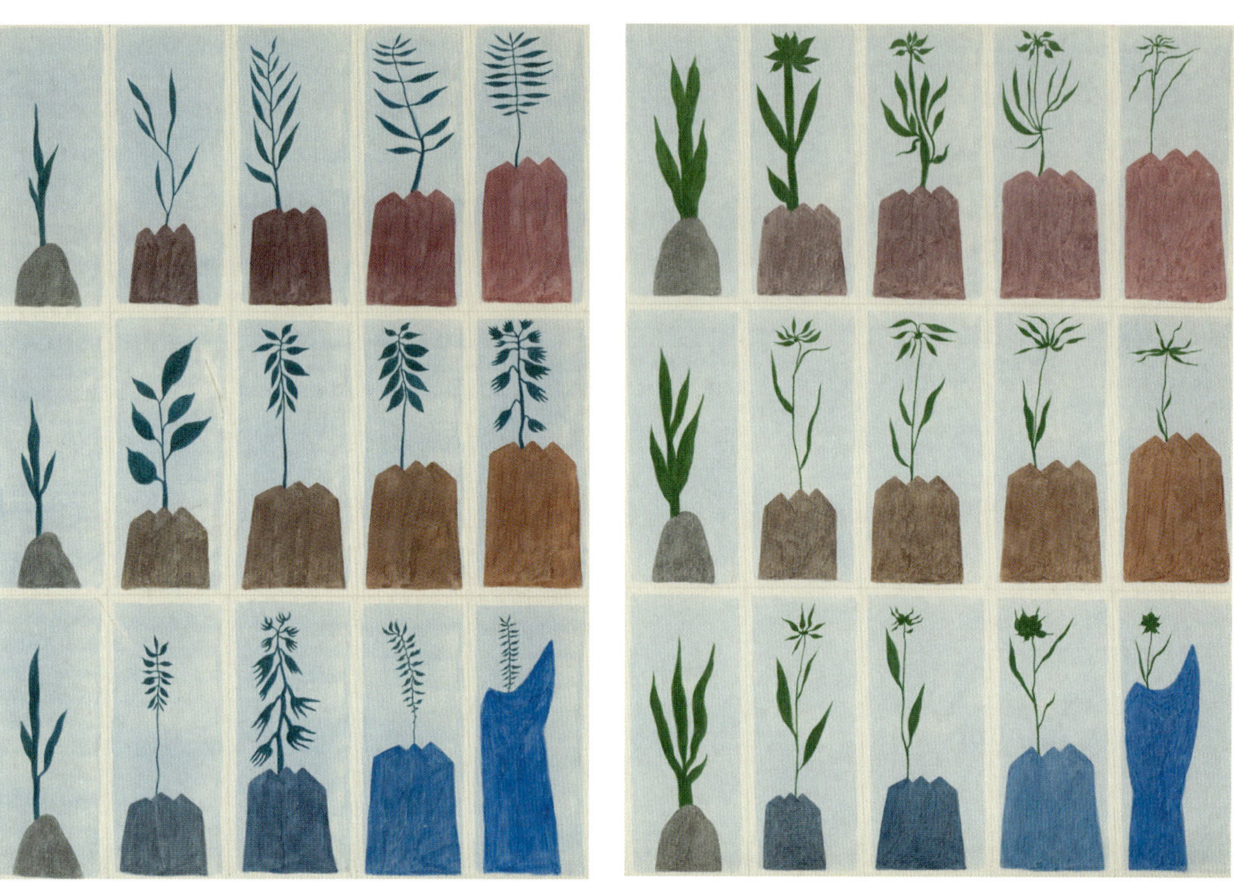

Plates 37–38: In this experiment the colour of the black/grey mound, seen in the first picture of each row, changes in four steps. In the first row, cool red (carmine) is added to the black; in the second row, warm red (vermillion), and in the third row blue. Cool green is the second colour in picture a. A warmer green is the second colour in picture b.

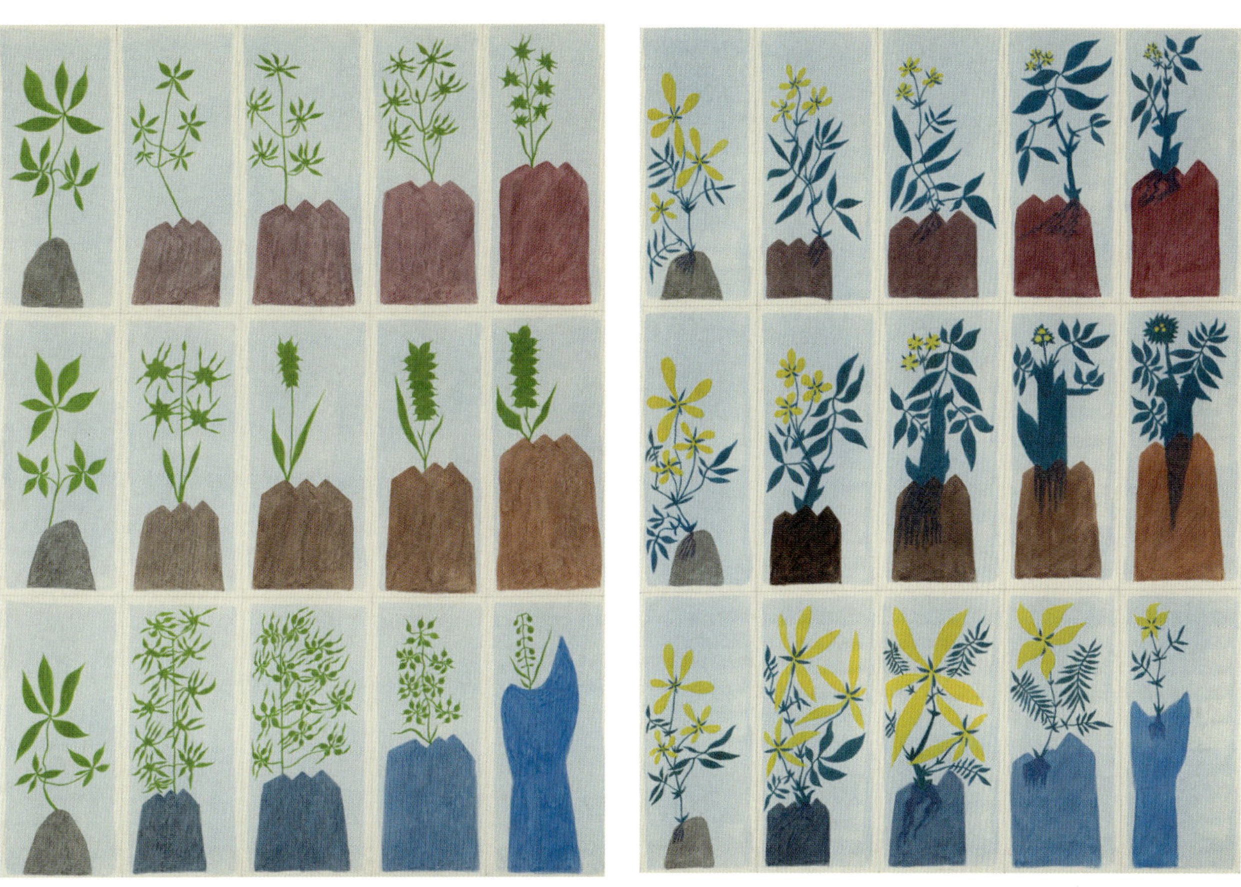

Plate 38: Yellow-green is the second colour in picture c.
Yellow is the second colour in picture d. Green is the third colour.

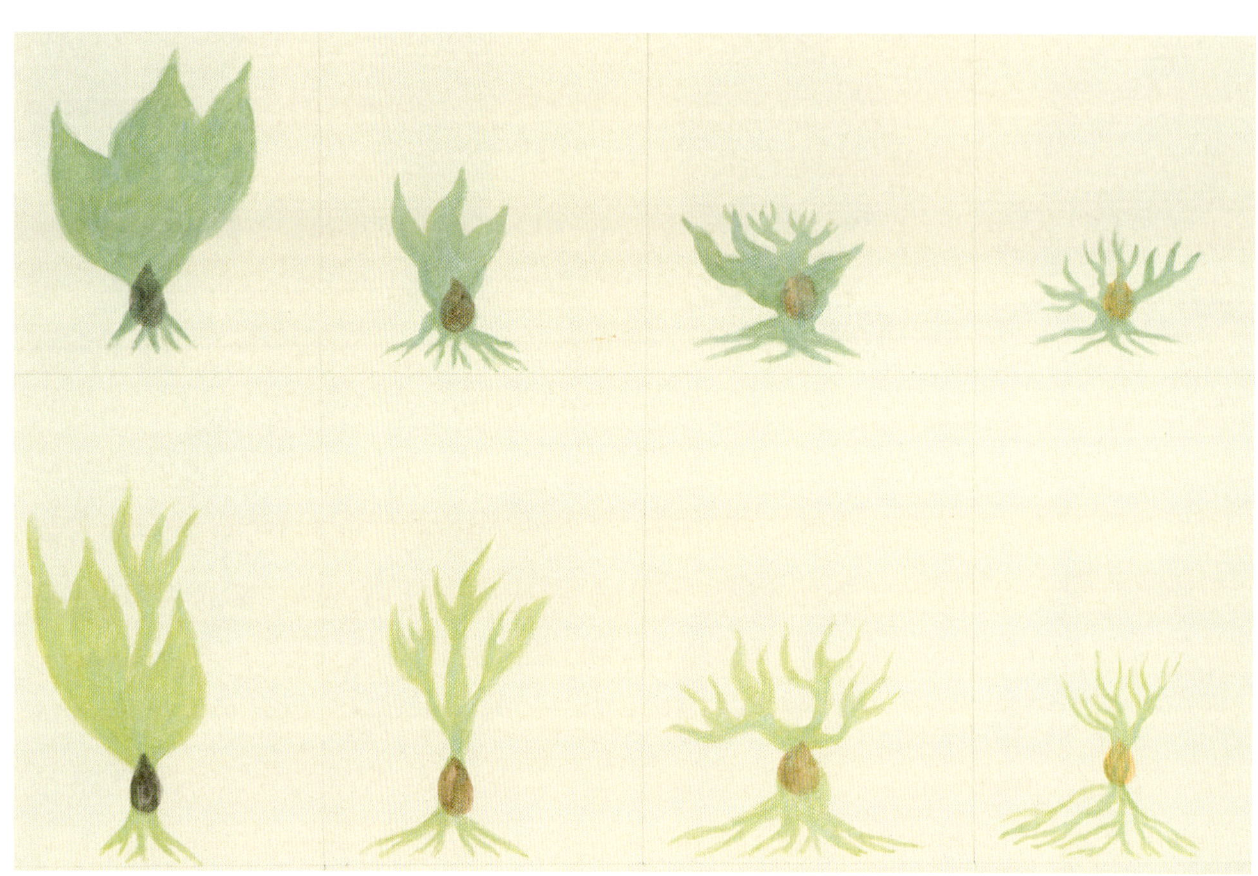

Plate 39: In this sequence the seed colour changes from black to brown, to red-brown and to yellow-brown. The form of the plant changes according to the tension between the green and the seed colour.

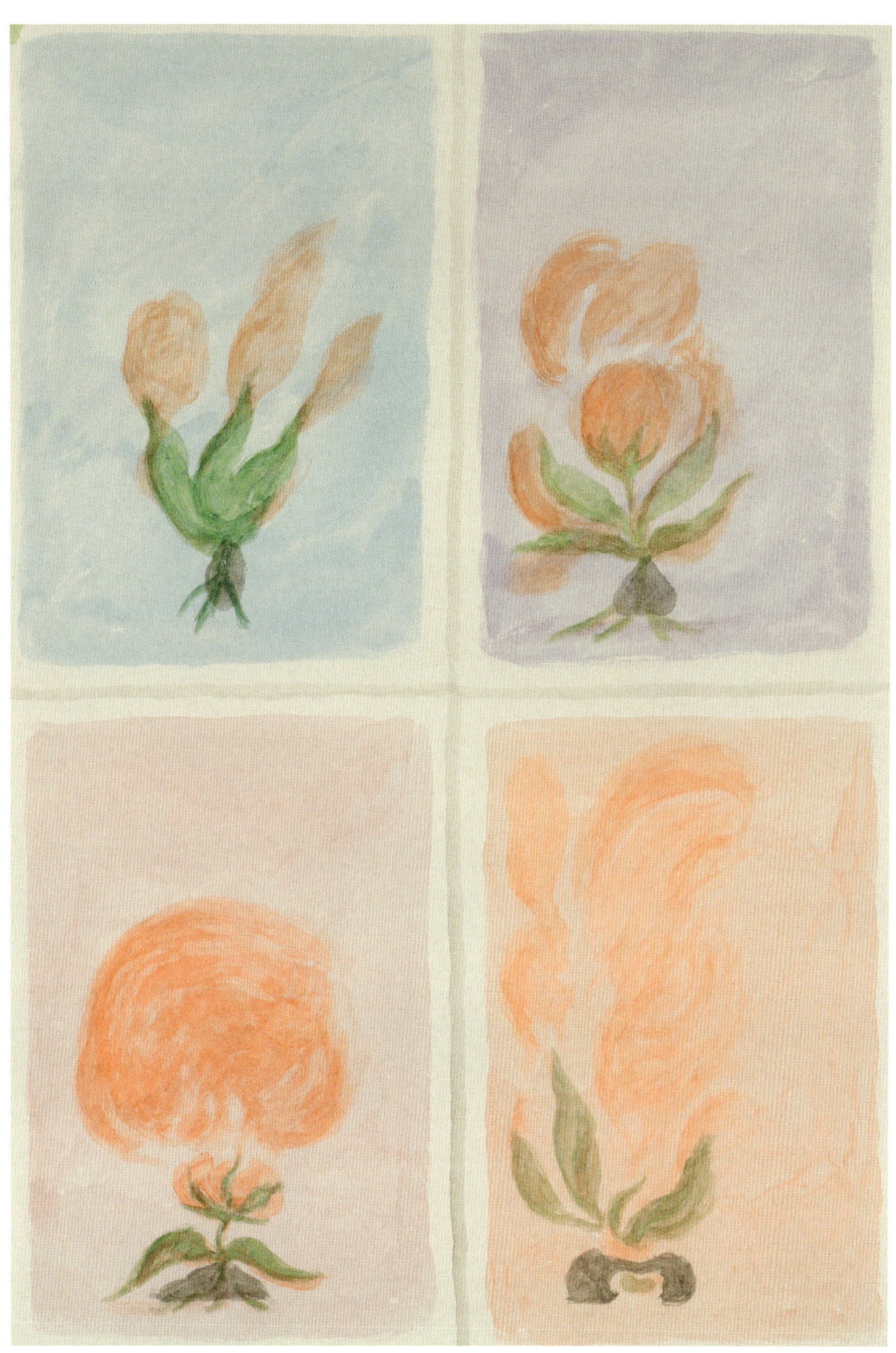

Plate 40: Red enlivens the green and black and seeks its place in relation to them.

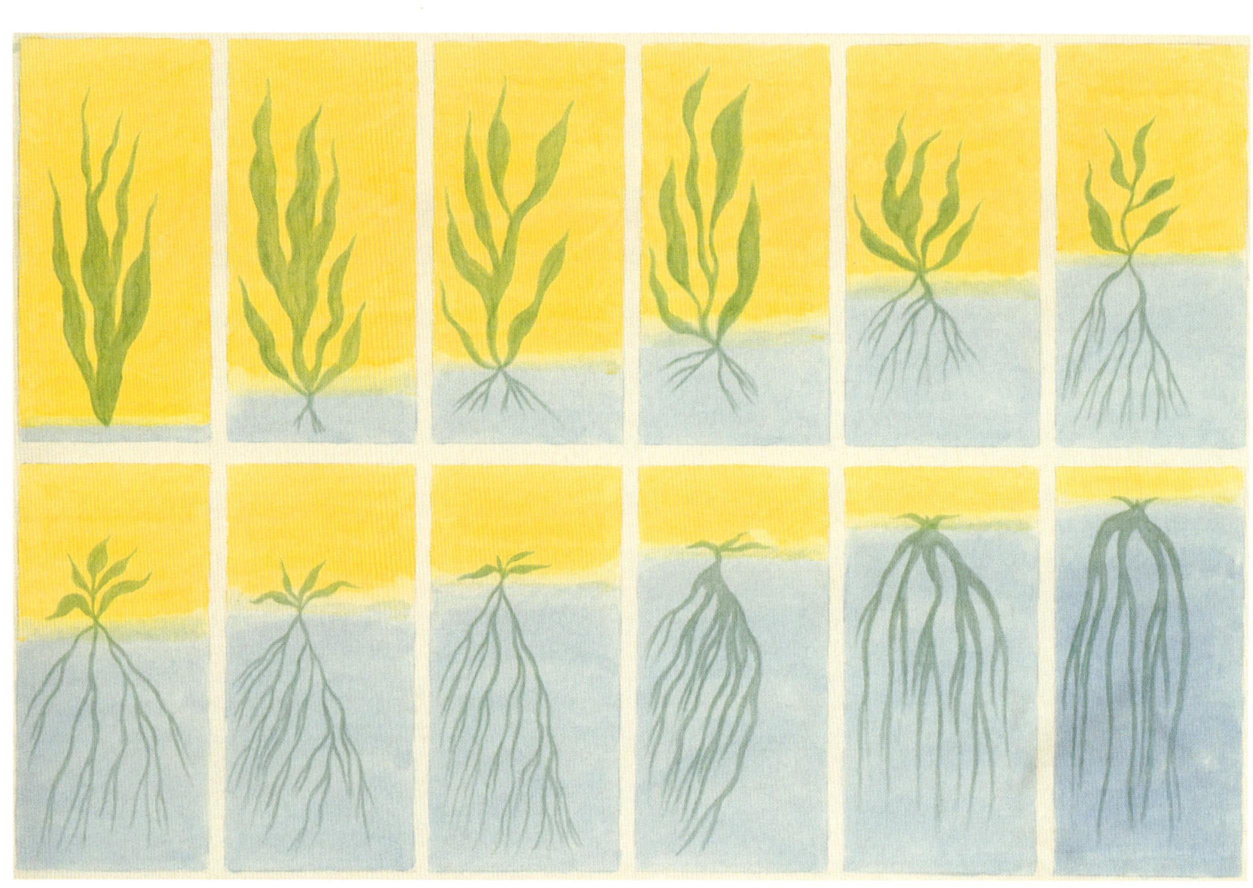

Plate 41: Green seeks balance between the yellow and blue background colours.

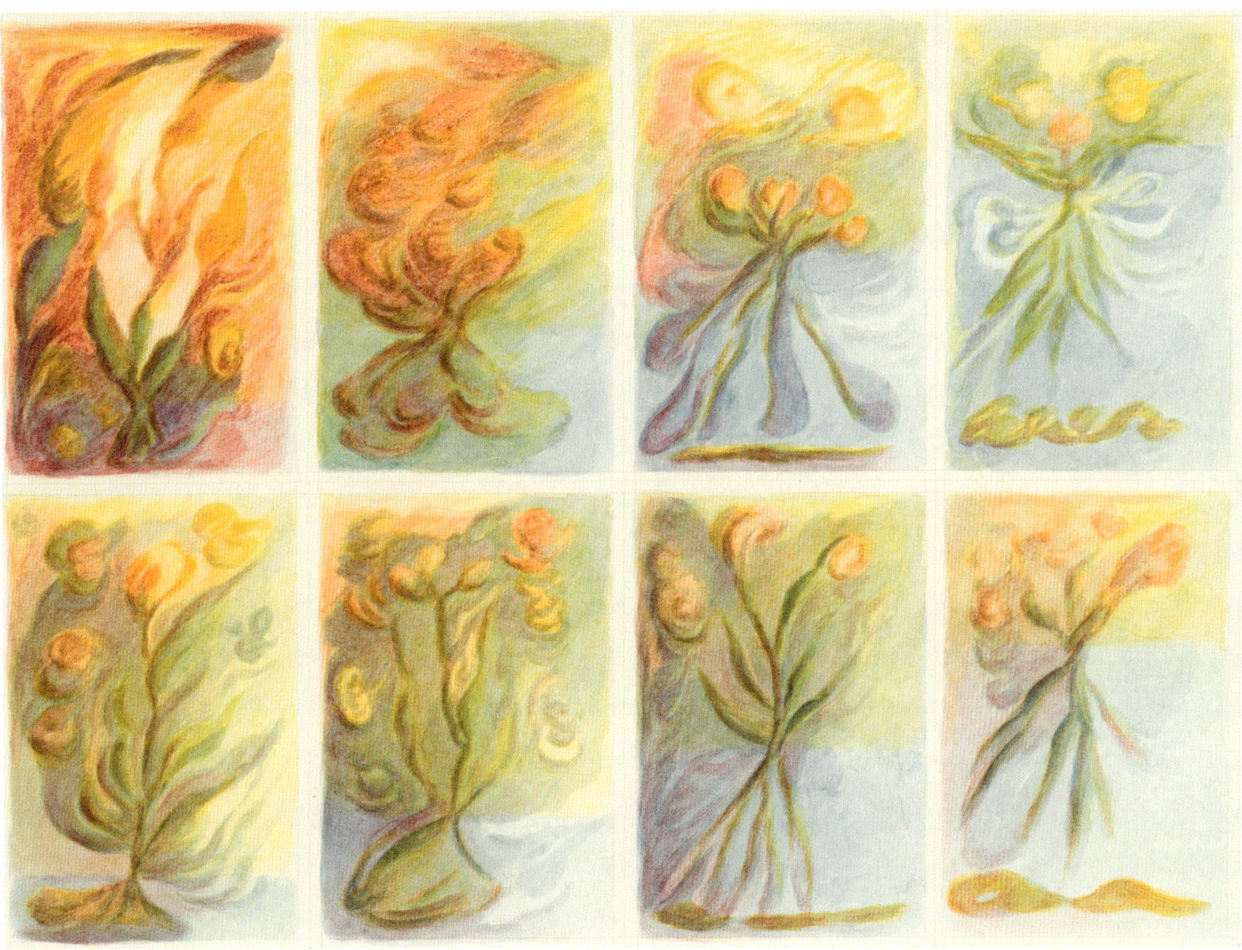

Plate 42: A painting developed from the experiment on the opposite page with yellow and blue background colours.

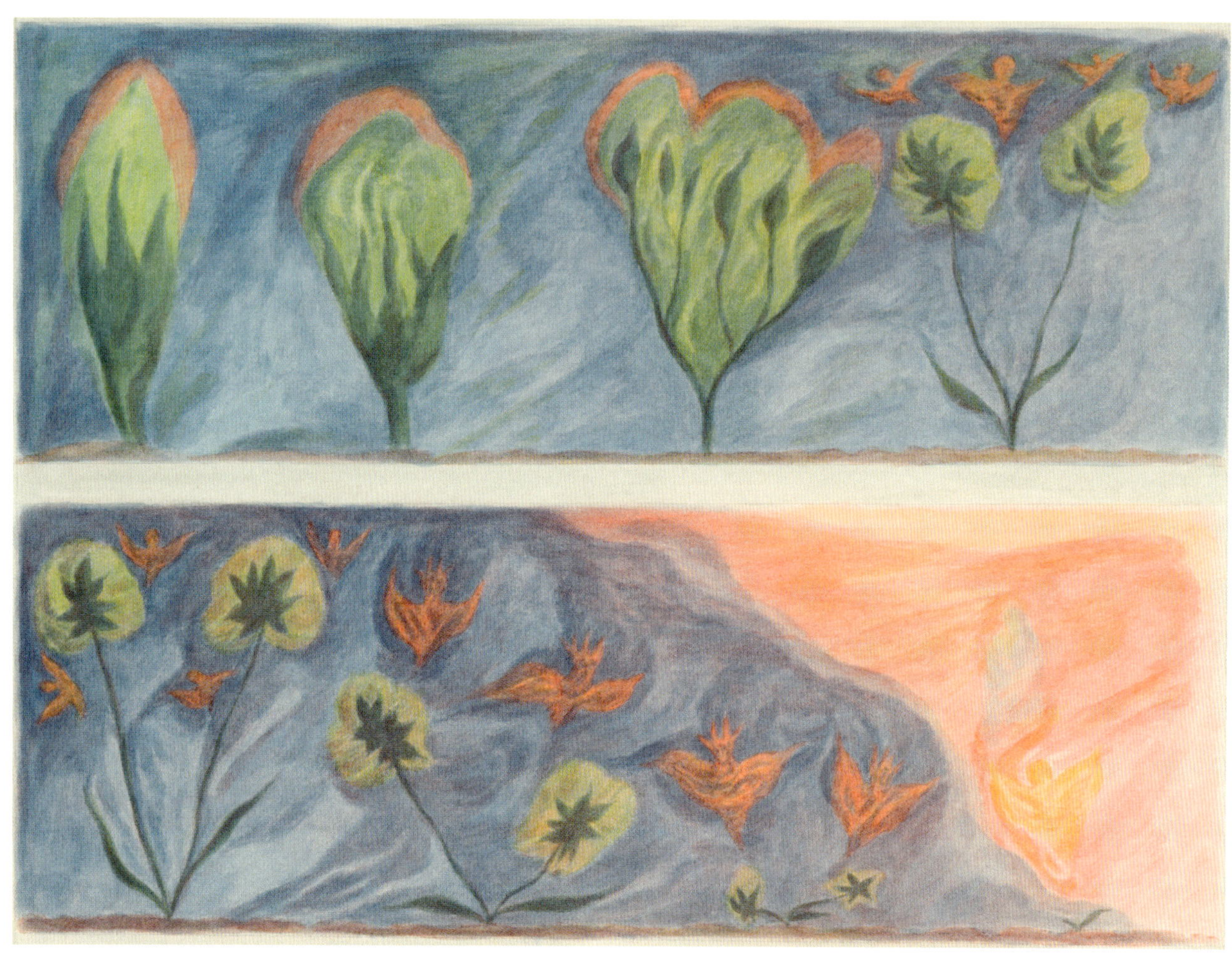

Plate 43: Gerard Wagner made experiments with the wide format used by Rudolf Steiner in the two Friedwart Sketches *Trees in Storm* and *Trees in Sunny Air.* This format allows a vista suitable for showing more phases of plant development in continuous movement. The background colour changes from cool to warm colours.

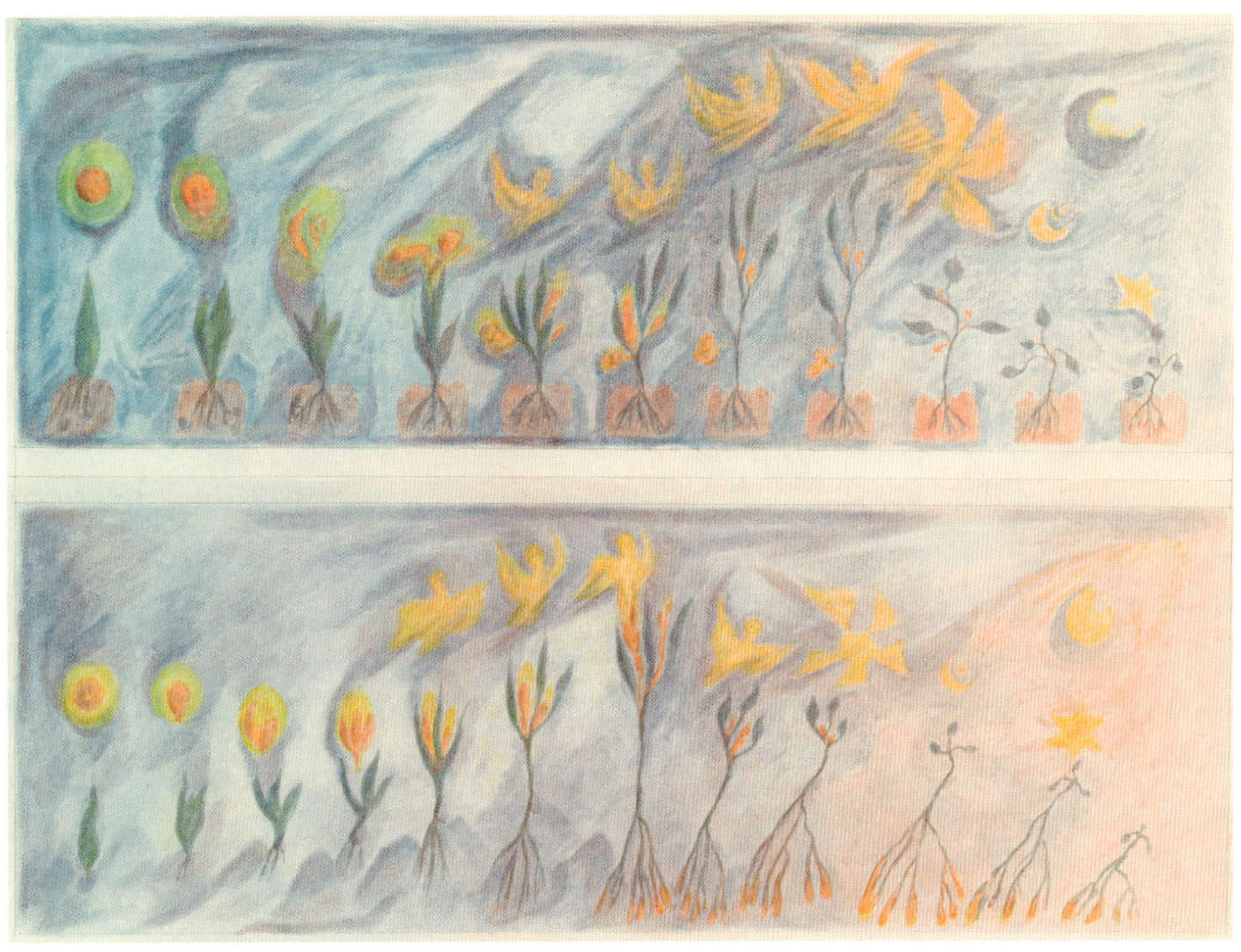

Plate 44: The background colour changes from cool colours to warm colours. Red, which begins as the colour of the blossoms, moves downwards to the roots of the plant.

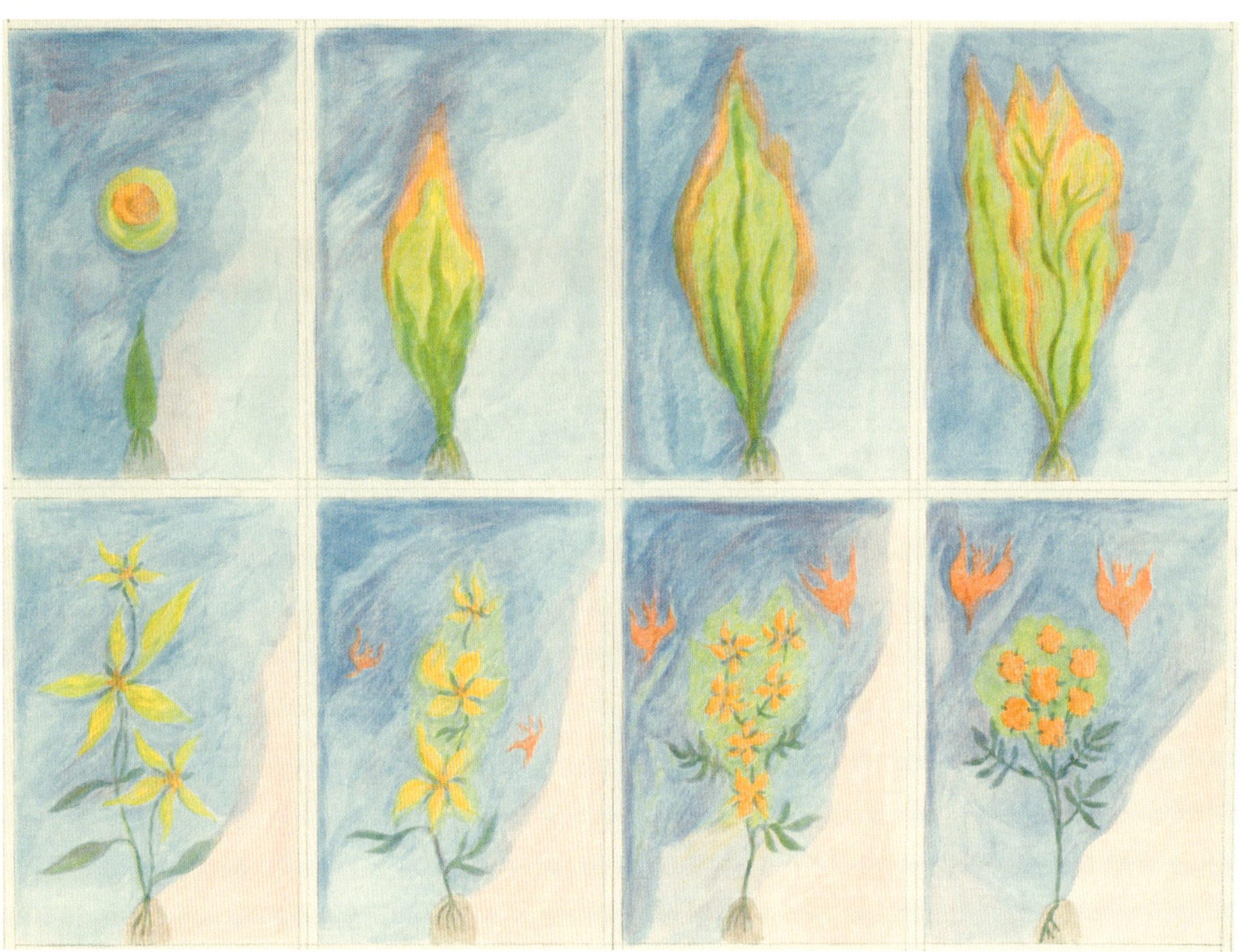

Plate 45: The colour of the blossoms changes from yellow to warm red.

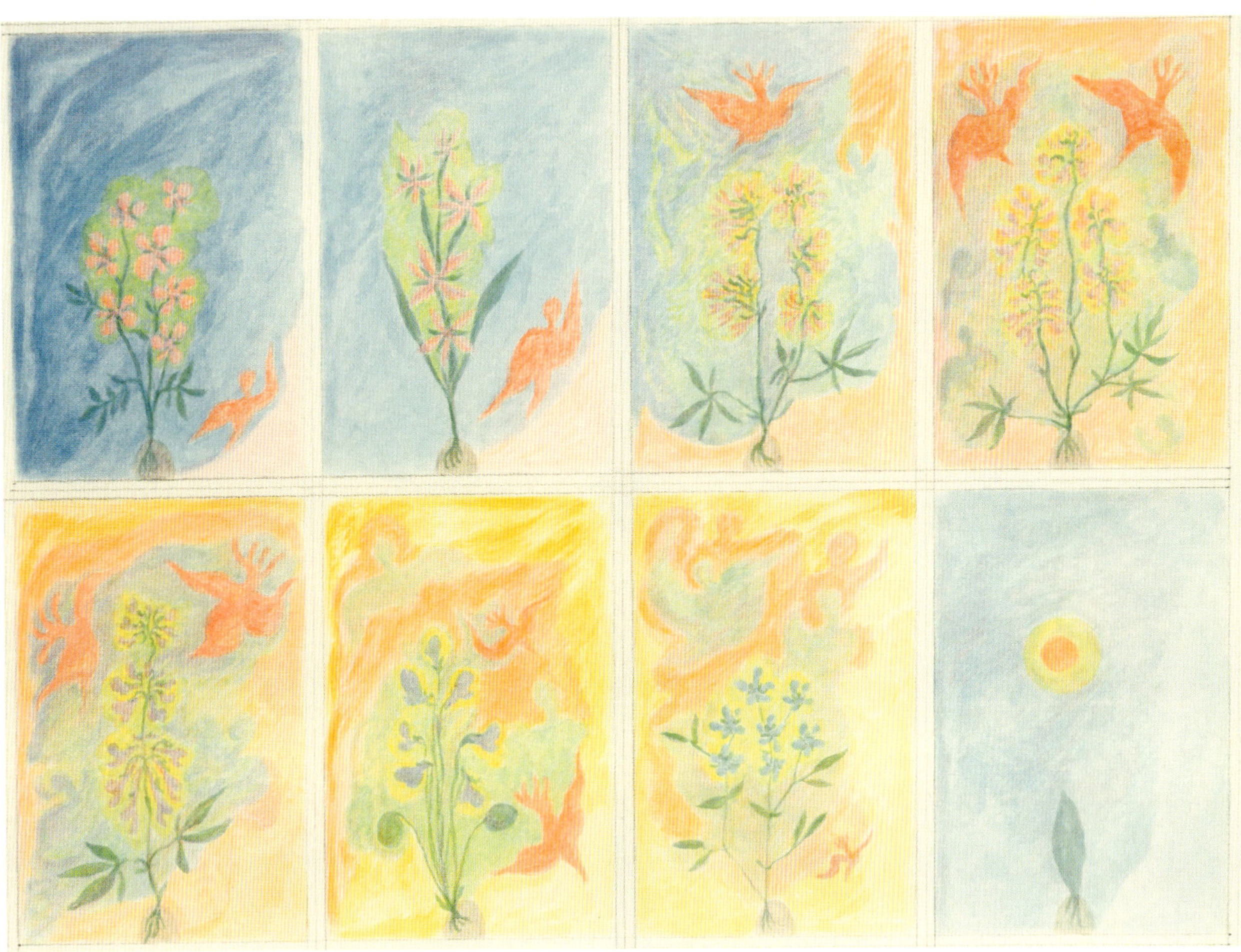

Plate 46: The colour of the blossoms changes from cool red to blue.

In addition to the indications gleaned from the *Archetypal Plant* painting, Gerard Wagner studied the sketch of the *Elemental Beings* which gave him insight into the colours and forms of the four types of elemental beings, and of the elements in which they live. The elemental beings work in all stages of plant growth: in root development, leaf formation, blossoming, fruiting, wilting, and seed formation. Wagner painted many single plants showing the activities of the elementals but also sequences showing their workings during the process of plant metamorphosis. The four elemental beings involved in this interaction are:

Fire-spirits (salamanders)
Beings of air and light (sylphs)
Water-spirits, (undines)
Root-spirits (gnomes)

A series of seven paintings (plates 47 to 53) shows a metamorphosis that begins with the dormant seed and ends with new seed formation.

1 In the first painting the seed is surrounded by the gnomes who are preparing it for growth. The higher beings above in red and yellow are taking an active part in the process.
2 The second painting shows heightened activity: the gnomes with their hands of red 'flame' are causing the green shoot to grow upwards. The undines hovering nearby seem to be eager to begin their work. The crystal world – the home of the gnomes–is visible below.
3 In the third painting the green shoot grows further with the help of the undines who are active around the leaves of the plant. The gnomes have finished their work for the time being. Above, the sylphs and salamanders are visible.
4 In the fourth painting the action of the sylphs is visible in the light-filled area around the top of the plant where the forming of the blossom begins.
5 In the fifth painting the plant has grown further; the salamanders can be seen above in their characteristic curved shapes of red.
6 In the sixth painting the plant has reached its full growth – a stage of completion has been reached. All four elemental beings are visible; it is as if they are celebrating together, rejoicing in their creation.
7 In the seventh painting the plant withers and new seeds are formed.

Rudolf Steiner describes what is made visible through this sequence of paintings in the wonderful lecture series *Man as Symphony of the Creative Word.*[27] Some excerpts from lecture seven, beginning with the activity of the root-spirits, are quoted here:

> 'Plants send their roots into the ground. Anyone who can observe what they really send down and can perceive the roots with spiritual vision [...] sees how the root-nature is surrounded, woven around, by elemental nature spirits. And these elemental spirits, which an old clairvoyant perception designated as gnomes and which we may call the root-spirits, can actually be studied by an imaginative and inspirational world-conception [...].
>
> [...] The gnomes are really that element within the earth which represents the extra-terrestrial, because they must continually reject a growing together with the earthly; otherwise, as single beings, they would take on the forms of the amphibian world. And it is just from what I may call this feeling of hatred, this feeling of antipathy towards the earthly, that the gnomes gain the power of driving the plants up out of the earth. With the fundamental force of their being they unceasingly thrust away the earthly, and it is this thrusting that determines the upward direction of the plant's growth; they push the plants up with them. It accords with the nature of the gnomes in regard to the earthly to allow the plant to have only its roots in the earth, and then to grow upwards out of the earth-sphere; so that it is actually out of the force of their own original nature that the gnomes push the plants out of the earth and make them grow upwards.'

Rudolf Steiner then moves on to a description of the elemental beings active in water, air and warmth:

> 'Once the plant has grown upwards, once it has left the domain of the gnomes and has passed out of the sphere of the moist-earthly element into the sphere of the moist-airy, the plant develops what comes to outer formation in the leaves. But in all that is now active in the leaves other beings are at work, water-spirits, elemental spirits of the watery element, to which an earlier instinctive clairvoyance gave among others the name undines. Just as we find the roots busied about, woven-about by the gnome- beings in the vicinity of the ground, and observe with pleasure the upward-striving direction which they give, we now see these water-beings, these elemental beings of the water, these undines in their connection with the leaves.
>
> These undine beings differ in their inner nature from the gnomes. [...] They live in the etheric element of water, swimming and swaying through it [...] They dream their own existence. And in dreaming their own existence they bind and release, they bind and disperse the substances of the air, which in a mysterious way they introduce into the leaves [...] So the plant develops its leaf-growth, and this mystery is now revealed as the dream of the undines into which the plants grow.

To the same degree, however, in which the plant grows into the dream of the undines, does it now come into another domain, into the domain of those spirits which live in the airy-warmth element, just as the gnomes live in the moist-earthly, and the undines in the moist-airy element. Thus it is in the element which is of the nature of air and warmth that those beings live which an earlier clairvoyant art designated as the sylphs. Because air is everywhere imbued with light, these sylphs, which live in the airy-warmth element, press towards the light, relate themselves to it. They are particularly susceptible to the finer but larger movements within the atmosphere.

[...] After it has passed through the sphere of the sylphs, the plant comes into the sphere of the elemental fire-spirits. These fire-spirits are the inhabitants of the warmth-light element. When the warmth of the earth is at its height, or is otherwise suitable, they gather the warmth together. Just as the sylphs gather up the light, so do the fire-spirits gather up the warmth and carry it into the blossoms of the plants.

[...] You see, when up above the fire-spirits are circling around the plant and transmitting the anther-pollen, they have only one feeling, which they have in an enhanced degree, compared to the feeling of the sylphs. The sylphs experience their self, their ego, when they see the birds flying about. The fire-spirits have this experience, but to an intensified degree, in regard to the butterfly world, and indeed the insect world as a whole. And it is these fire-spirits which take the utmost delight in following in the tracks of the insects' flight so that they may bring about the distribution of warmth for the seed-buds. In order to carry the concentrated warmth, which must descend into the earth so that it may be united with the ideal form, in order to do this the fire-spirits feel themselves inwardly related to the butterfly-world, and to the insect-creation in general. Everywhere they follow the tracks of the insects as they buzz from blossom to blossom. [...]'

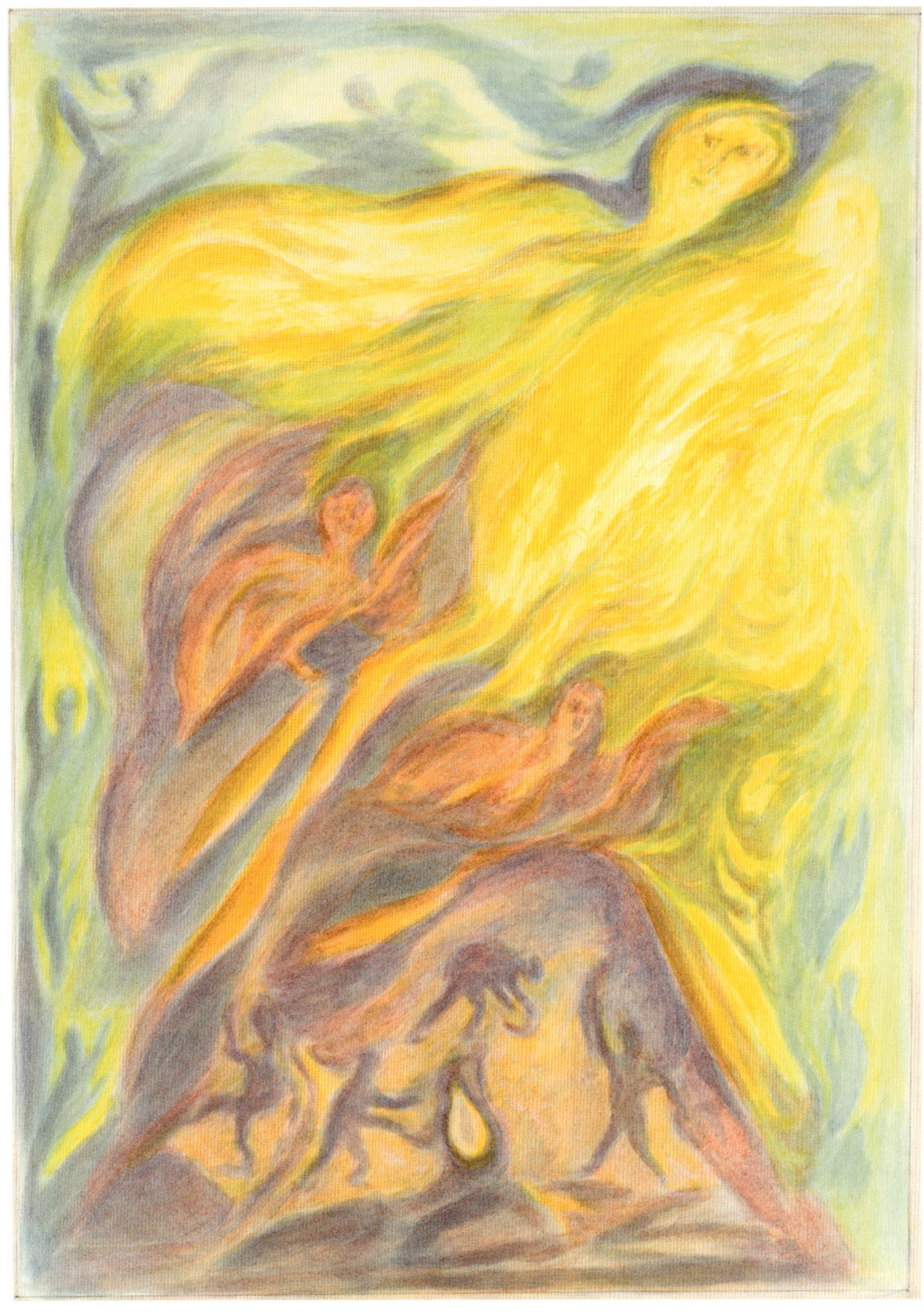

1

Plates 47–53: Plant and Elemental Beings Metamorphosis

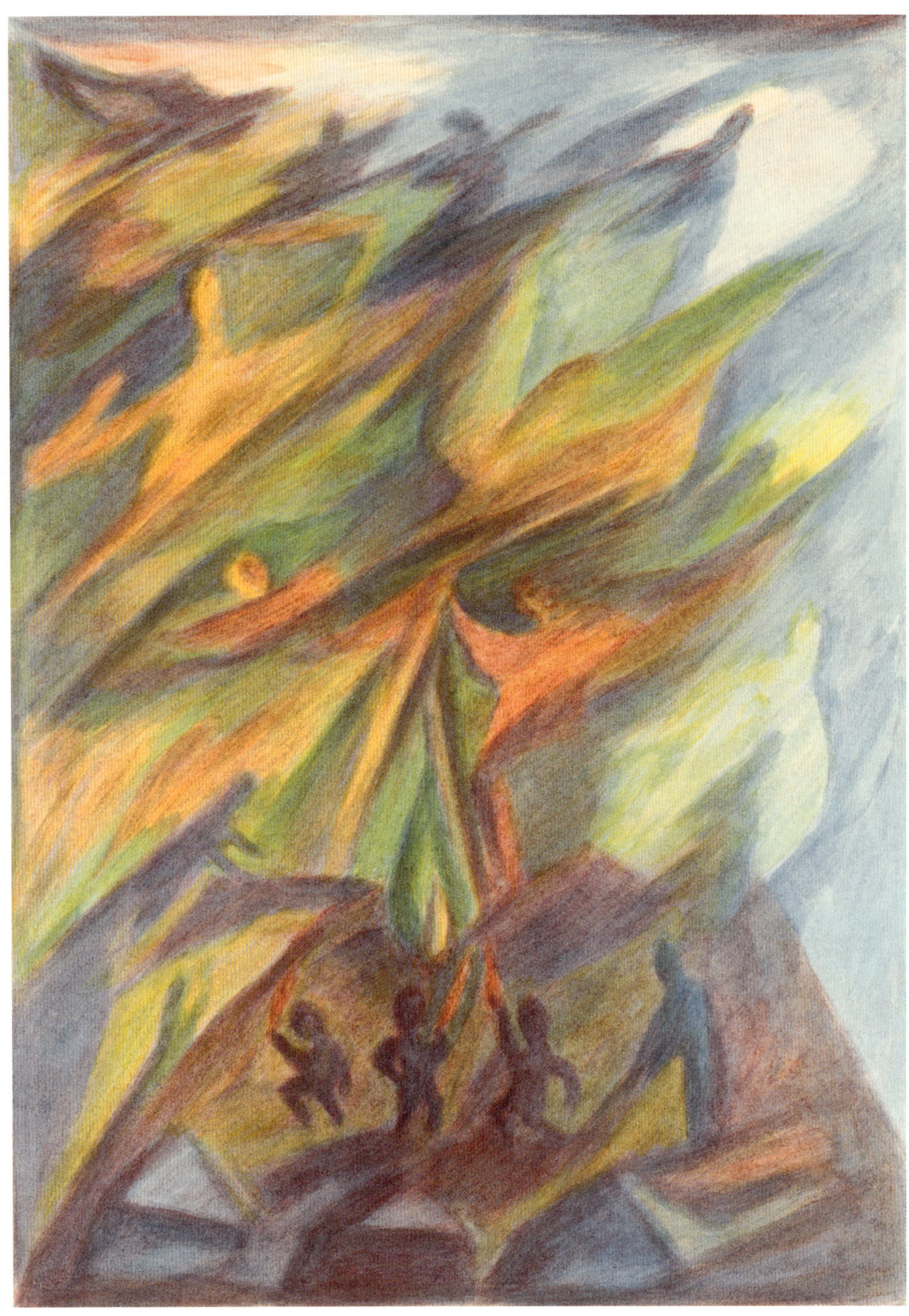

2

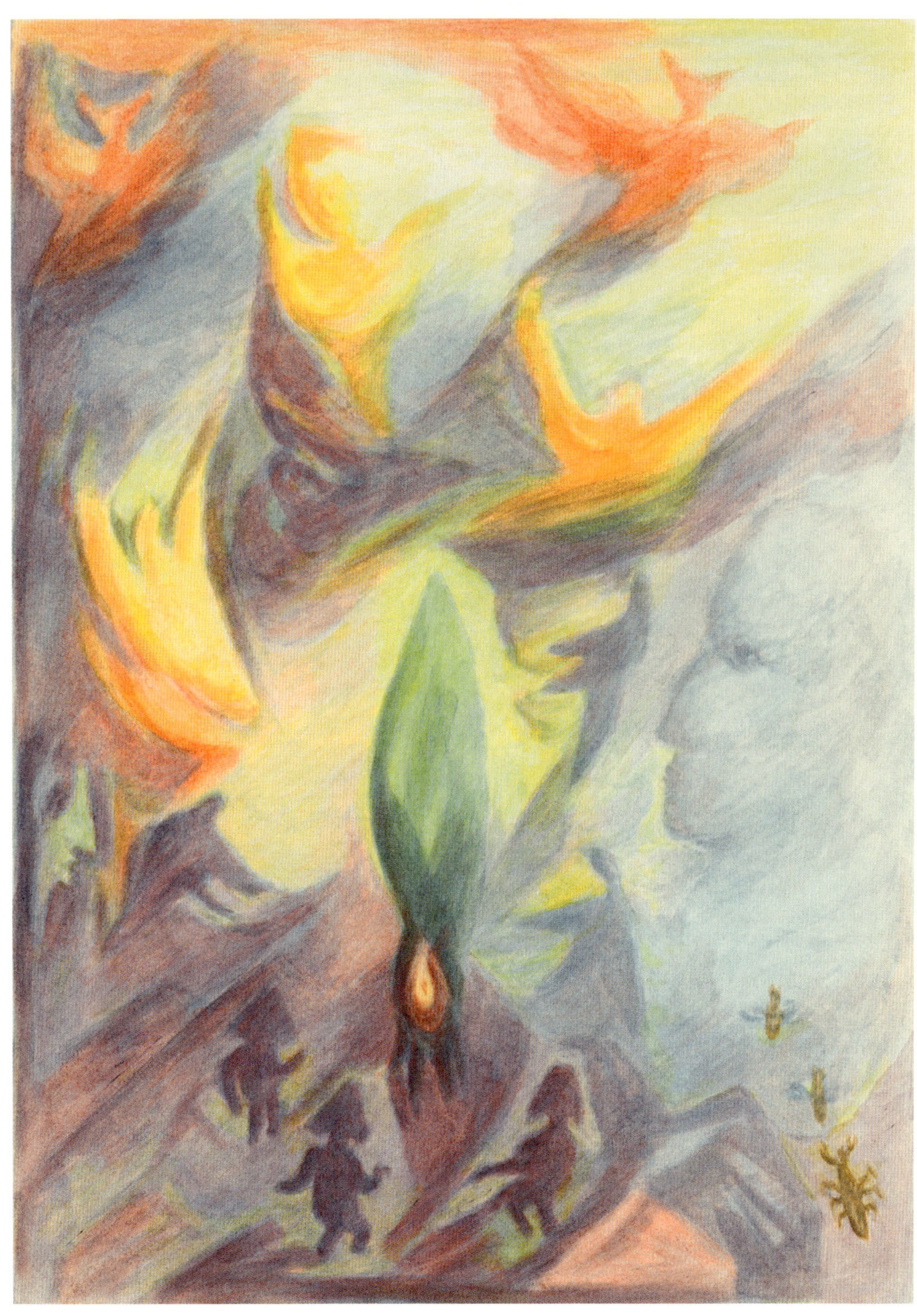

3

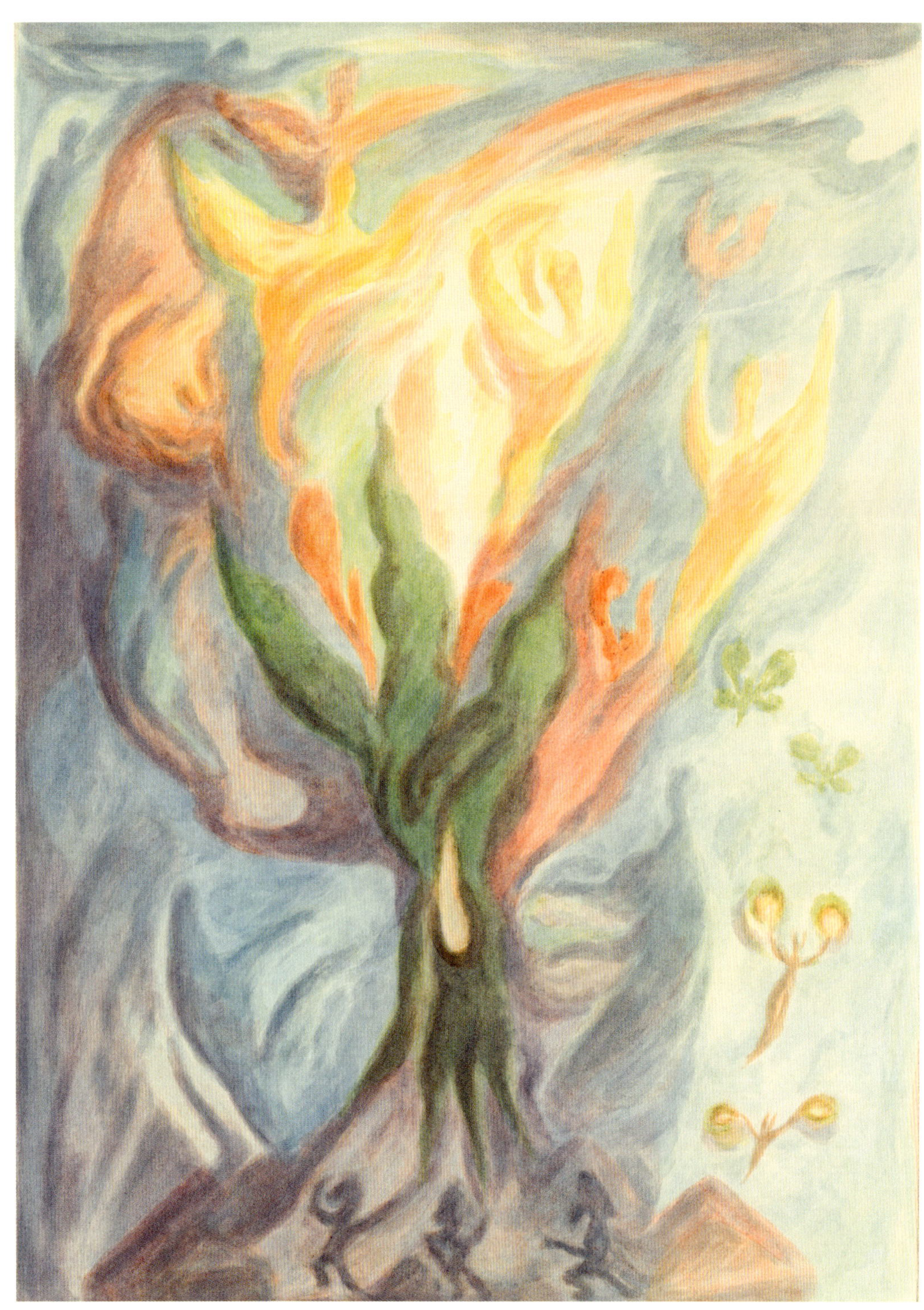

4

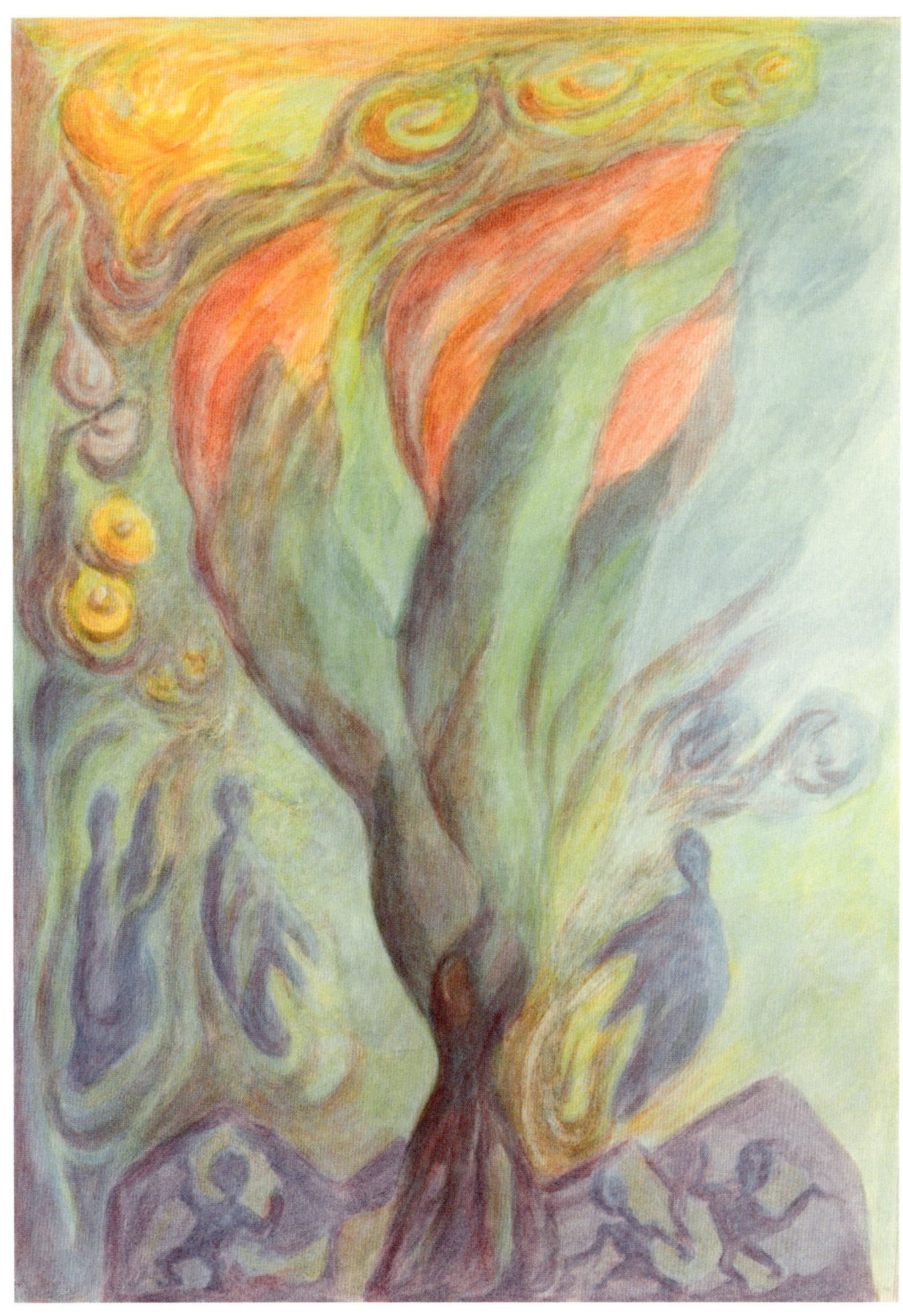

5

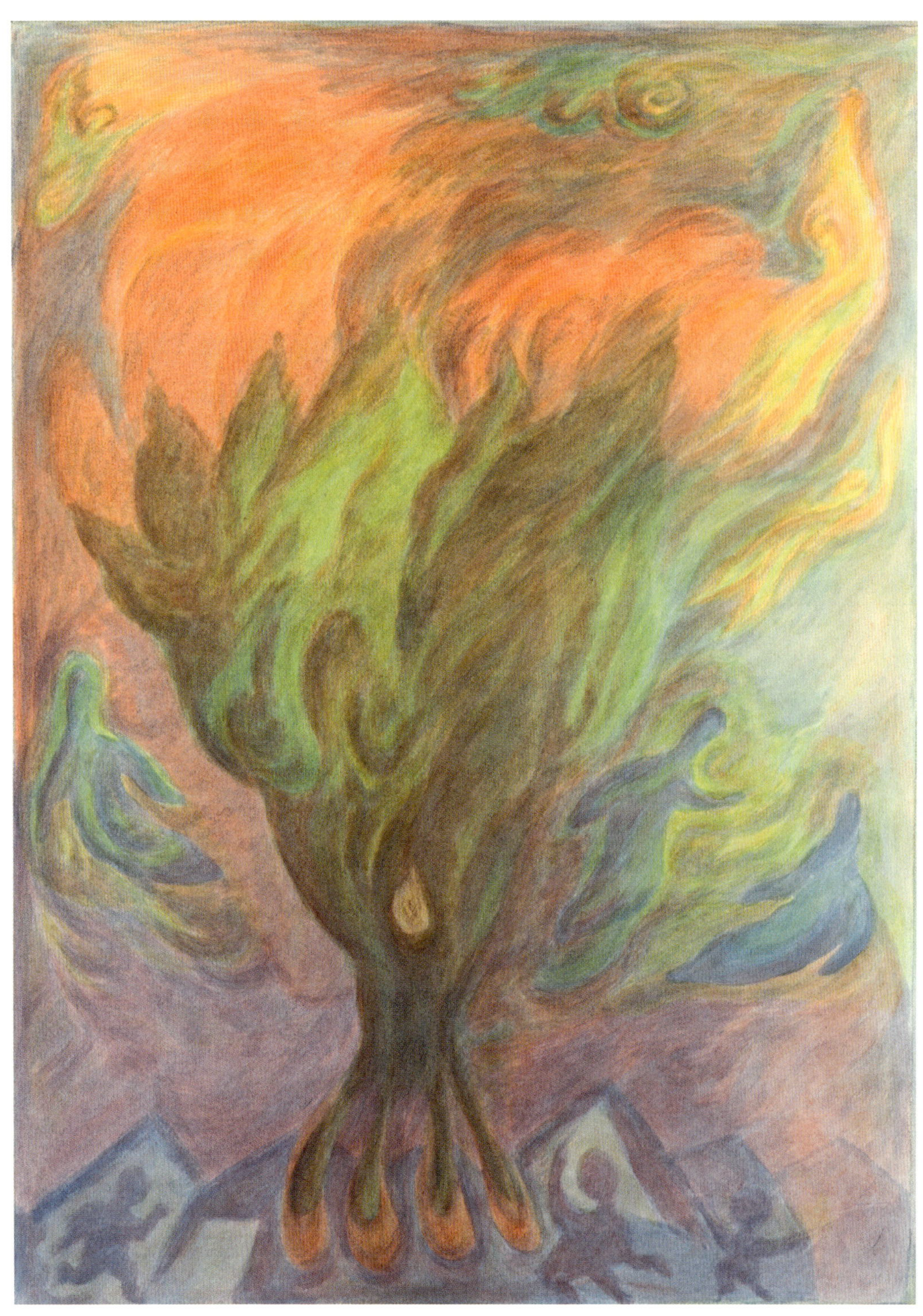

6

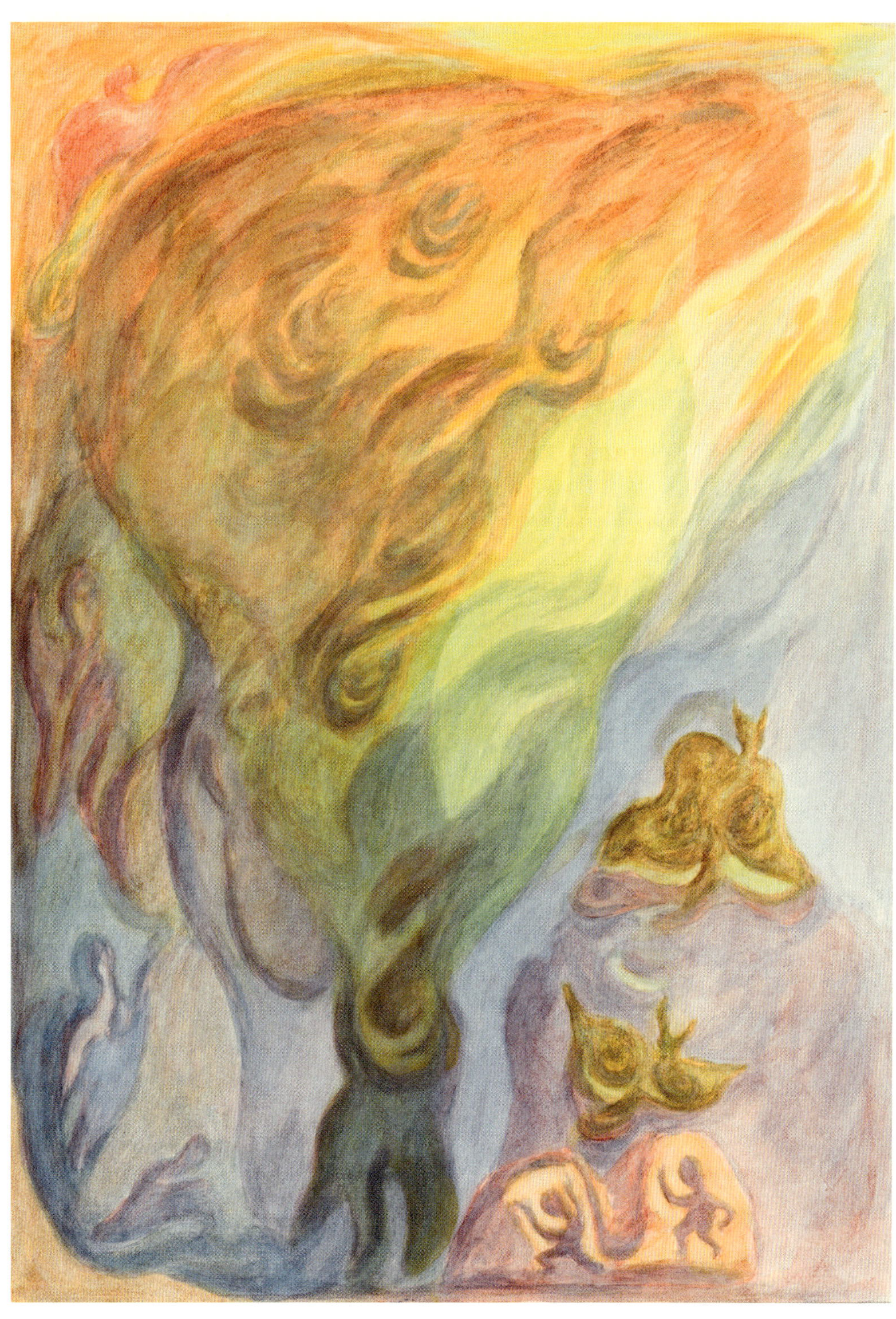

7

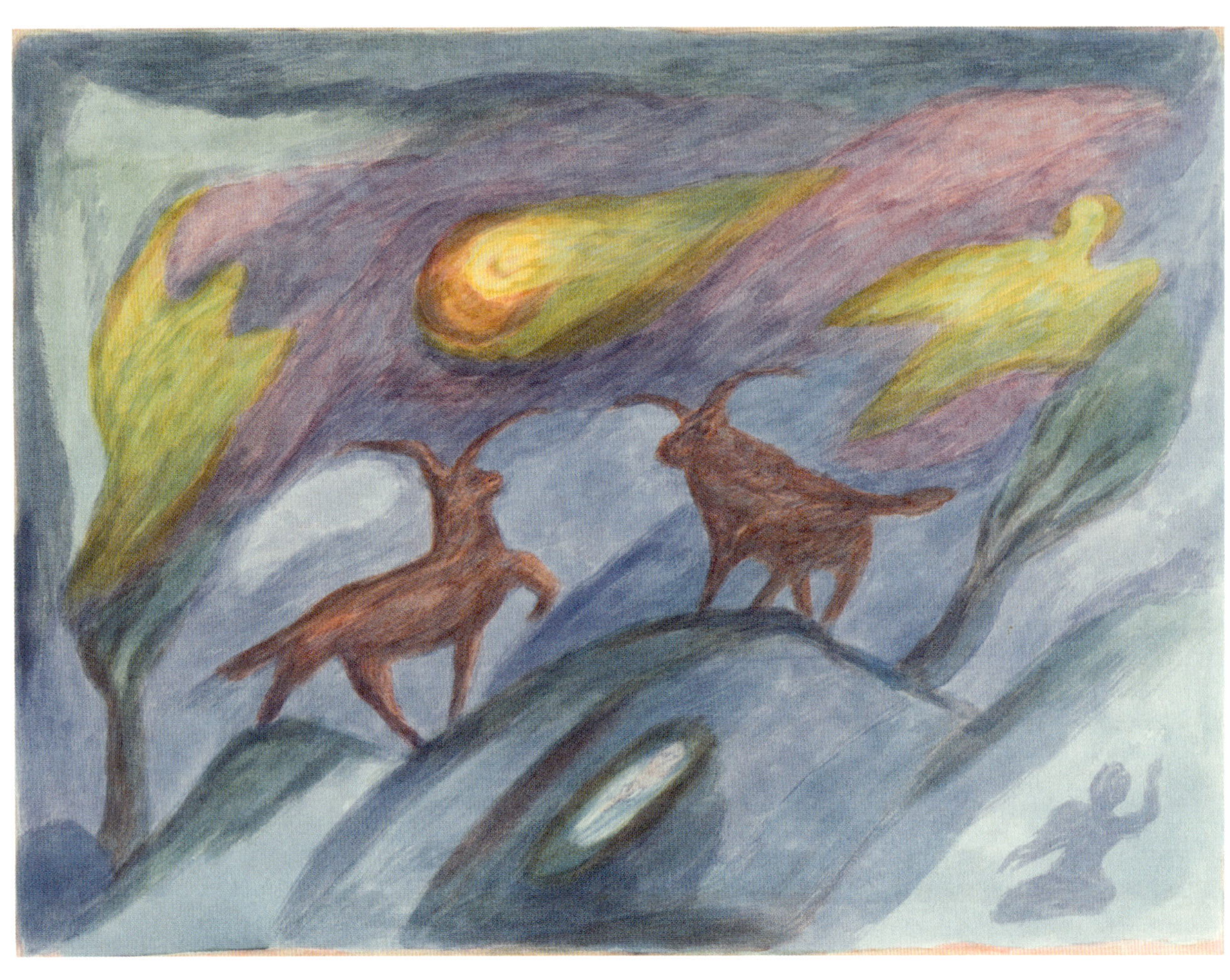

Plate 54: Animals in Moonlight

Animals

Just as the *Archetypal Plant* was a doorway into the life of the plant, preoccupation with the *Archetypal Animal/Archetypal Human Being* sketch gave Gerard Wagner orientation for his painting of the animal motif. Based on numerous studies of Rudolf Steiner's painting, Wagner gained insight into the connection between animal and man and into processes of human evolution. His paintings of sequences beginning with the *Archetypal Animal/Archetypal Human Being* show diverse animal forms evolving out of it. They also show development from the archetypal form, shown in the sketch, towards the image of the human being.

Gerard Wagner experimented with the animal motif in his usual way. By changing the colour of the animal, the ground, and the background colour countless variations of animal forms arose. It is rare to see an animal alone in his paintings, they are usually in pairs or in groups indicative of the group-soul or group-I (ego) in which animals are united and guided from the spiritual world. According to spiritual science each animal is part of a 'group soul'. Whereas the 'I' of the human being can be experienced as being on the physical plane, the 'I' of an animal exists on the astral plane as part of a group-I. Rudolf Steiner described in the following way how animals are directed from higher realms by the group-I:[28]

> '[...] The human I is found in the physical world; although we may not see it with our eyes it is present, so to say, within the skin of every human being. This is not the case with animals. We do not find their group-I in the physical world. In order that you may form an idea of such a group-I imagine that there is a partition before me, and in this partition ten holes. I put my ten fingers through the holes and move them. You see my fingers but not myself, and without much deep thought you say that these ten fingers do not move of themselves, but something hidden must be causing the movement; in other words you presume a being that belongs to the fingers. This comparison brings us to the group-nature or soul-nature in the case of animals.'
>
> 'The many lions on the physical plane are beings which, in a certain sense, have also something hidden behind them. Just as the central being belonging to the ten fingers is hidden by the partition, so something is also hidden which is common to all lions. [...] These group-egos live as single individuals on the astral plane, just as human individual-egos do here on the physical plane. [...]'

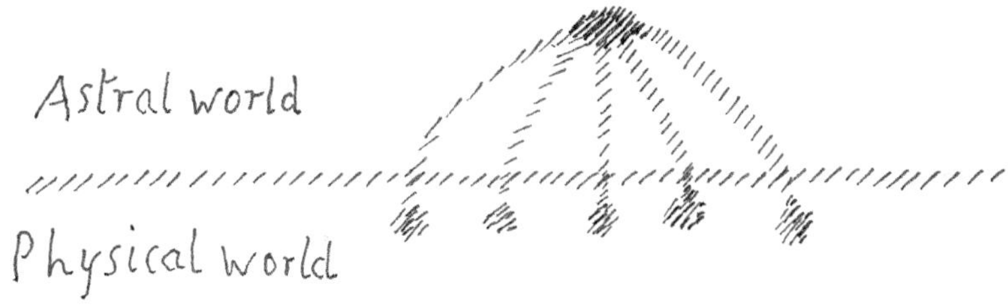

Animals in Gerard Wagner's paintings appear as part of the astral soul mood that surrounds them: lions in a vibrant red; deer in a deep shining blue. A recurring theme of Wagner's early period was the ‚St. Hubertus motif'. The 8th century legend tells of Hubertus, the son of Bertrand the Duke of Aquitaine, who went through an inner conversion after experiencing a vision of the crucified Christ between the antlers of a stag he was hunting. He gave up his privileged life, took holy orders and was known for his miraculous healing powers. Wagner also included horses, for instance, in such significant motifs as the 'Baptism in the Jordan' or the 'Mystery of Golgotha'. (See plate 101)

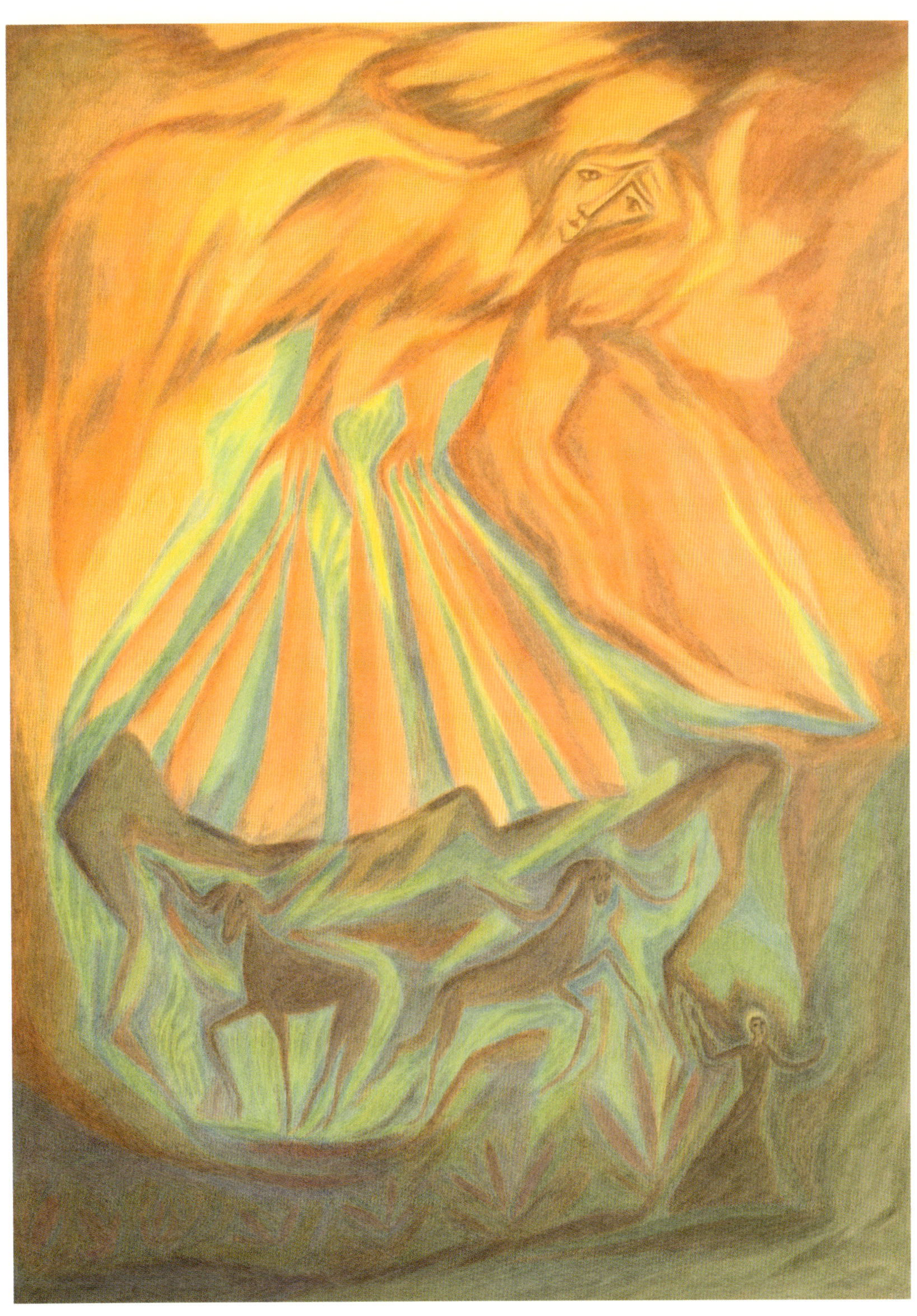

Plate 55: Animals (Group Soul)

Transformation from Moonrise or Moonset to Fruiting and Blossoming Trees

An interesting discovery of Gerard Wagner's in relation to animals came about through his study of the moon motifs of the Nature Mood Sketches. He found that the motif of the rising or setting moon develops naturally into motifs of animals, and further to trees and plant growth. He painted sequences of this motif-transformation in eight or 16 steps beginning with *Moonrise* or *Moonset* and ending with *Fruiting and Blossoming Trees.*

How does this change of motif come about? It has already been shown that Gerard Wagner was interested in how the *order* in which he painted the colours influenced the creation of the motif; and how by changing one colour in a sequence of colours, the motif would change.

- In the series of eight paintings seen on the opposite page he began by painting a violet background.
- The first colour in all eight paintings was brown which was painted at the bottom of each picture.
- The second colour was changed from red to green in gradual steps in the following manner: a little green was added to the red in the second picture, more green to the red in the third picture and so forth.
- In the last picture the second colour was green without any red in it.

This caused the second colour to change through the sequence of eight paintings as follows:

1 Red
2 Dull red
3 Red-brown
4 Brown
5 Dark brown
6 Greenish-brown
7 Olive green
8 Green

Red loses its brightness with the addition of green and changes in stages to a dark brown; then green enlivens the brown which changes in steps to a pure fresh green. The experience of the changing colours in relation to each other is the reason for the change of motif.

This is just one example of how the Nature Mood Sketches are related to each other. It is as if they all exist together as *one* family within the living forces of nature.

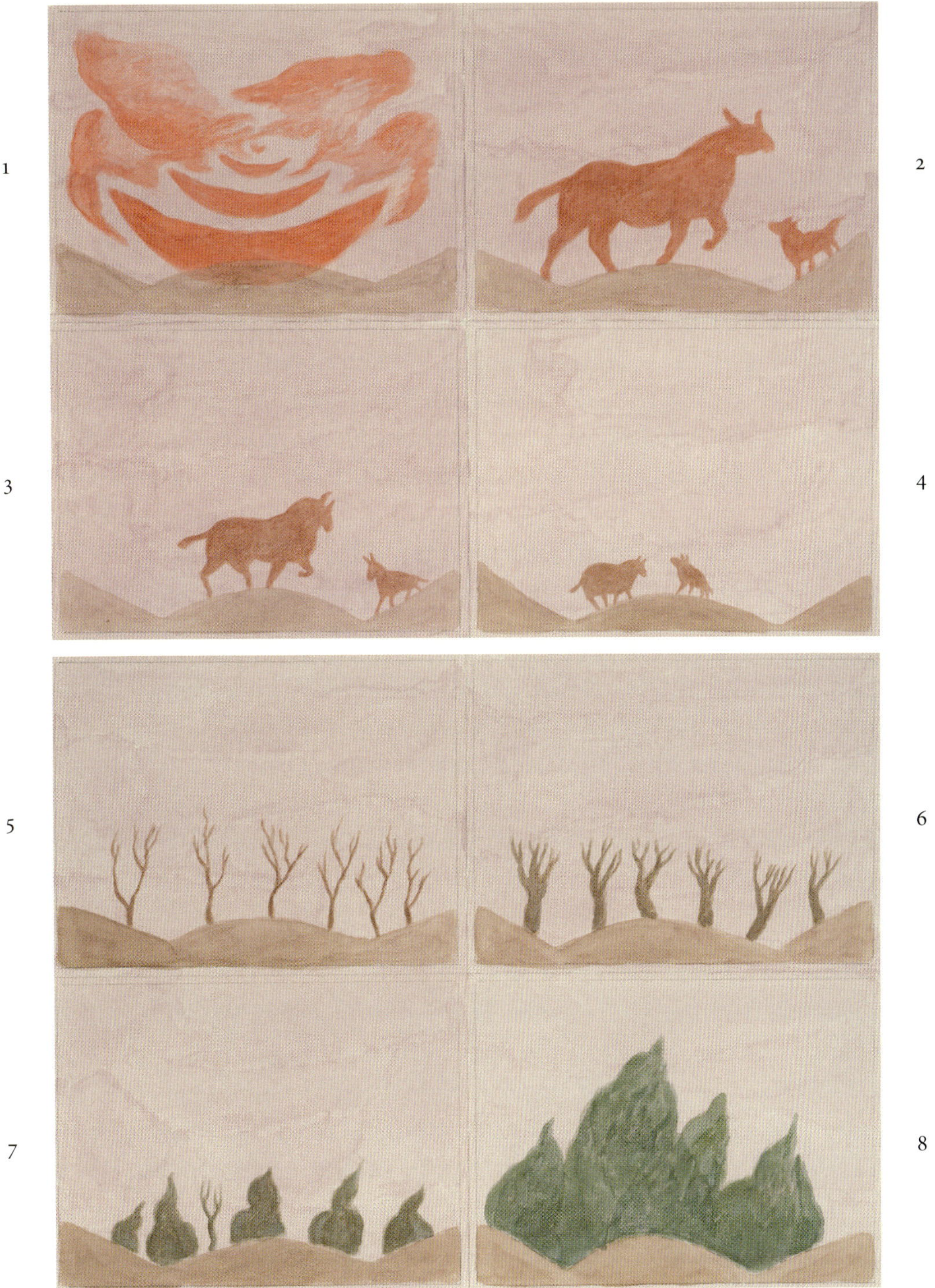

Plate 56: The *Moonset* motif transforms into the motif of the *Fruiting and Blossoming Trees;* the background colour is violet.

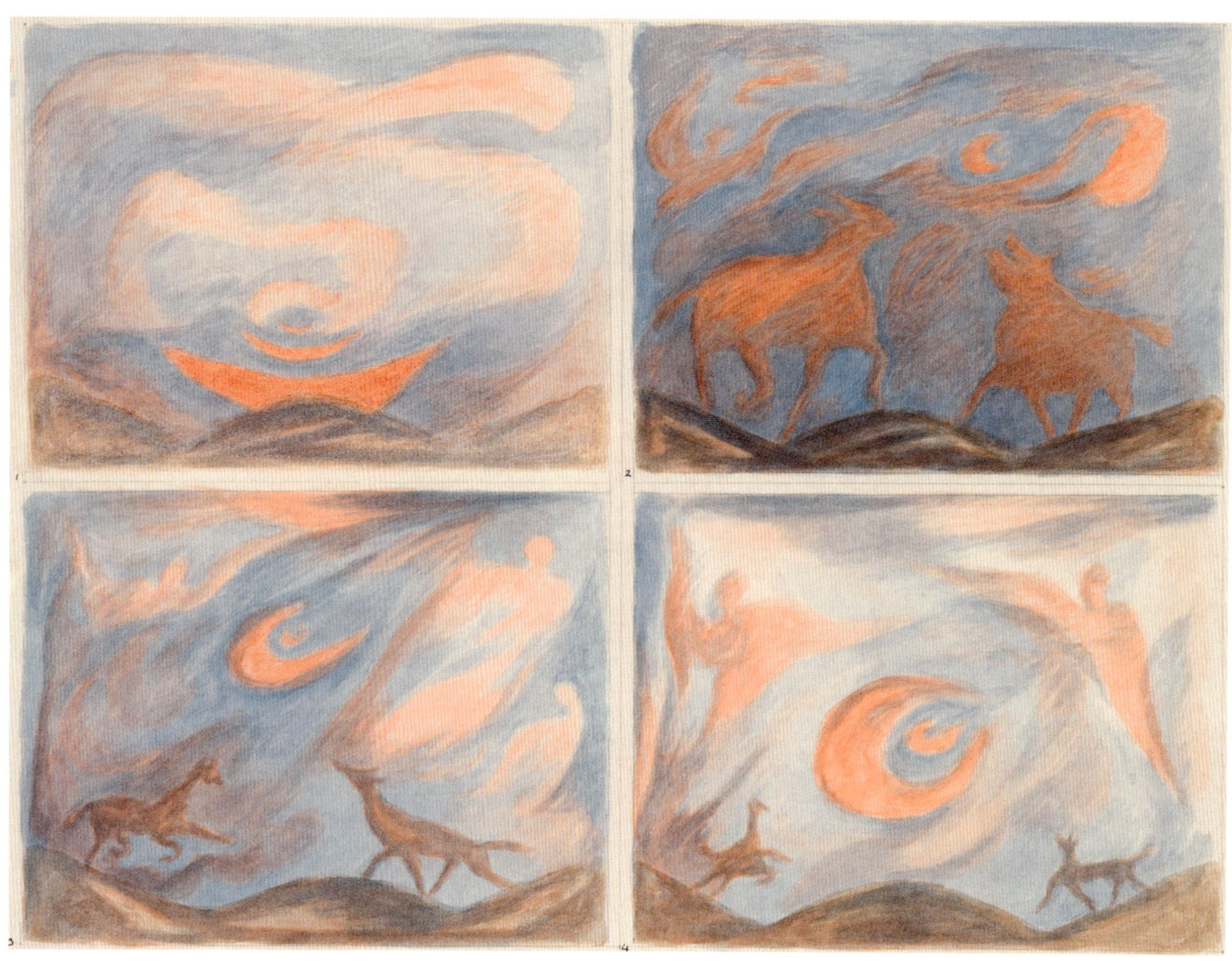

Plate 57: The *Moonset* motif transforms into the motif of the *Fruiting and Blossoming Trees;* the background colour is violet.

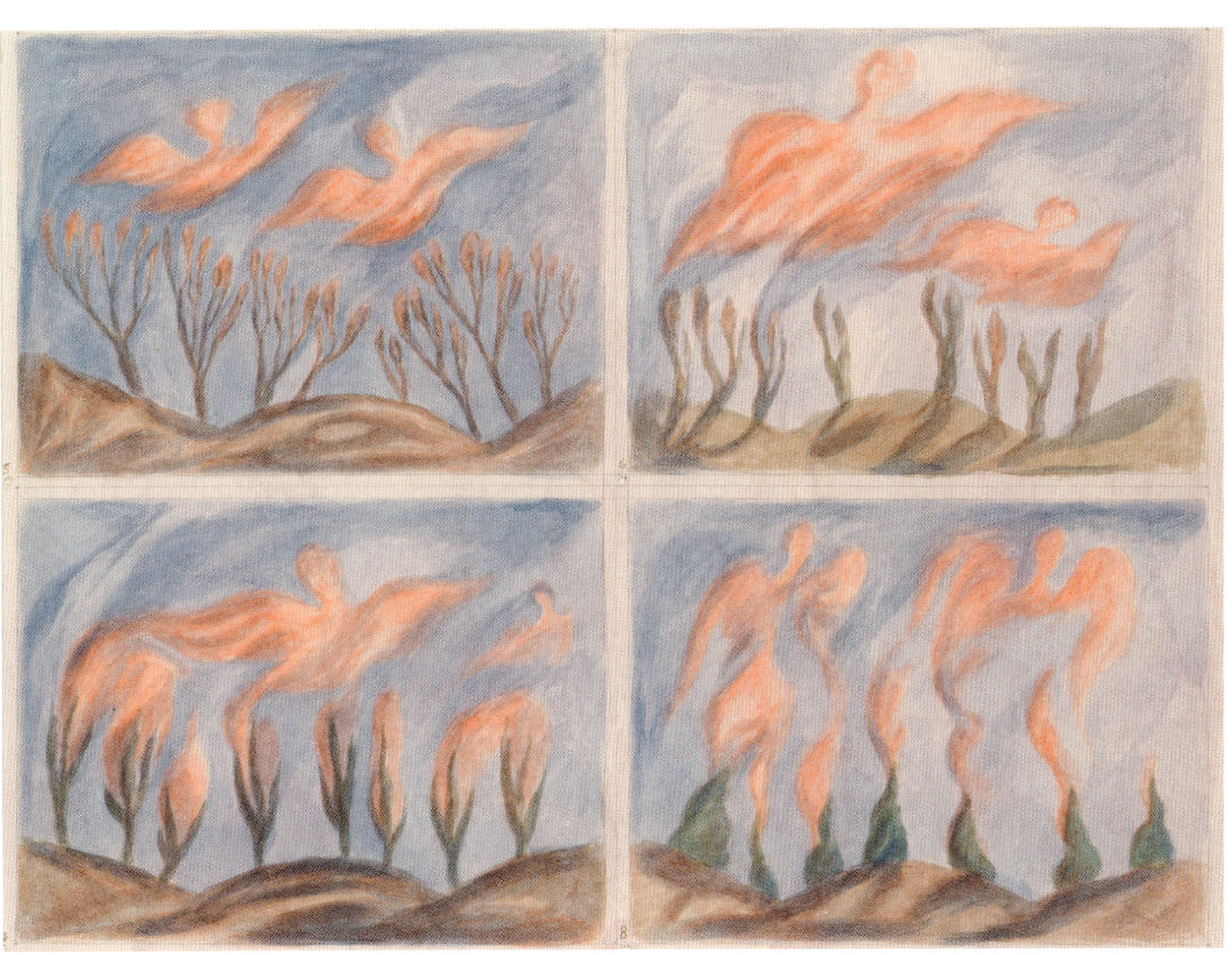

Plate 58: The *Moonset* motif transforms into the motif of the *Fruiting and Blossoming Trees;* the background colour is violet.

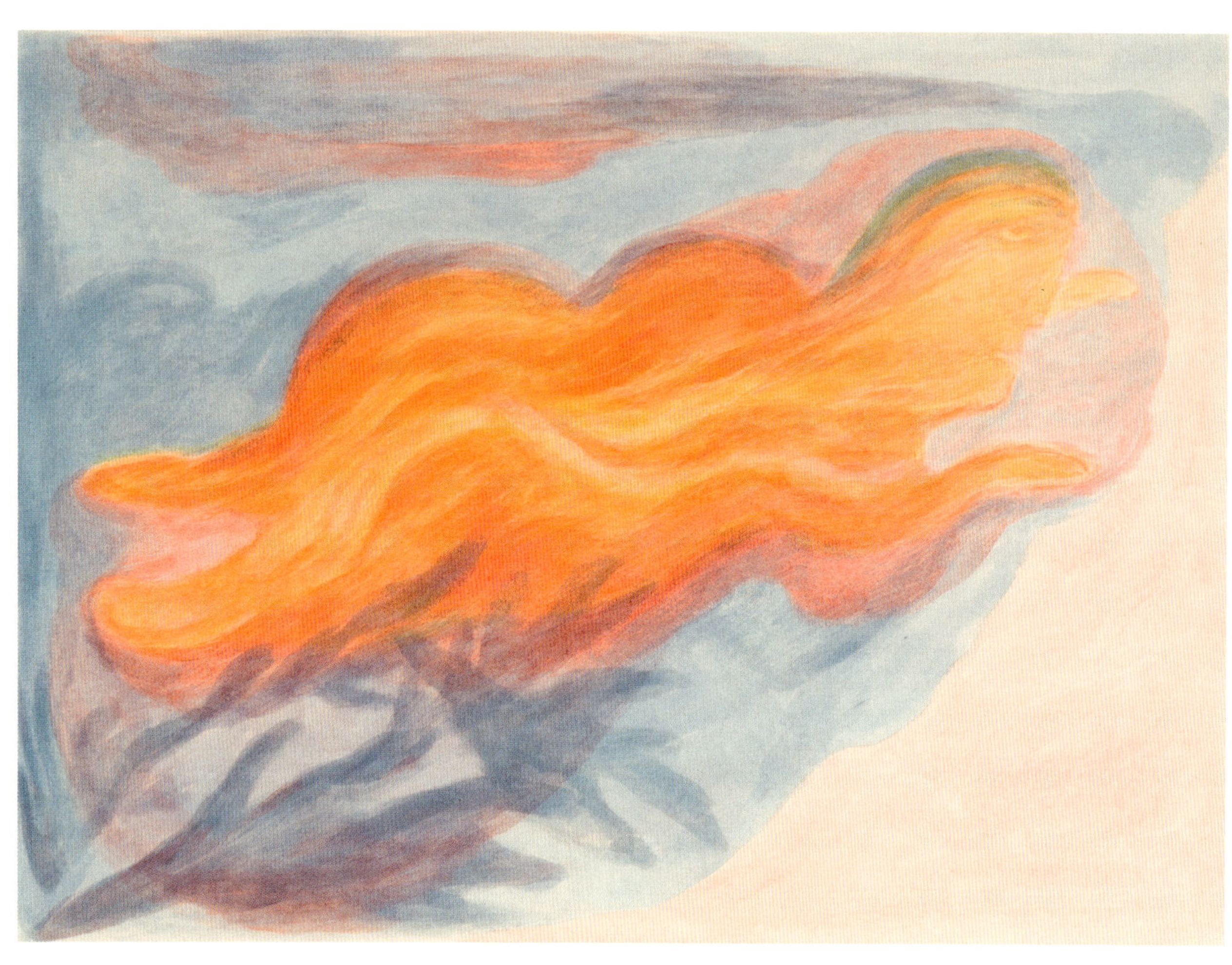

Plate 59: *Archetypal Animal / Archetypal Human Being* after Rudolf Steiner

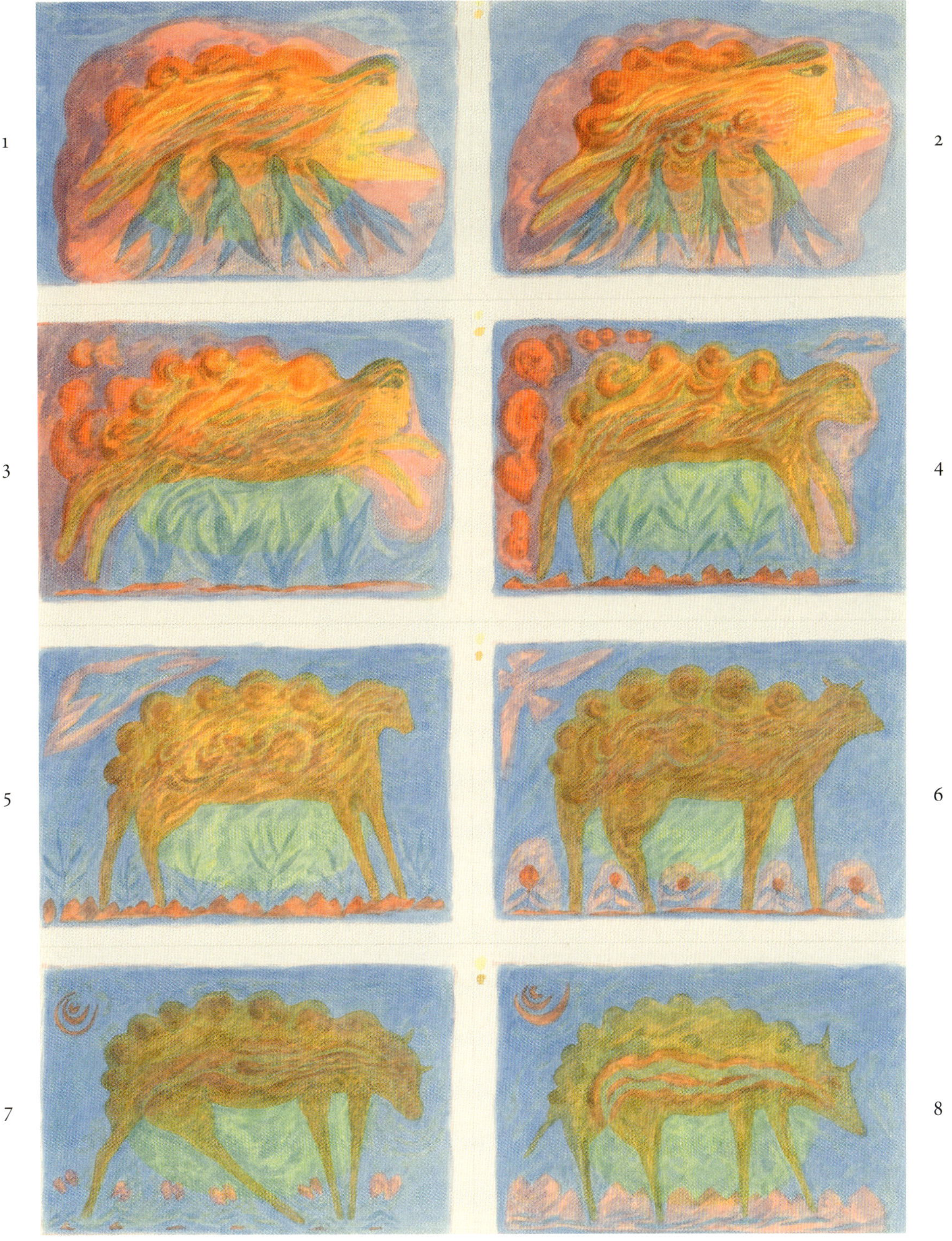

Plate 60: Metamorphosis of the *Archetypal Animal/ Archetypal Human Being* motif

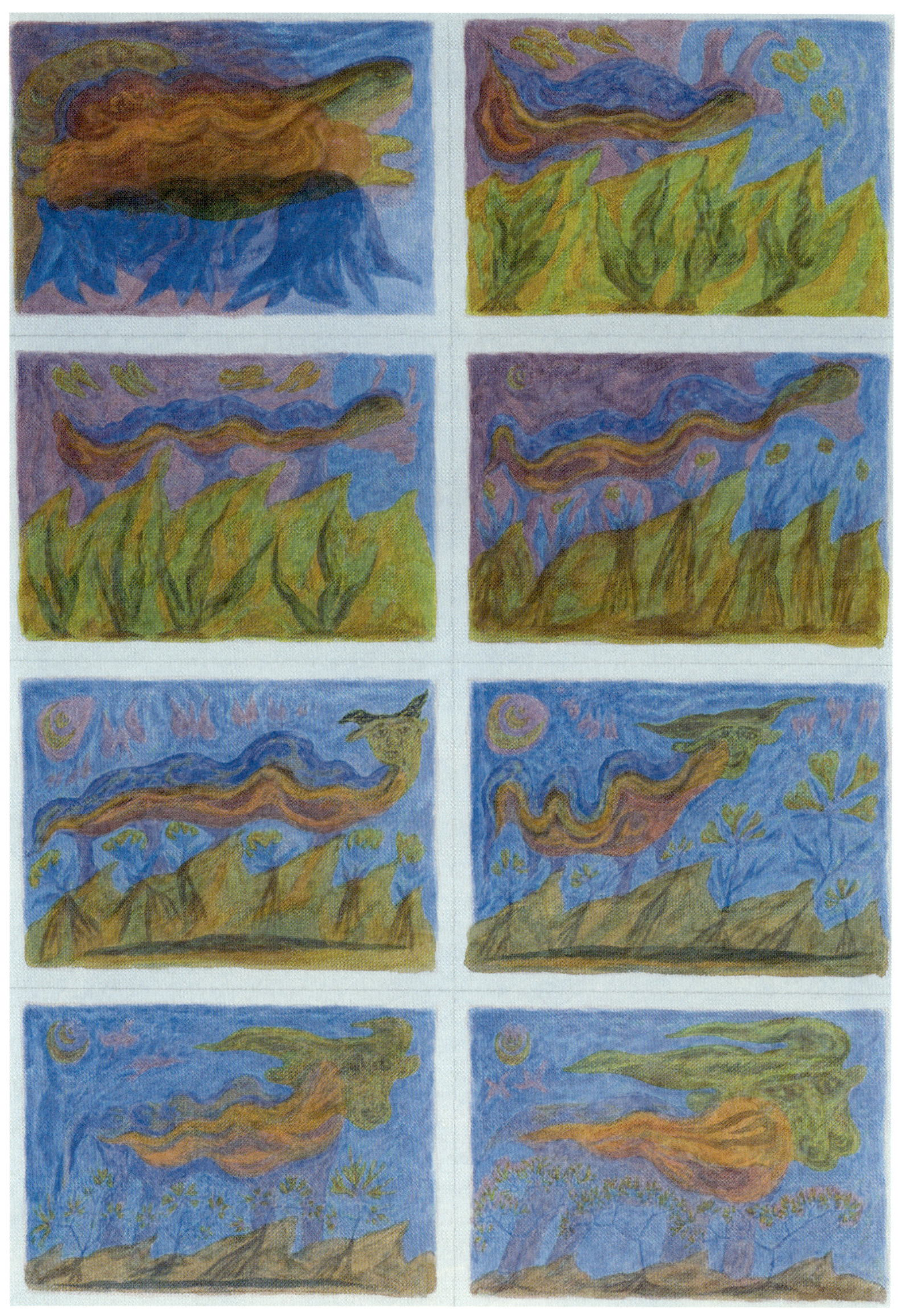

Plate 61: Metamorphosis of the *Archetypal Animal / Archetypal Human Being* motif

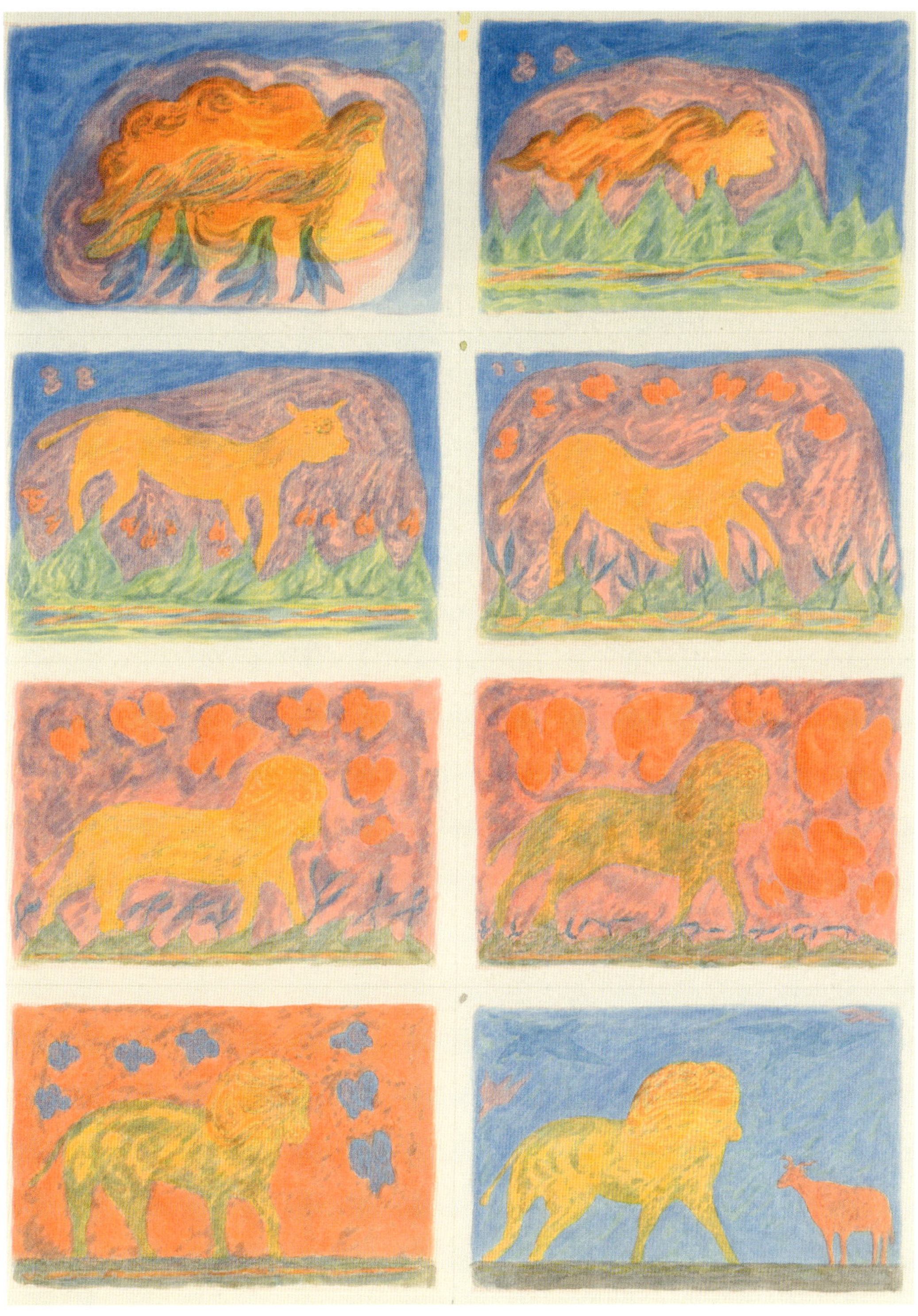

Plate 62: Metamorphosis of the *Archetypal Animal / Archetypal Human Being* motif

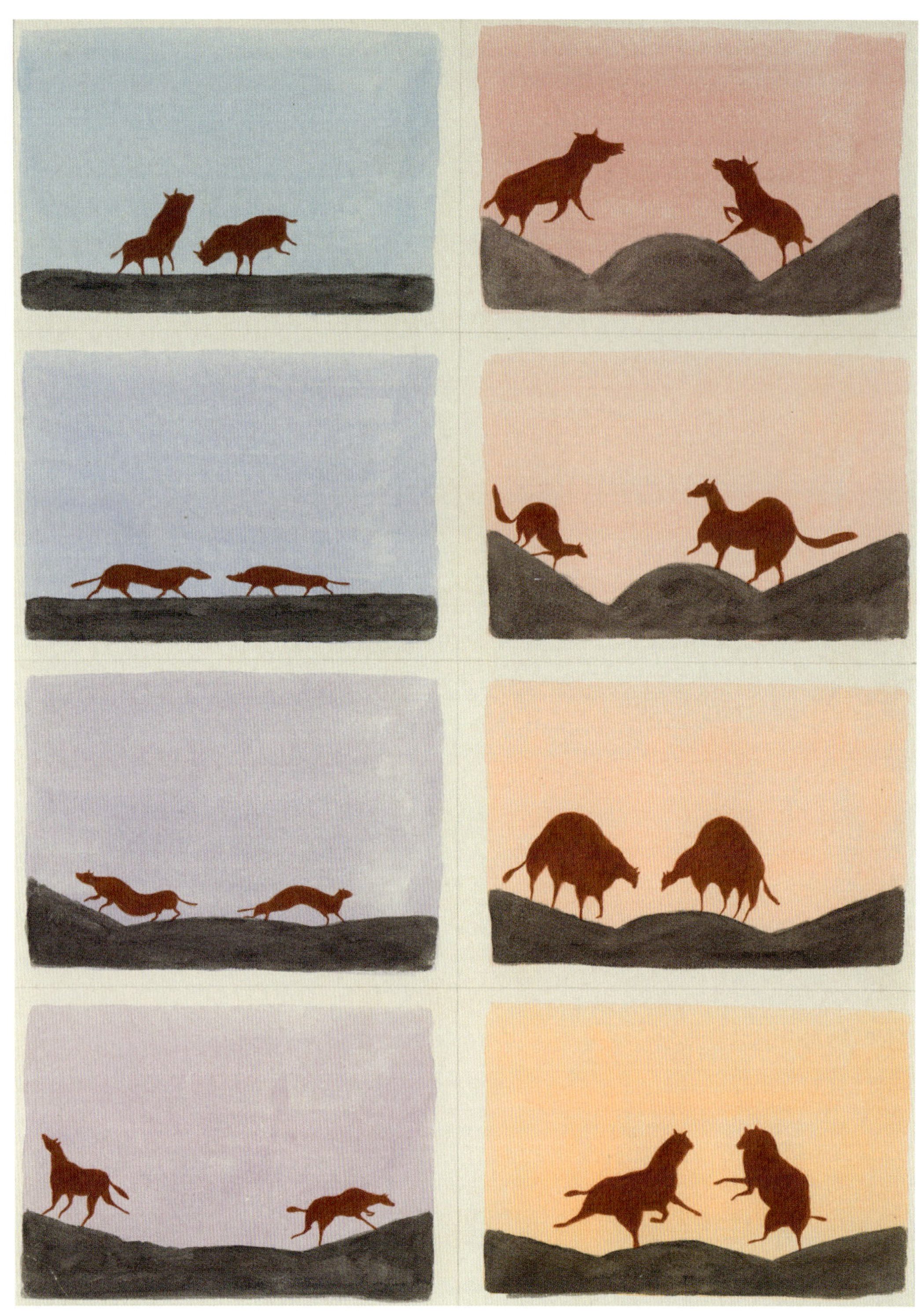

Plate 63: The background colour changes; the colour of the animal and the ground remains constant.

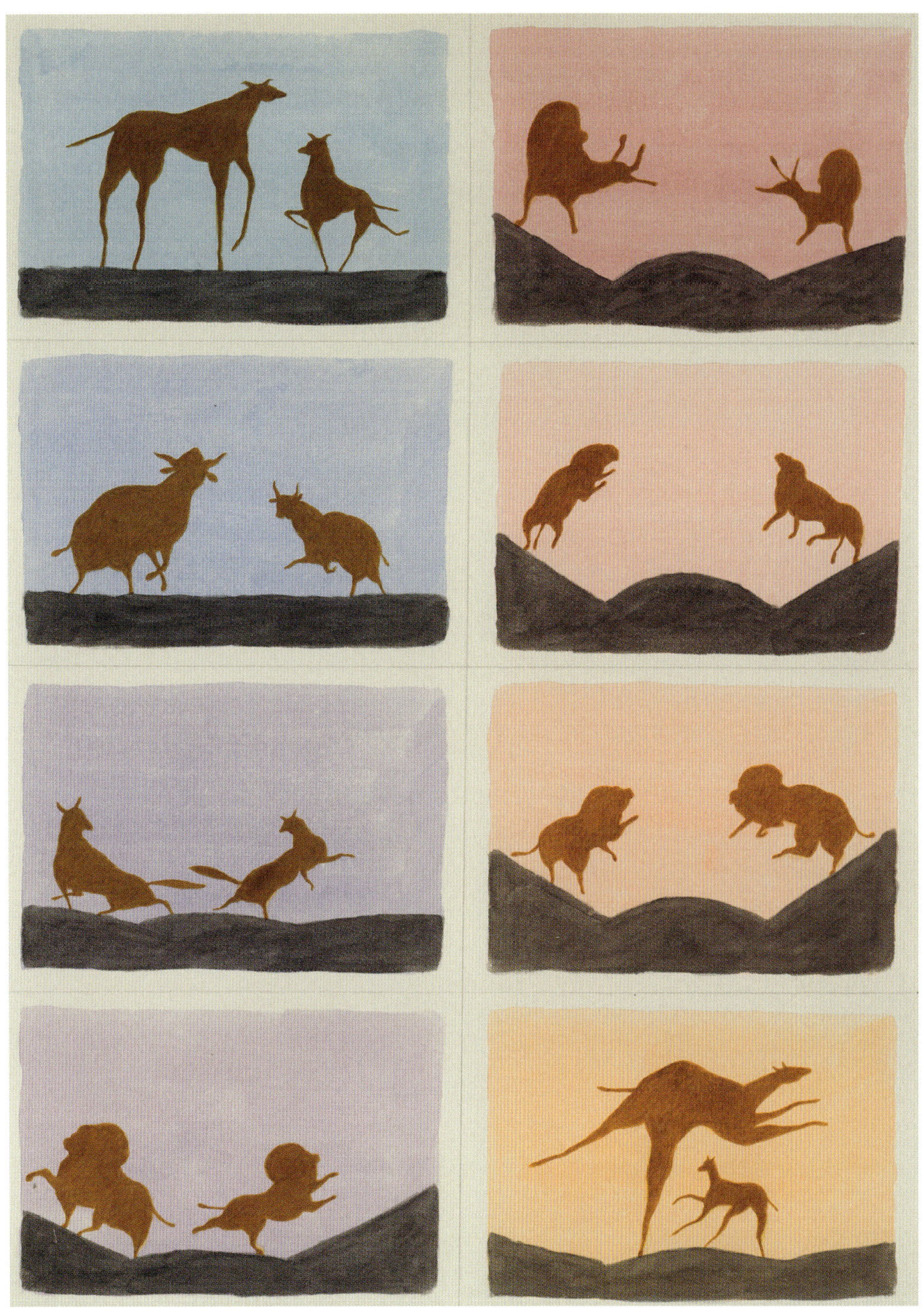

Plate 64: The background colour changes; the colour of the animal and the ground remains constant.

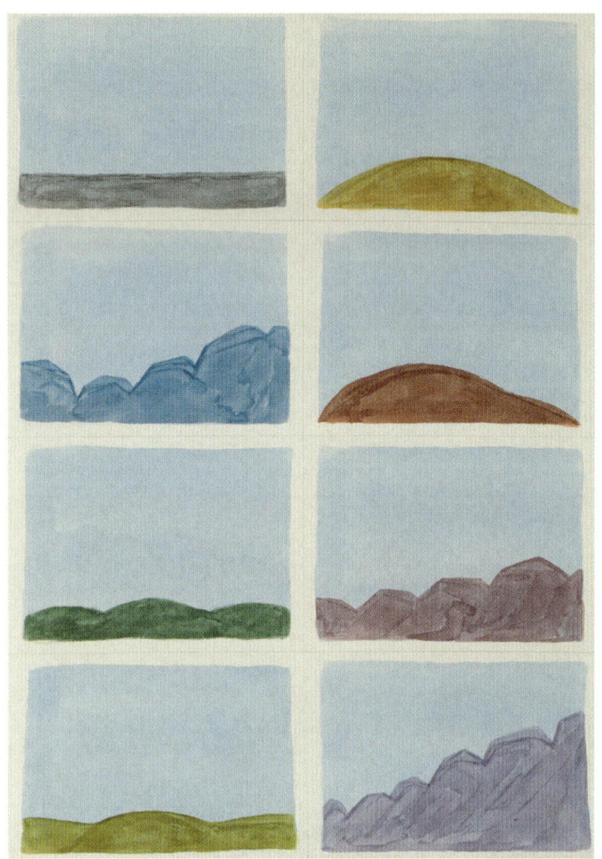

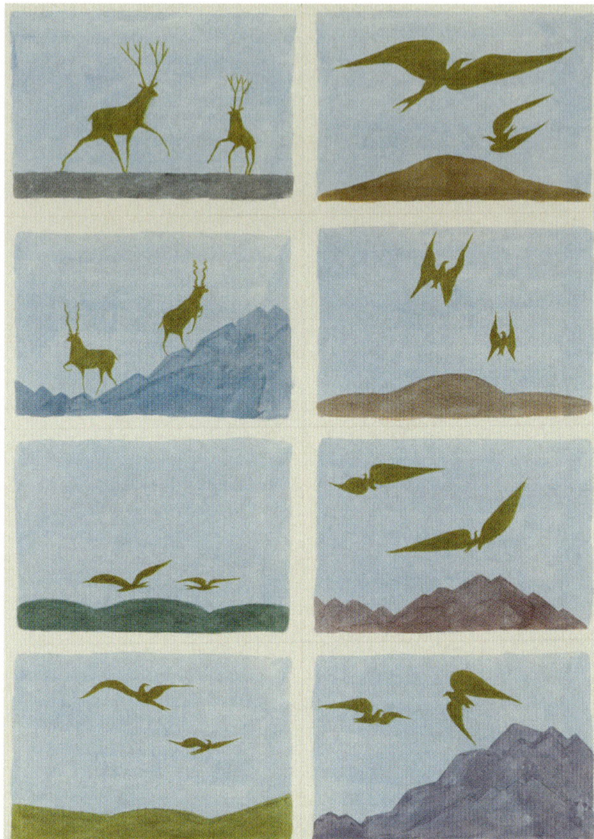

Plate 65: The background colour is blue; the colour of the ground changes, the animal colour is unchanged.

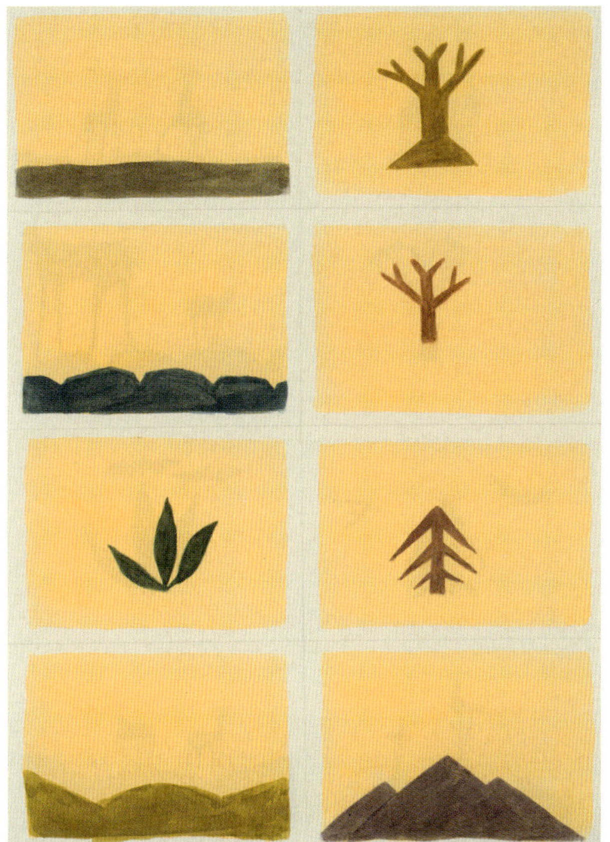

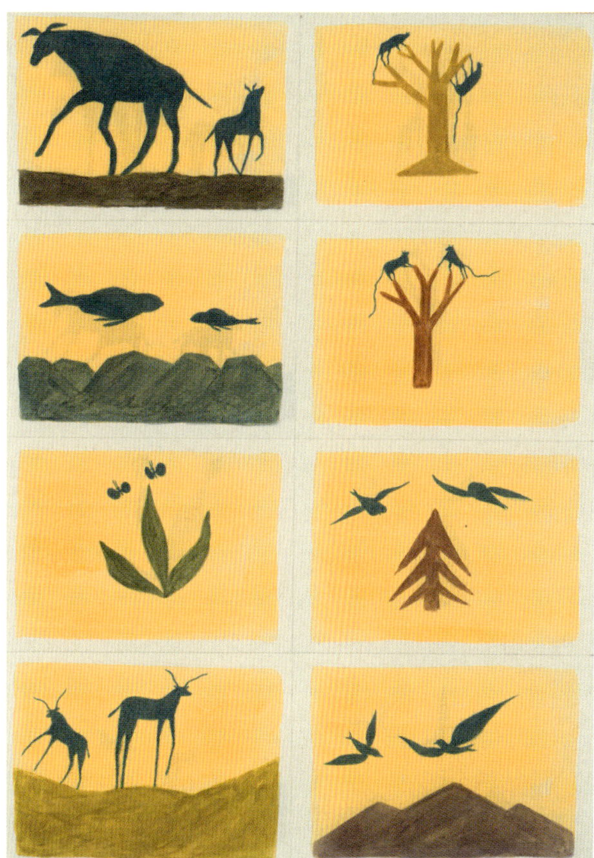

Plate 66: The background colour is orange; the colour of the ground changes, the animal colour is unchanged. The orange background is the reason for the change in the form of the first colour.

The Human Being

The Threefold Human Being sketch was central to Gerard Wagner's understanding of colour in relation to the human being. It also gave further insight into the art of composing a picture. Whether a basic or an elaborate motif, a balance of threefoldness can almost always be found in Rudolf Steiner's art works. (It goes without saying that a living threefold composition comes about by way of an inner process and not from an abstract division of the picture into three parts.)

The composition of the *Threefold Human Being*, as Rudolf Steiner created it, is embedded in a sequence of spectrum colours. This approach to the creative source of the rainbow colours can also be found in other Motif Sketches. They show how Steiner was able to connect this lawful unity of colours artistically with the various themes he painted.

In this sketch the upper part of the picture shows the thinking human being (as head only) in yellow and white, both colours of the spirit. Green holds the middle position in the picture, and just as feeling lives in the middle realm of the human being where the activity of heart and lung interact, so yellow and blue, both 'breathing' colours, interact to create green – the image colour of life.[29] The upper part of a figure can be seen in the green.

In the lower part of the picture a small figure can be seen as if supported by blue, the colour close to darkness which is connected with the sphere of the will. The figure has a red sphere as its centre revealing the heart through which the blood pulsates. The red in the upper part of the picture and the red 'heart' relate to each other as centre and periphery, – as interaction of human and cosmic will. Black seen in the lower figure brings the necessary wakefulness and tension to the picture, and is a balance to the white above. Peach blossom, the unification of all colours in Goethe's 'colour circle', appears at the bottom of the picture consolidating the whole motif.

The Threefold Human Being sketch was the starting point for some mysterious and deeply esoteric themes painted in sequences by Gerard Wagner. His work with the Motif Sketches show that they too are interwoven with each other as well as with other art works created by Rudolf Steiner, for instance with the Goetheanum glass window motifs.

*

The Friedwart Sketches gave inspiration for painting themes of nature, particularly sun motifs and tree motifs but also for painting the human being. The *Head Study*, for example, which shows a human head in profile, was the starting point of some interesting areas of research. Gerard Wagner explored the relation of the head to what is around it: how the 'surroundings', in a far-reaching sense, determine and reflect the momentary

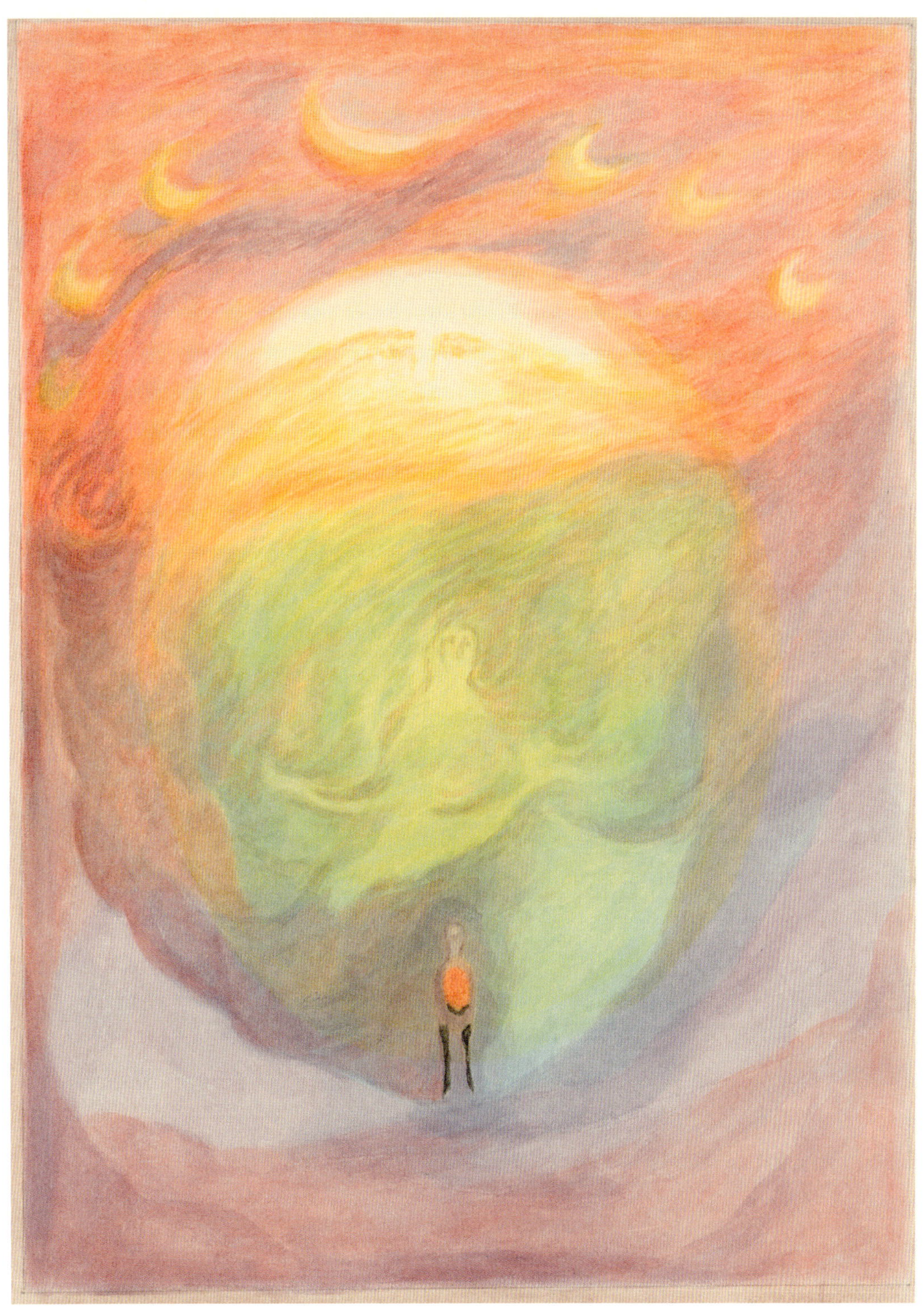

Plate 67: *The Threefold Human Being*

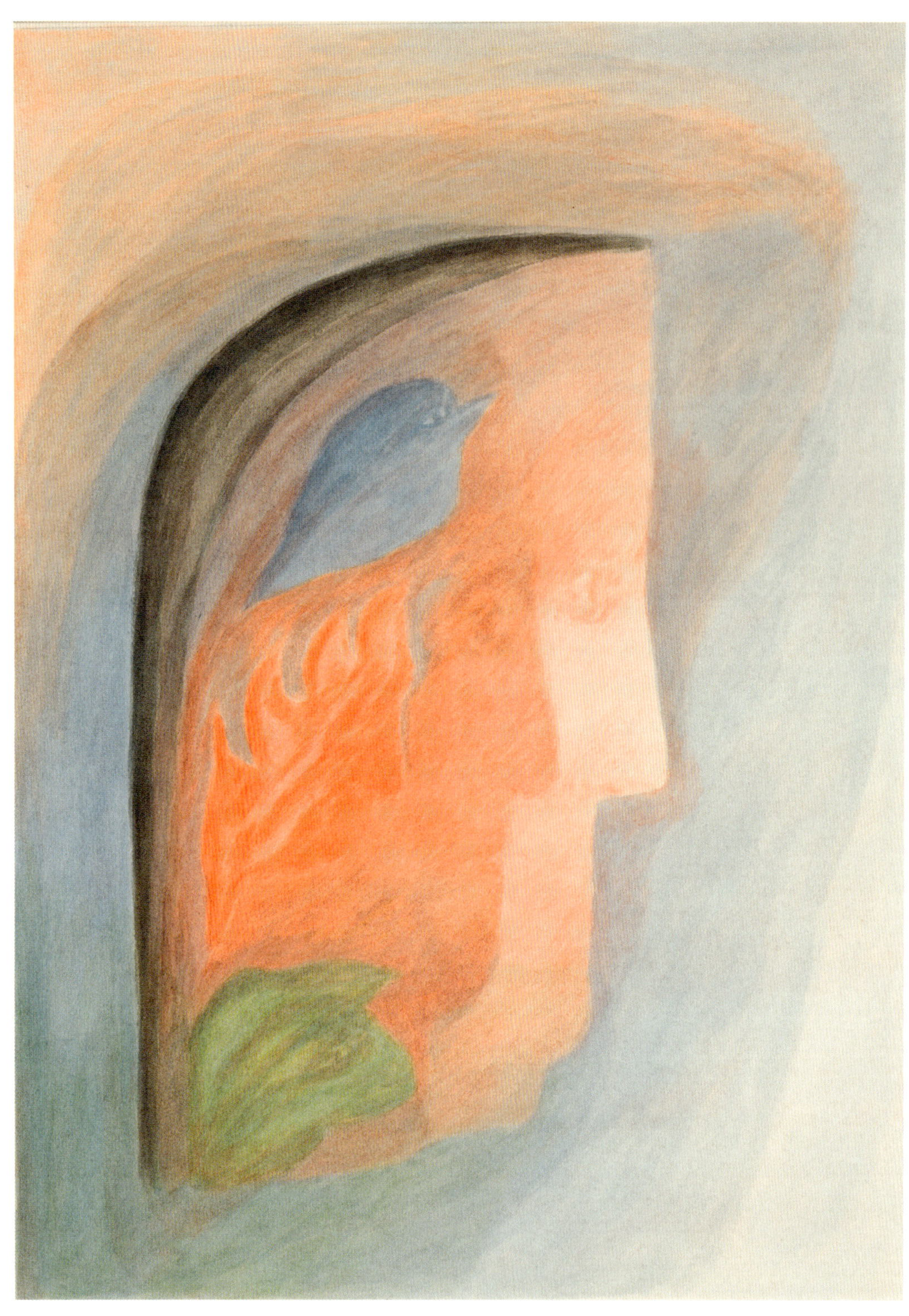

Plate 68: *Group Souls – The Human Being*

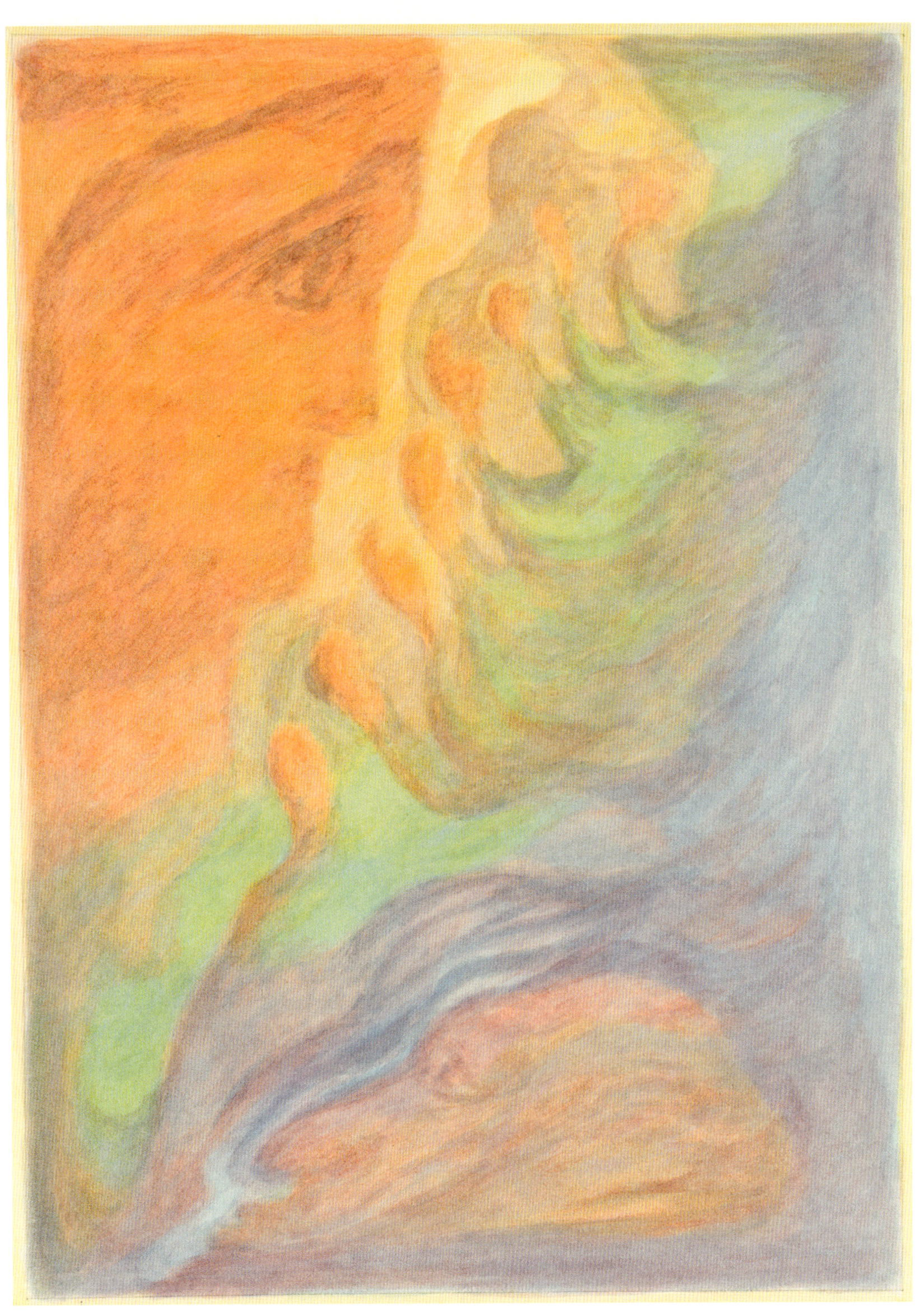

Plate 69: *Light and Darkness / Lucifer and Ahriman*

inner standpoint of the person revealed in the countenance. This interaction, spoken of by Rudolf Steiner in a lecture given in 1914 in Dornach,[30] led Wagner to a new art of portrait painting. In the quote below, Steiner is continuing the theme of the two aspects of painting, – drawing and colouration:

> 'But actually any good painter would not try to use colouration of the face to express vital relationships within the human organism. Anyone who painted a pale face – let us consider an extreme example – in order to indicate by this pallor that the person being painted was perhaps inwardly ill, would actually be pursuing something that is not genuinely artistic. Not to mention how inartistic it would be to paint a wine drinker with a red nose!
>
> Anyone who attempts to capture a being's stationary characteristics colouristically is not working in a genuinely artistic way. But if on the other hand we paint a cloud, let us say, and bring to expression in the cloud the whole magic of nature – of the morning sun, for example, and the way in which the morning mood affects the nuances of the clouds – then we have captured something that is fleeting in nature, not something that proceeds from the single being, from the cloud. What one captures is something fleeting, brought about by its relation to the entire environment, to the cosmos, to the extent that comes into consideration. If we paint a perfectly illuminated cloud at a specific time of the day, we are painting along with it the whole world as it exists at that time of the day. If we paint a person and want to reproduce the whole of that person's inner constitution, then, as I have said, we are actually leaving the realm of art. *But if we succeed in bringing to expression what this person experienced – if we can depict what caused the person to blush, for example, then we are already standing more within the realm of art, and even more so, if we ourselves can gather from the picture what the experience actually is, – if the red of the cheeks can tell us something about what the person in the picture must have lived through. So again, the important thing is not what is within the separate entity but rather what is in the surroundings, in the whole cosmos.* [Italics C. C.]
>
> What I'm saying now is related in a certain way to what I said in my lectures on 'Occult Reading and Occult Hearing'[31] There I described how, in waking consciousness, the soul is actually always outside the body, and our body is only a mirror that we use to bring to consciousness what lives outside in the cosmos. The only way to be a real artist is to live with things out in the cosmos; for the real artist, the motif is only an occasion for representing his own life within the larger cosmos.'

Gerard Wagner's explorations led to some interesting figuration and facial expressions which are not always appreciated by those art lovers who still feel more comfortable with pleasing Greek aesthetics! By putting the emphasis in the first place on the colour and allowing the drawing element to follow, he certainly made steps in freeing the human form from naturalistic representation. He approached the motif of the *Head Study* in various ways, for instance by placing two profiles facing each other. This and further research gave insight into colour as the language of the human soul.

The *Head Study*, as profile, arises by virtue of the colour blue which in its enclosing gesture creates the spherical cosmic form of the human head. The contour of the profile emerges from a certain artistic encounter between the first colour yellow, and the second colour blue, which is how Wagner built up the motif. He also investigated how Rudolf Steiner's indication of a head in profile could lead to a face seen from the front, enfaçe. This found its justification when yellow and blue, as the first and second colours in the build-up of the *Head Study*, was changed to yellow and red. And of course, other ways were investigated and found to be justified in the search for painting the human countenance out of the laws of colour.

Other areas of research included the four temperaments, the different ages, the influence of the opposing powers on the human being, and the question of the origin and configuration of the human form.

The Friedwart Sketch of the *Mother and Child* as also the Motif Sketch *New Life/Mother and Child* gave inspiration for many variations of this intimate archetypal image that accompanied Gerard Wagner throughout his life and to which he had a special connection. This motif of the 'eternal feminine' evolves out of the archetypal blue form, which, by being darker on its borders,[32] creates an inner space for the incarnation of the child. The Madonna is the image of the purified soul that gives birth to the new human being, – that higher being that wishes to reunite with its true home in the spiritual world. Rudolf Steiner speaks of this new birth in the lecture *Isis and Madonna* as follows:[33]

> '[...] What we are as human beings and how we are connected as human beings with the world faces us in pictures of the Madonna. Hence, these pictures of the Madonna are so holy to us, completely apart from any religious trend and any religious dogma. [...] The Madonna contains what can be born out of the human soul: the true, higher human being who slumbers in every human being, the humanely very best, and what as spirit flows through the world.'

This image of the Madonna and Child has been known in different cultures worldwide since antiquity, for instance in Ancient Egypt as the image of Isis with her child Horus. The legend tells that Isis was fructified from the spiritual world by Osiris and gave birth to the higher human being. Steiner continues as follows on the subject of Isis:

'This Isis, when she is purified and has laid aside all she has received from the physical [world], is impregnated from the spiritual world and gives birth to Horus, the higher human, who is victorious over the lower human being. Thus we see Isis as the representative of the human soul, as the divine spiritual in us that is born of the universal Father and has remained within us, seeking Osiris and only finding him through initiation or death. [...]'

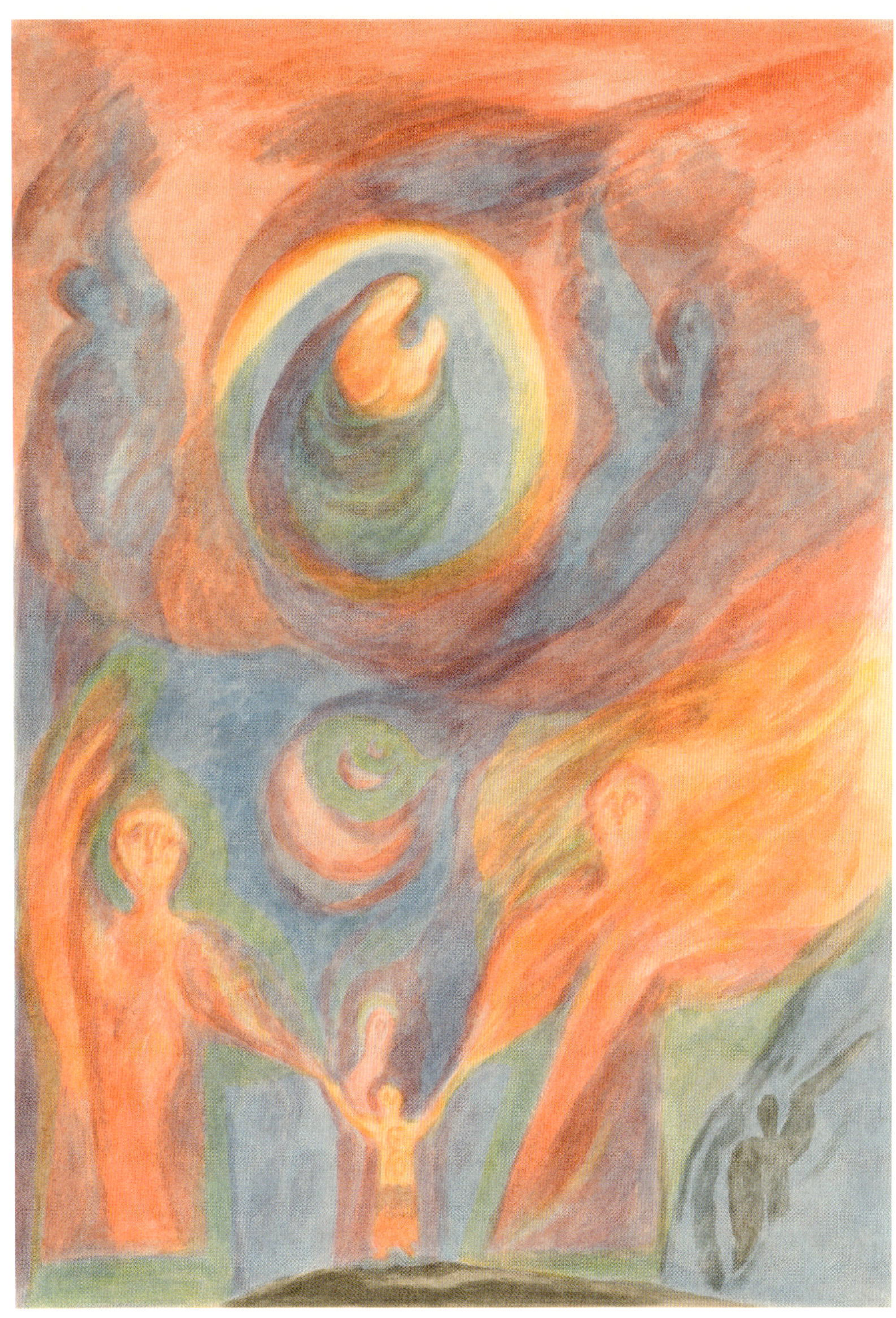

Plate 70: Birth

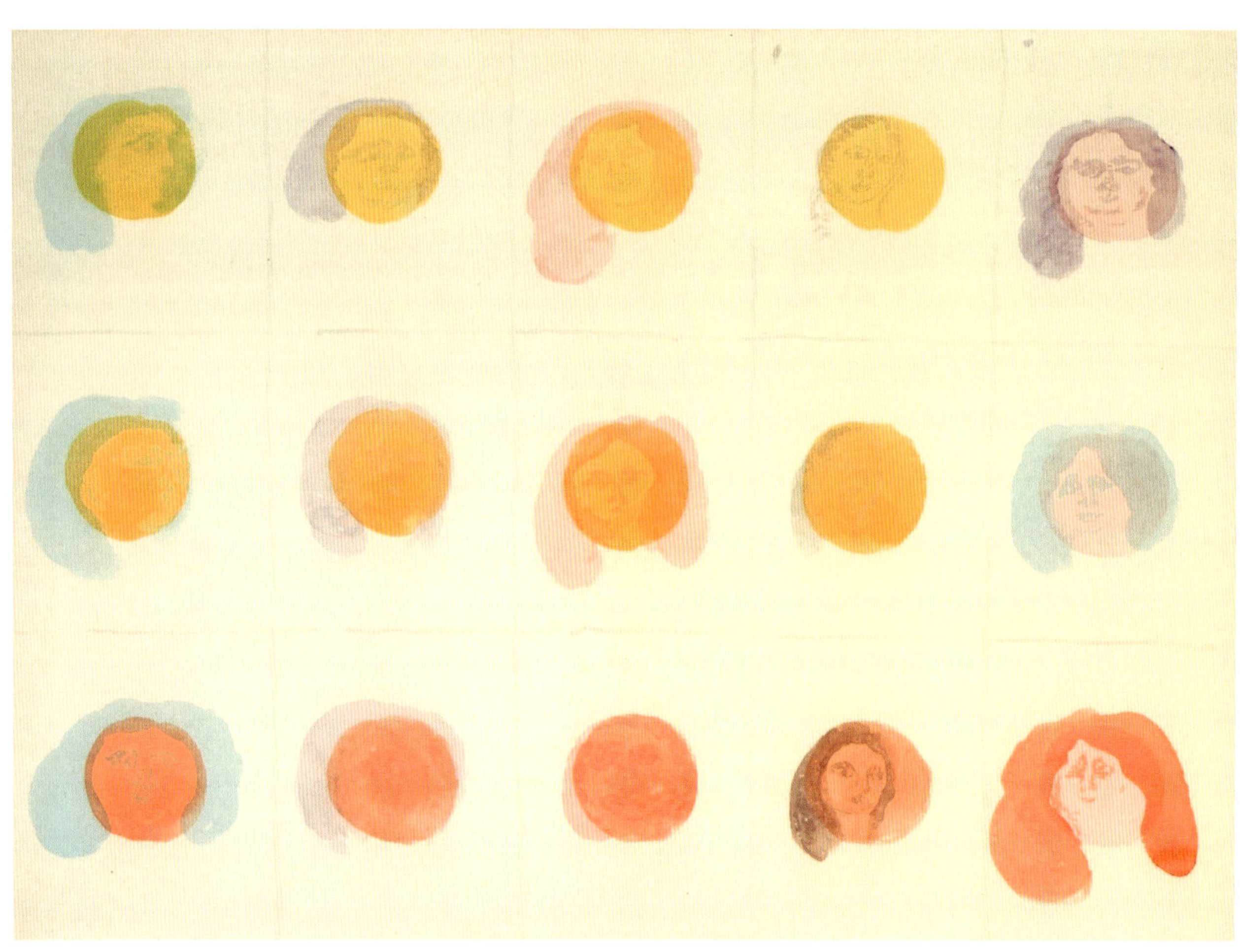

Plate 71: Head motifs: research of the *Head Study,* profile and enface

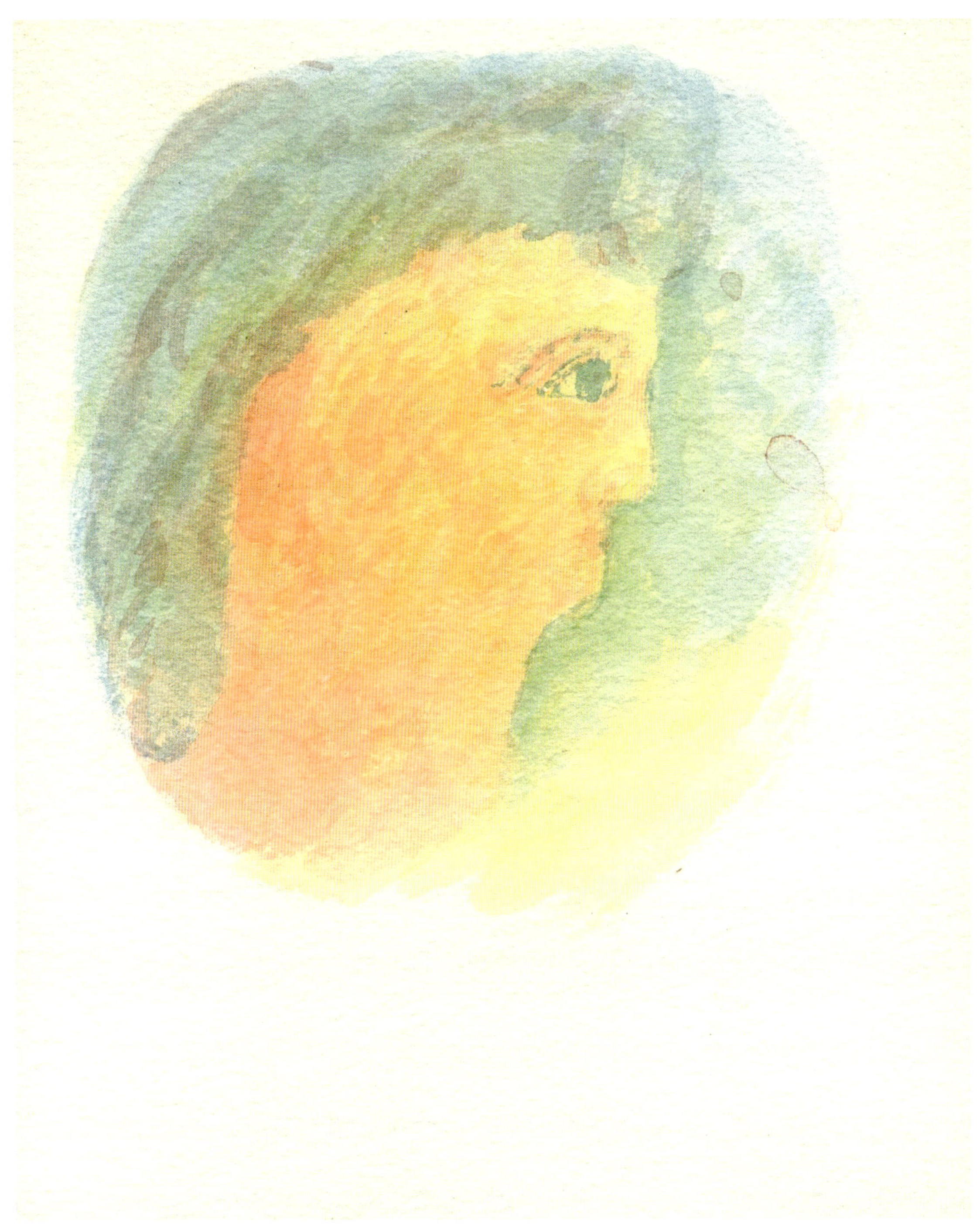

Plate 72: *Head Study* of the Friedwart Sketches

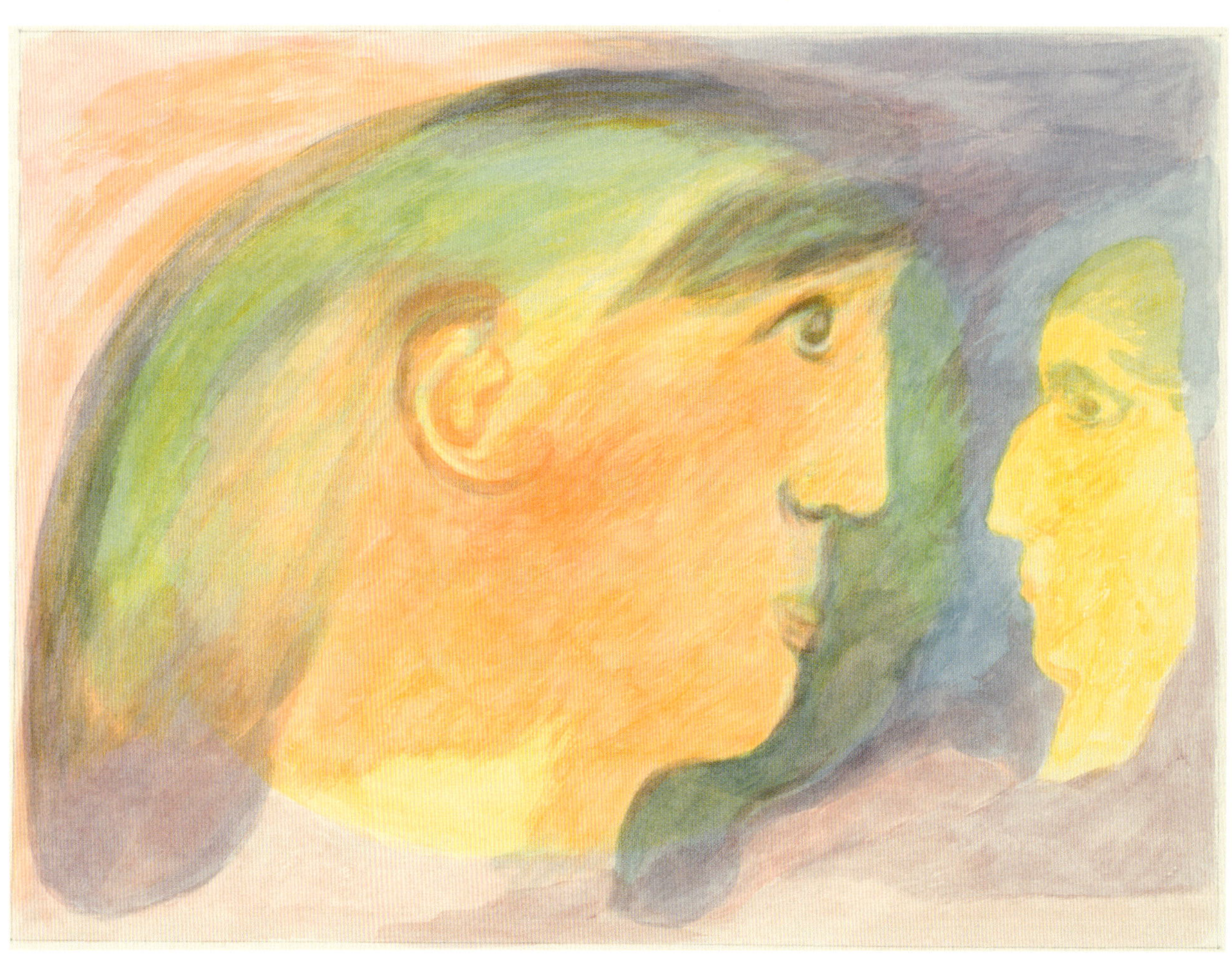

Plate 73: Meeting

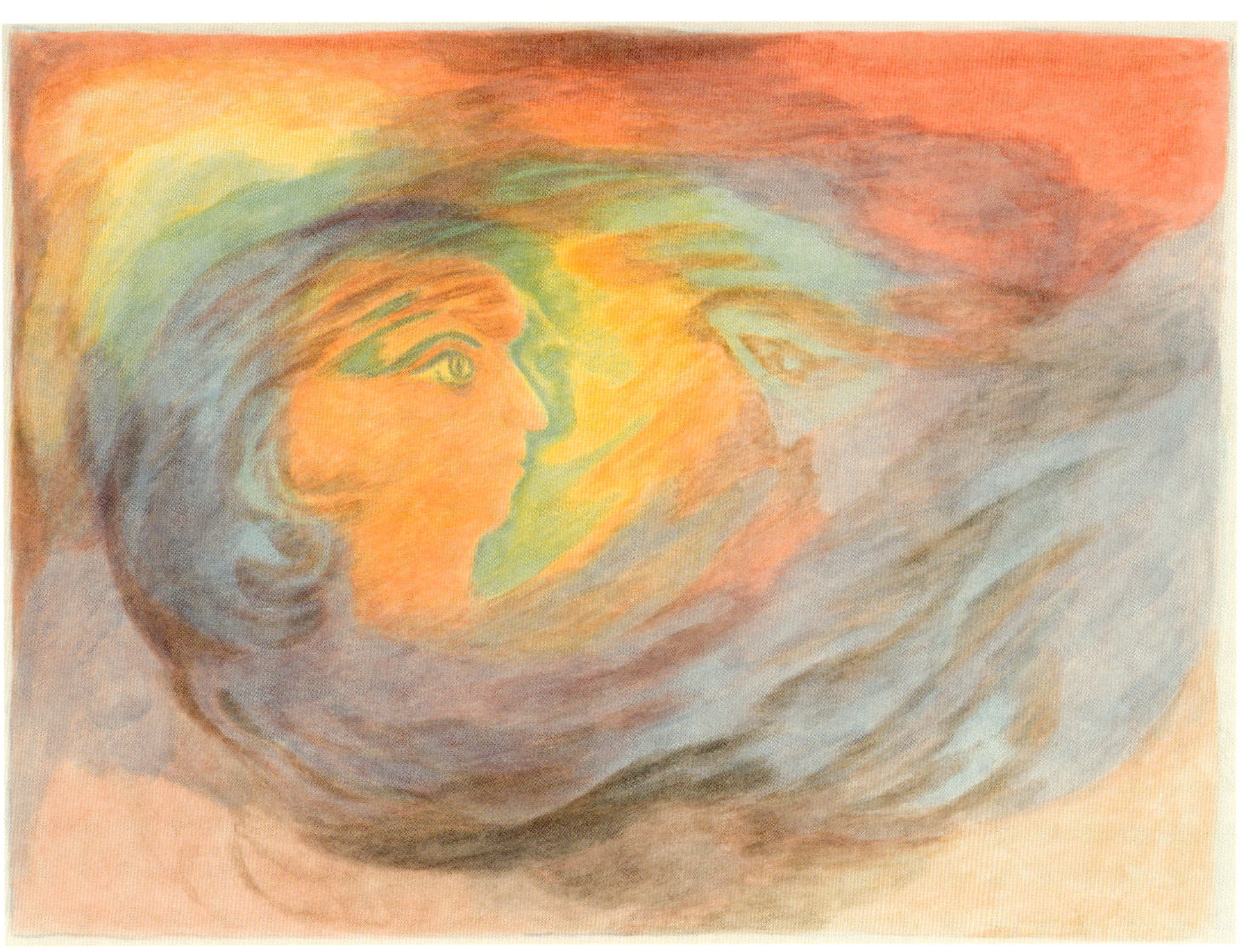

Plate 74: Conversation

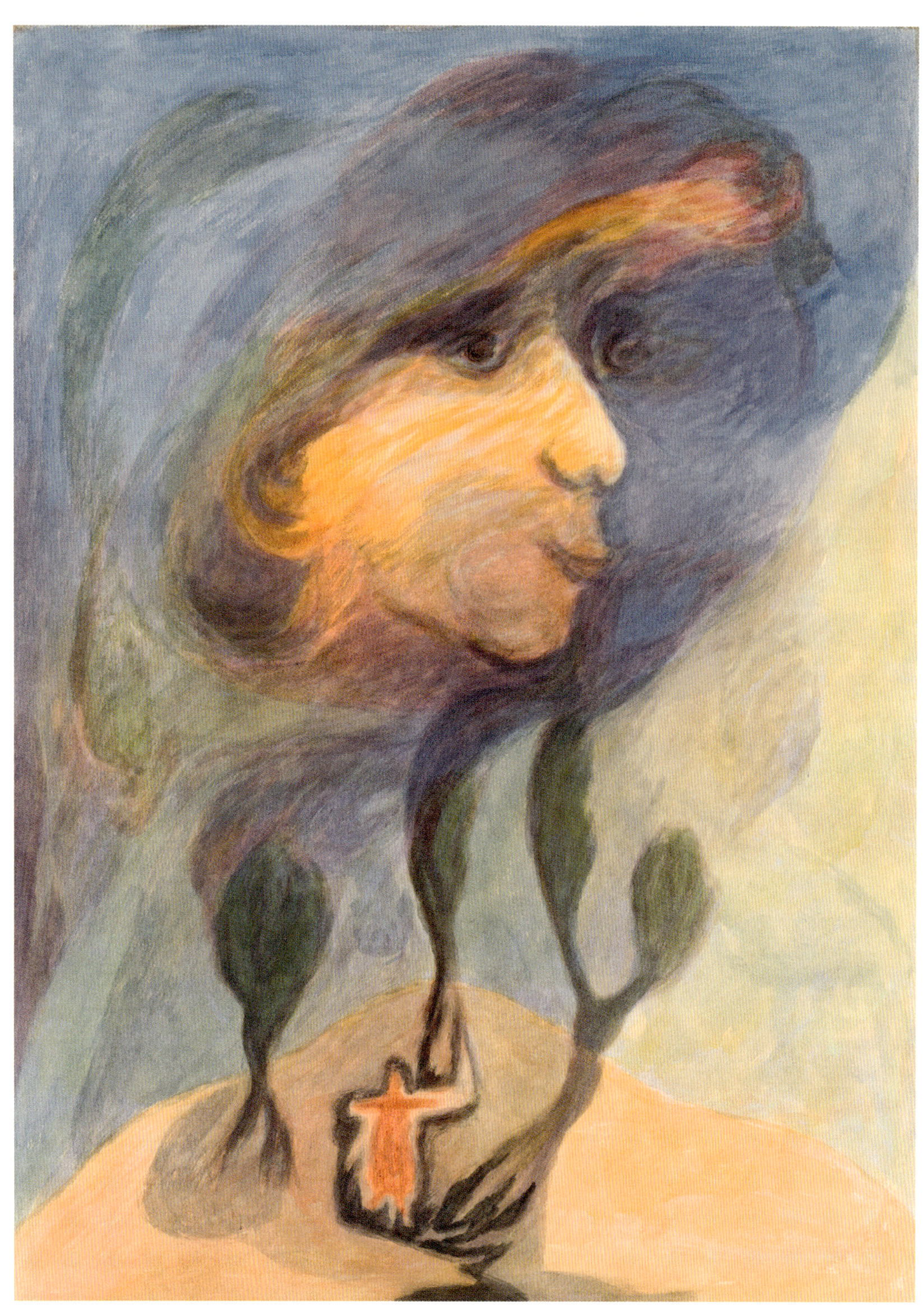

Plate 75: Laddie

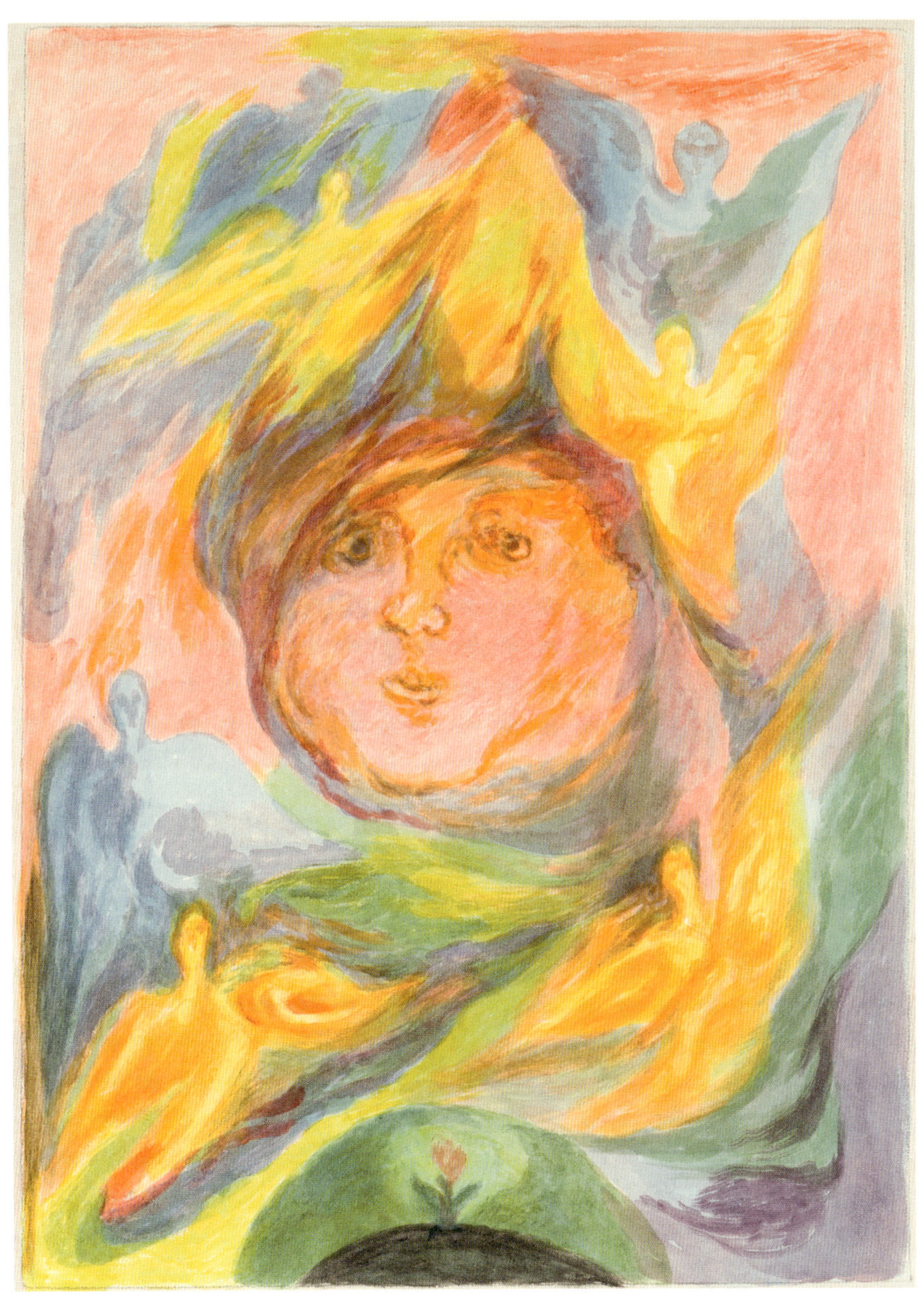

Plate 76: Flower Child

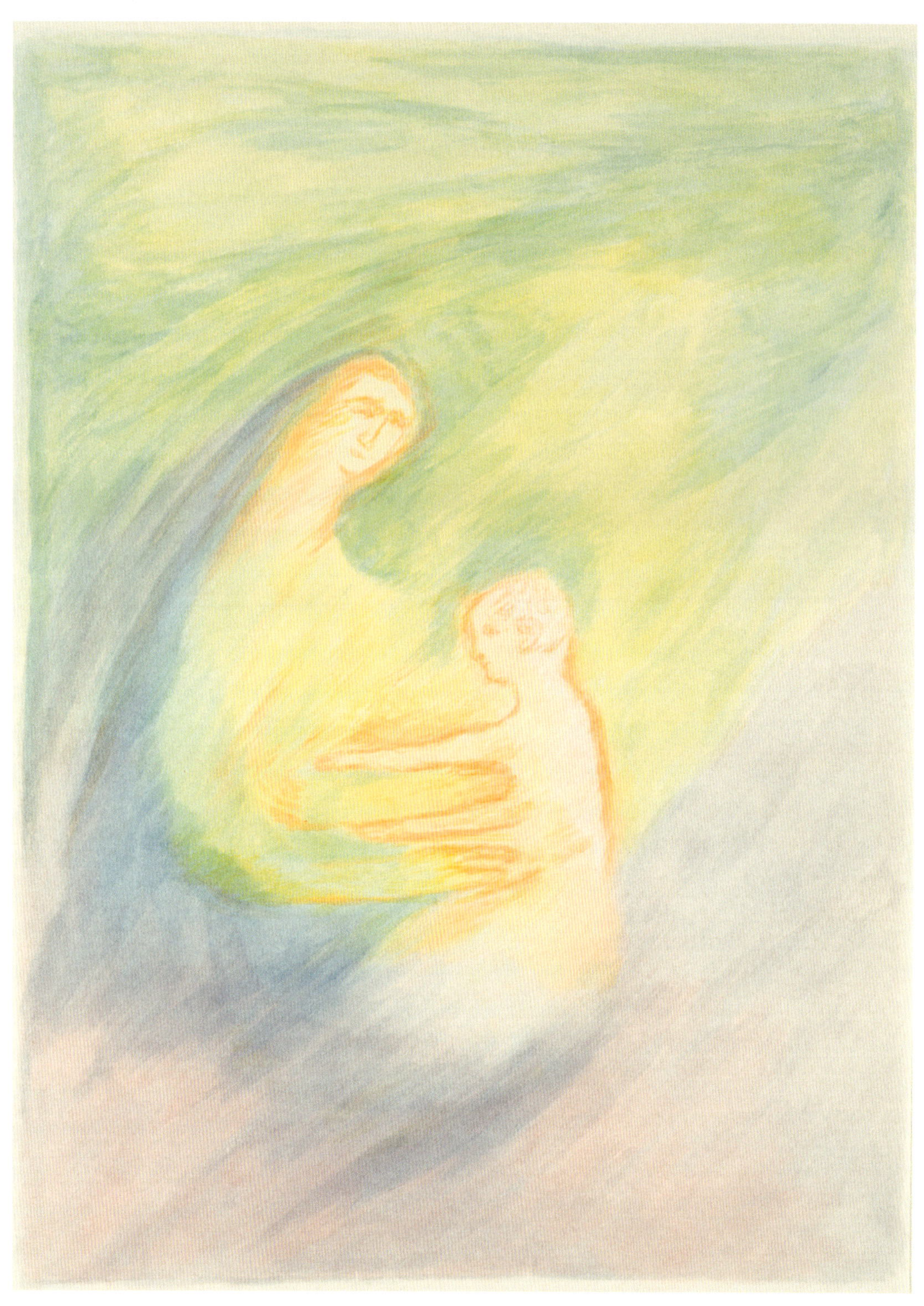

Plate 77: *Mother and Child* (Friedwart Sketch)

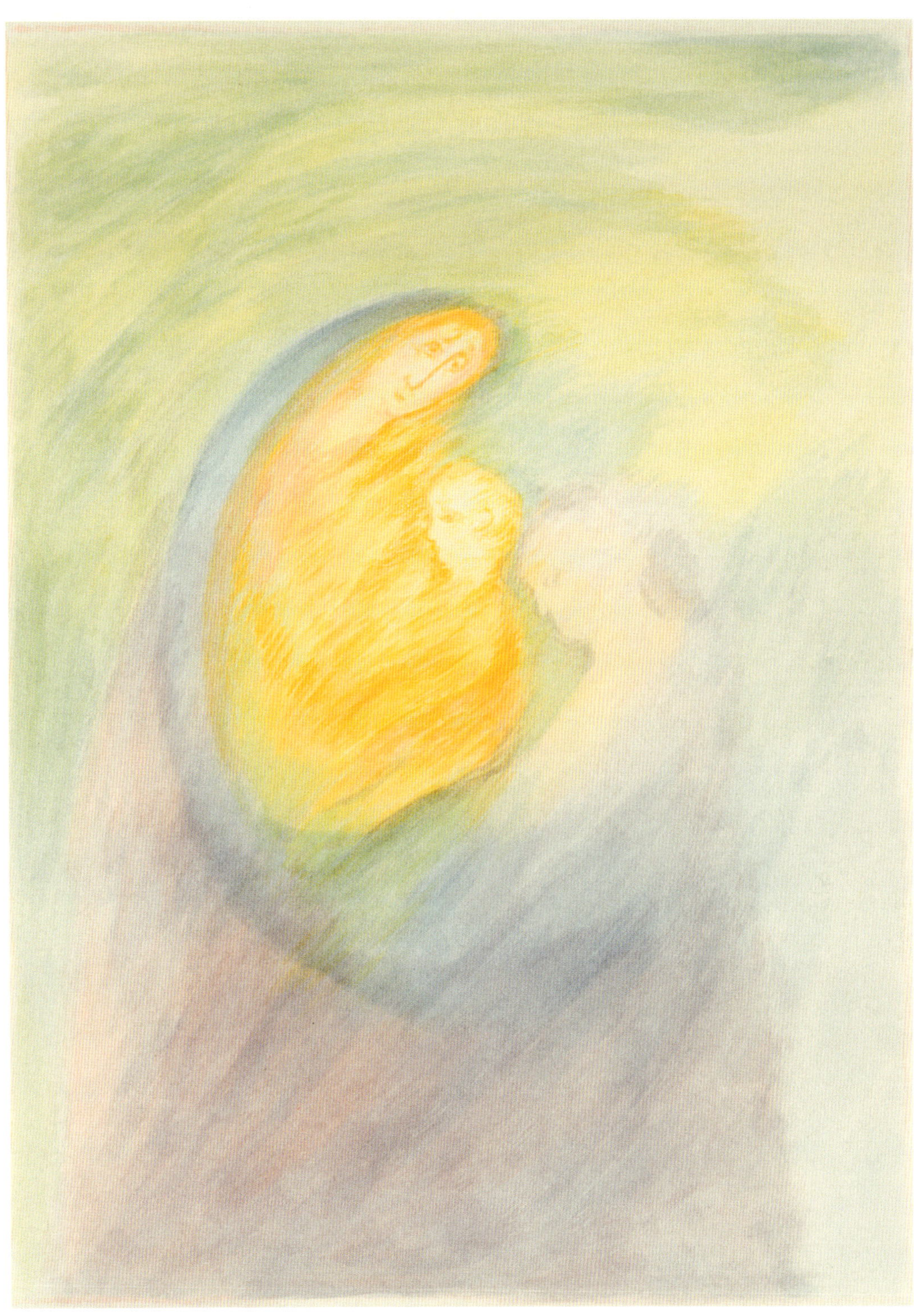

Plate 78: *Mother and Child*

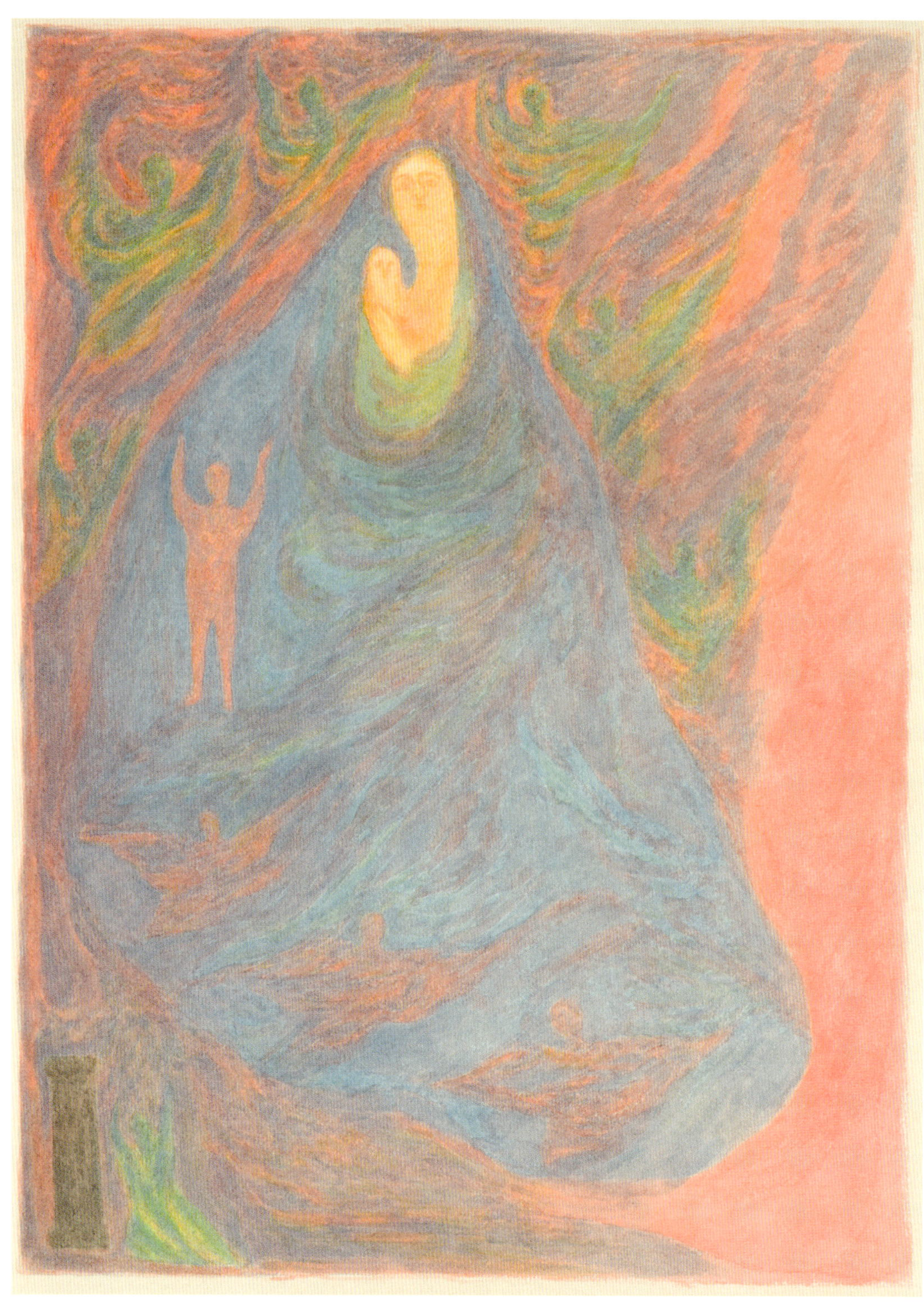

Plate 79: Mother and Child

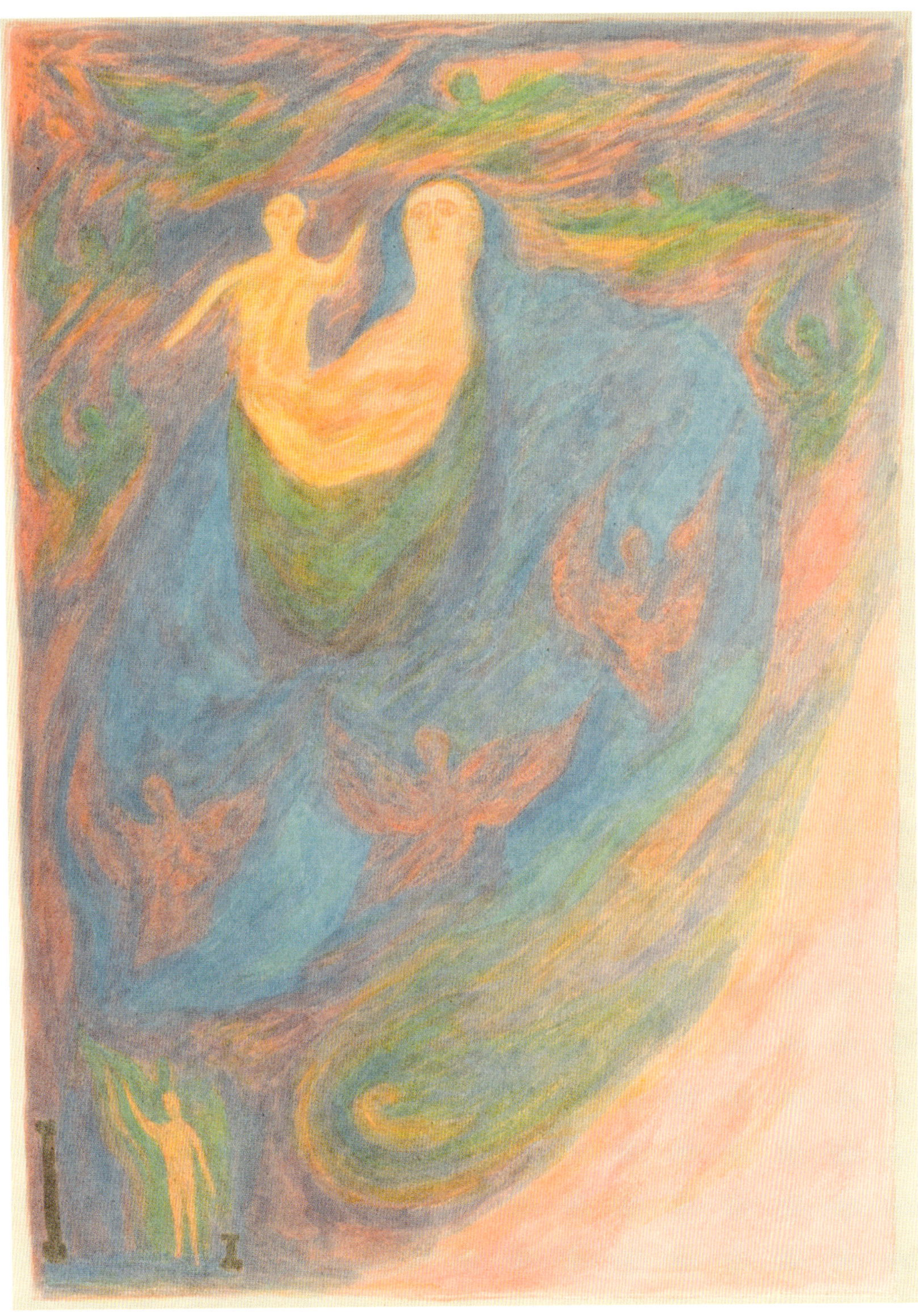

Plate 80: Mother and Child

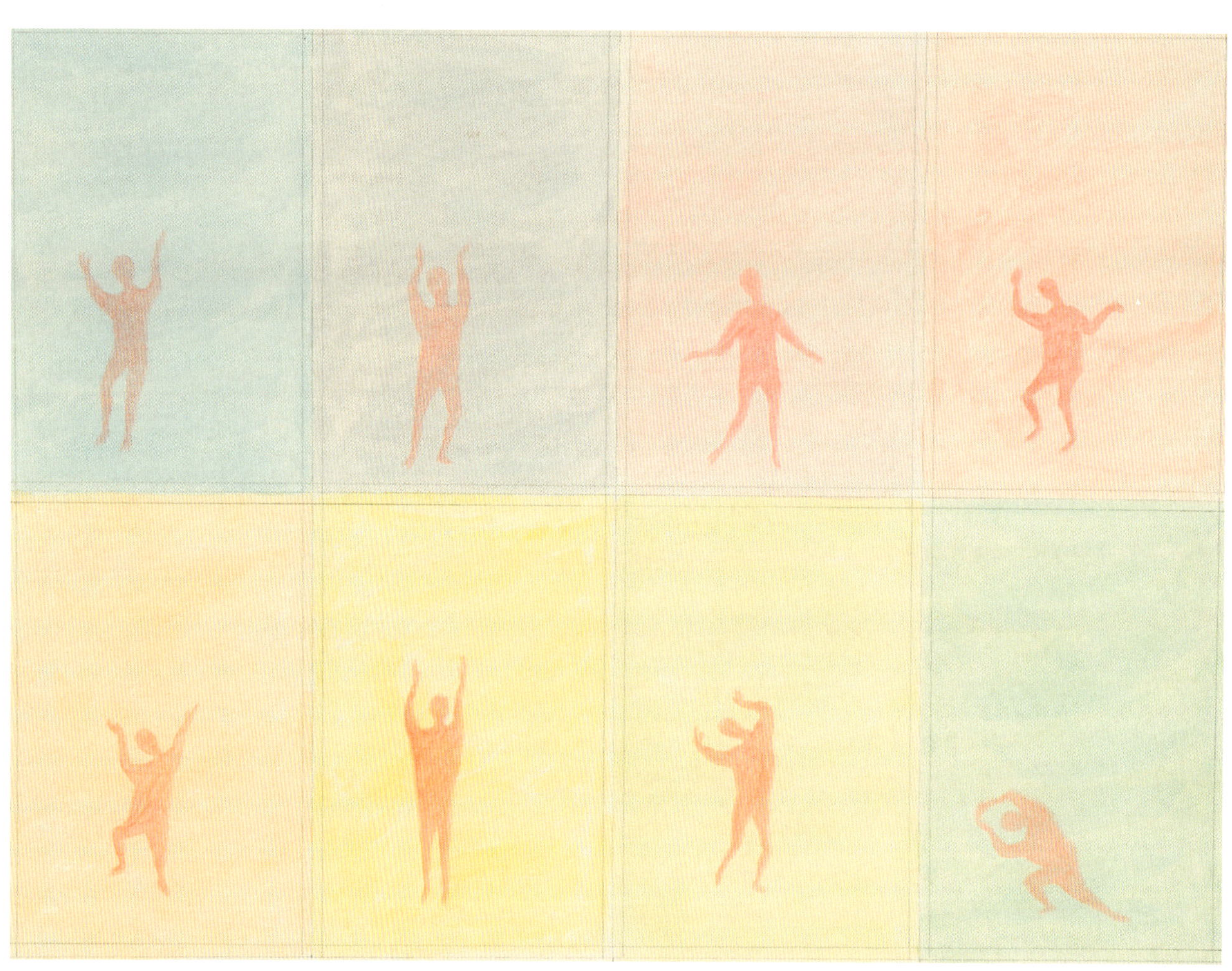

Plate 81: Incarnadine on different colour backgrounds

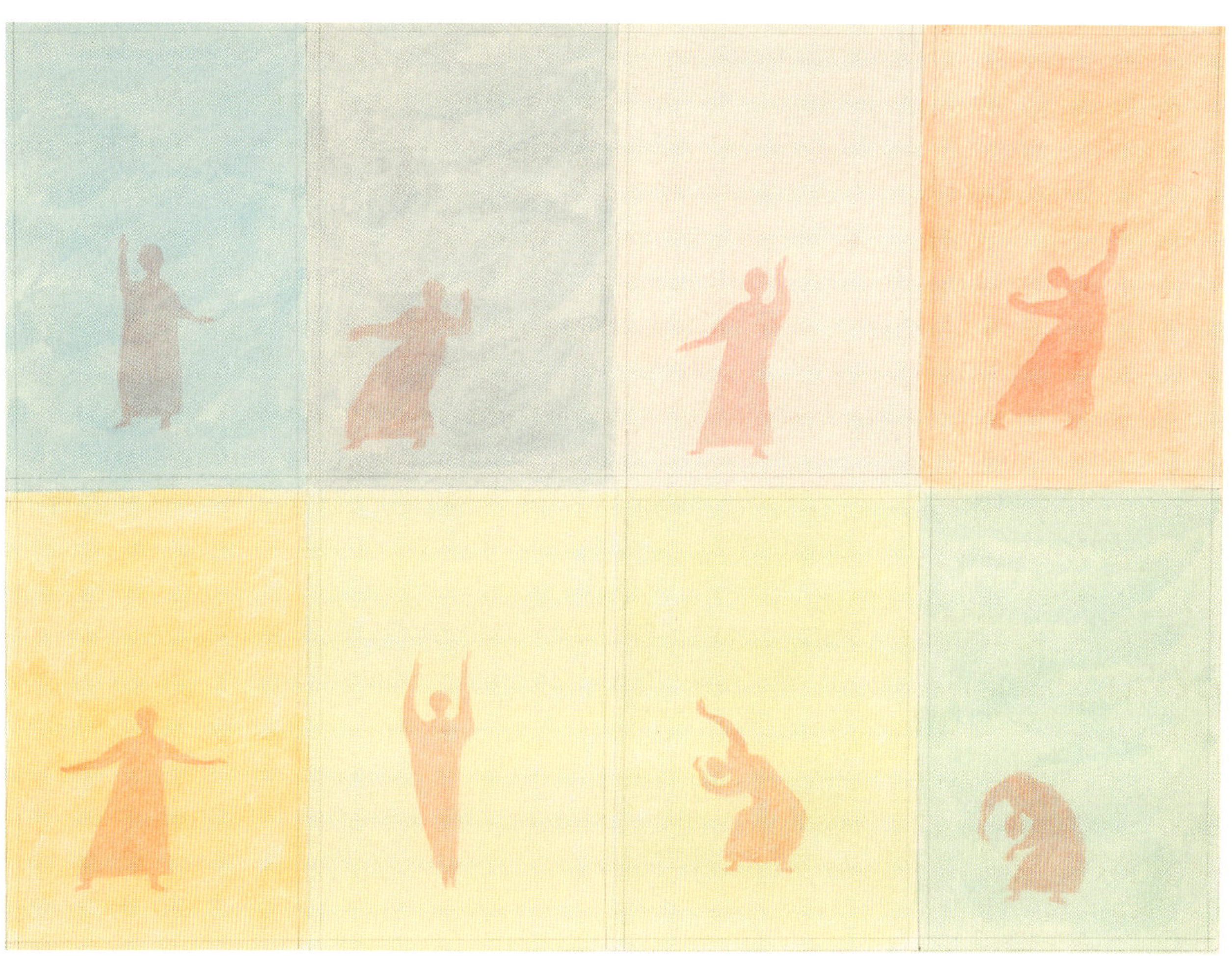

Plate 82: Incarnadine on different colour backgrounds

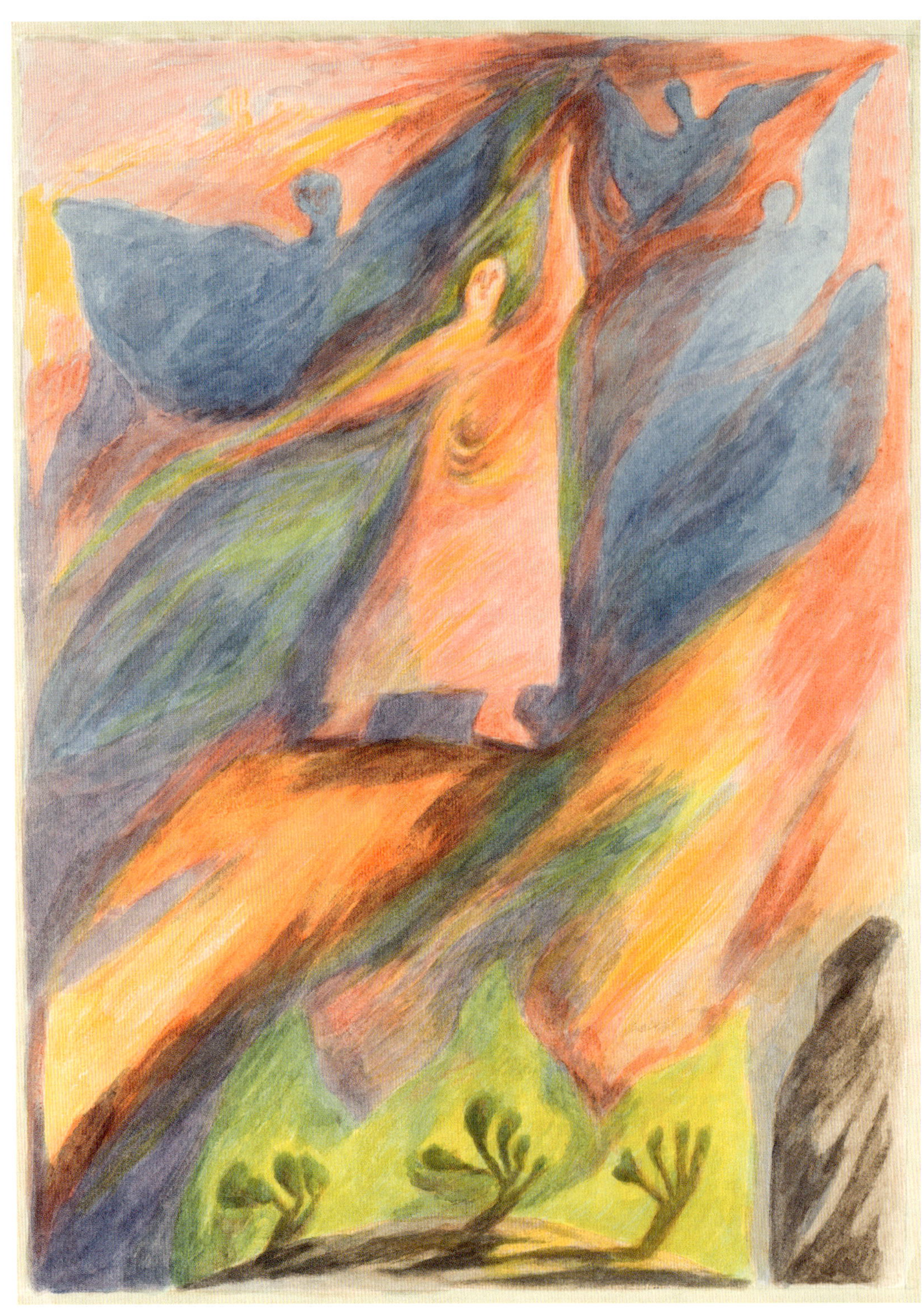

Plate 83: Youth

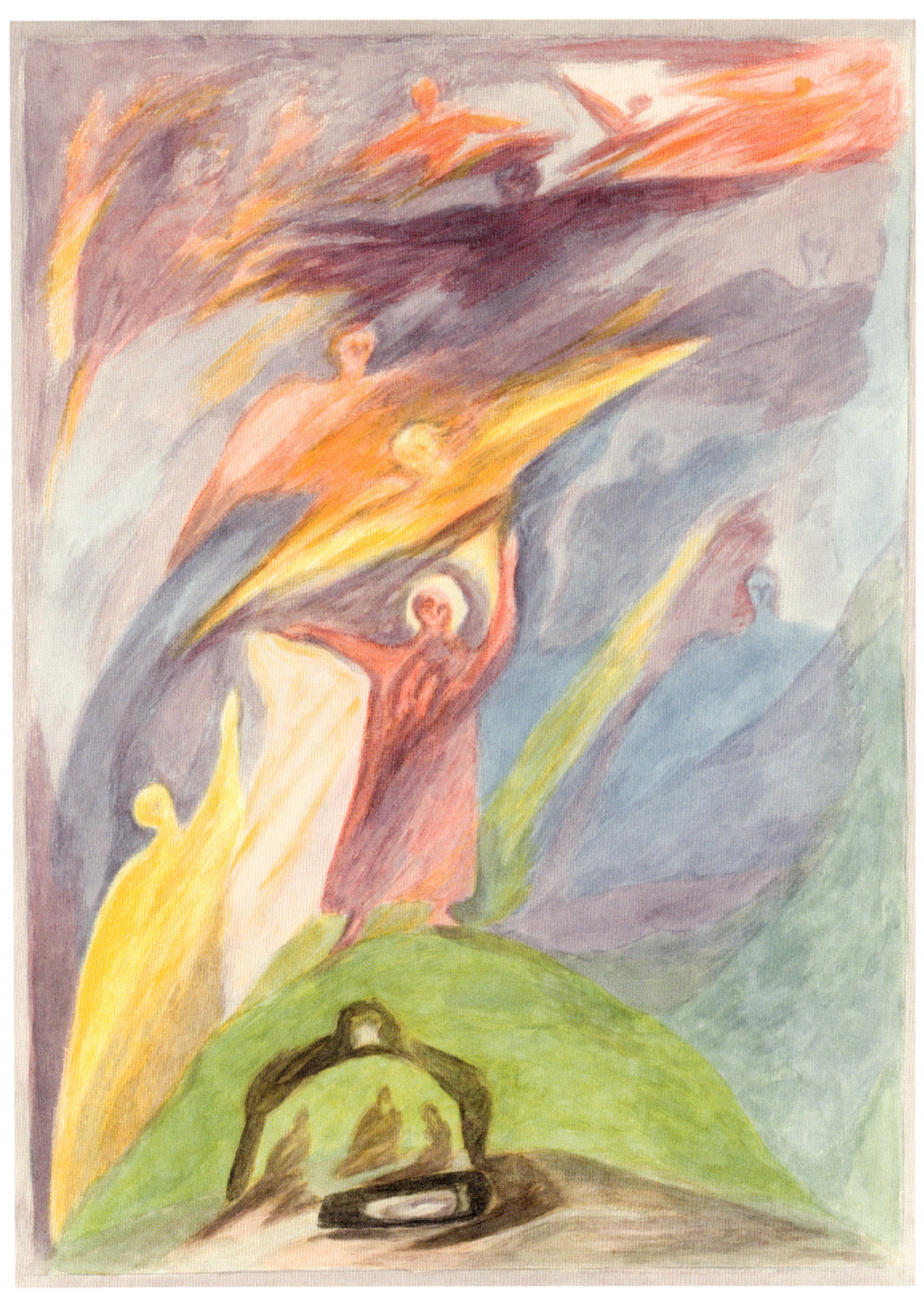

Plate 84: Age

THE CUPOLA MOTIFS

Sketches of the cupola motifs of the first Goetheanum were essentially the earliest picture-creations of Rudolf Steiner's. They were given as guidance to the artists who were preparing to paint the ceilings of the two cupolas in 1914.[34] The motifs of the large cupola show the evolution of the world, beginning with the creation of the earth by the Elohim and developing towards the four great Post-Atlantean culture epochs of Ancient India, Ancient Persia, Egypt and Greece. The motifs of the small cupola show the inner evolution of humanity and culminate in the central motif of the 'Representative of Humanity'.

Gerard Wagner's own words from the monograph *The Art of Colour*[35] give insight into how he approached the motifs of the large cupola which are painted on a rainbow coloured background. He describes how he found entry into the motif of *Eye and Ear*:

> 'The cupola motifs of the First Goetheanum were also models for constant inner research initially through their colour moods but later focusing on the necessity of their configuration, and on the connection between the motifs. They are painted out of the colour in the same way as the other motifs of Rudolf Steiner's. One can experience them as a single motif which, on the background of rainbow colours that covered the cupola, changes accordingly depending on the background colour on which it is painted. One needs to have the influence of the background colour in one's consciousness for an understanding of the figuration of the motif. Like the Training Sketches, the cupola pictures are filled with the same objective life-element. They also carry within them the principle of metamorphosis.
>
> To avoid entering into an inartistic copying, the motif 'Eye and Ear' was approached in the following way: I painted a small surface of black and placed it opposite a small surface of brown – enveloped in a blue mood – in a similar way to how it appears in the sketch of Rudolf Steiner's. I then asked myself in which order the colours would need to be painted to be able to enter into the formative forces which would lead to this motif? How would the colour crystallize in relation to the black and brown? And I tried: deep blue – light blue – red – green – until an order of colours gave me the feeling that it would out of necessity lead to the given motif, naturally with the help of the original sketch that I had constantly before me. In this way it became possible to follow one's own artistic feeling without copying but at the same time to have an impetus from outside that gave direction.

What arose in this connection often did not bear much resemblance to the pictures of Rudolf Steiner's; it was more important to me that what I painted should be able to stand for itself artistically, be artistically alive. How to choose the colours which would lead to Rudolf Steiner's result was a constant question for me. One might think that working in this way would create dependency on the model, on the original of Rudolf Steiner's, but it's exactly the opposite. In that one follows one's own experience of what one feels as artistic necessity, even if this leads to something different to the original, one becomes free, independent of it. The colour experience must become stronger than the mental image, must totally supplant it. Then we are led into the region of the living colour out of which the motifs form themselves ever new.

A life time of artistic work with the cupola motifs as a whole can lead to the surprising impression that the painter stands before quite new unresolved questions, and can come to the mysterious realisation that one motif, 'Eye and Ear' for example, which can be experienced as if within a mood of blue, can transform into the 'Paradise' motif when painted on a green background, and painted on indigo would lead to the 'Elohim' motif.

By deepening one's work with the cupola motifs as a totality, the conviction can arise that the various motifs are all transformations of each other, modified by the background colour, as also by the curvature of the cupola form. The motifs appear as a living being which in different times, conditions and places, 'incarnates' in various configurations.'

Gerard Wagner turned to the motifs of the Goetheanum cupolas again and again, right up until his last creative period. One of his late works is the outstanding metamorphic sequence (plates 90 to 93) that begins with the motif of *Eye and Ear*.

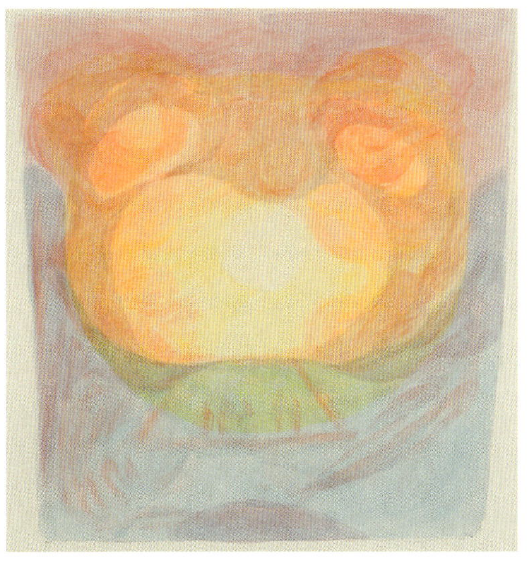

a

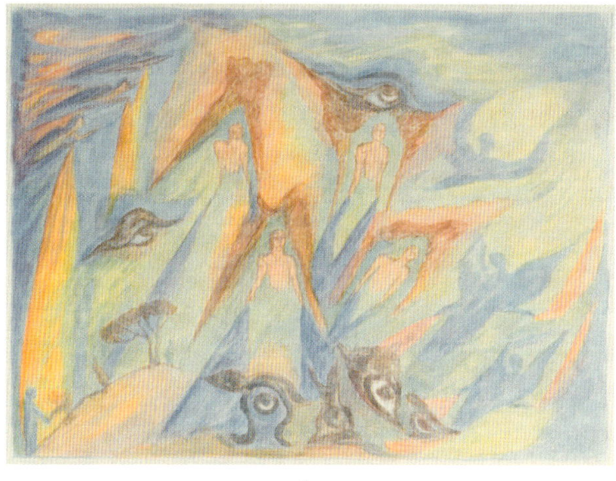

b

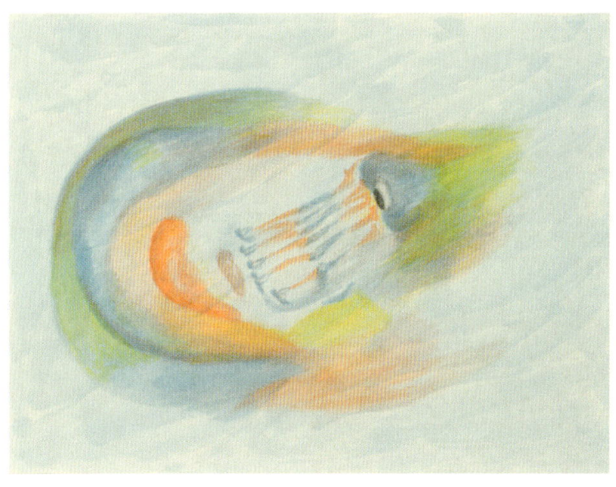

c

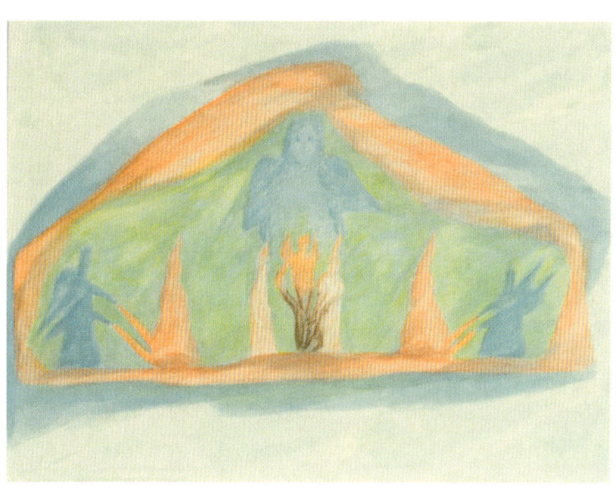

d

Plate 85: a) A sketch of the coloured background to the large Cupola in the trapeze form of the second Goetheanum,
b) *The Elohim work creatively into the Earth; Light-Beings radiate into it,*
c) *The Senses are Born (Eye and Ear),*
d) *Jehovah and the Luciferic Temptation / Paradise*

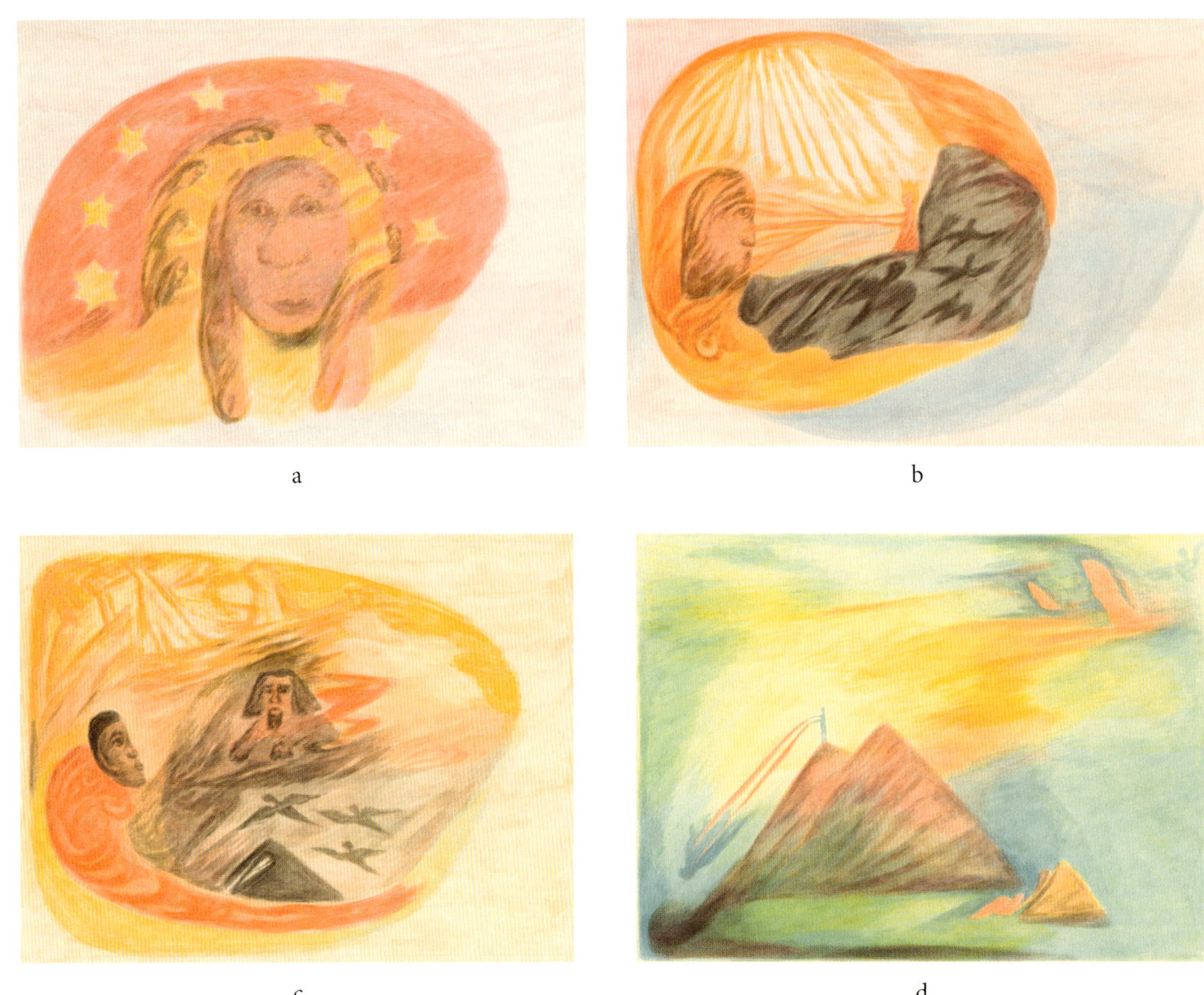

Plate 86: a) *The Ancient Indian,* b) *The Ancient Persian,* c) *The Ancient Egyptian,* d) *Greece and the Oedipus Motif*

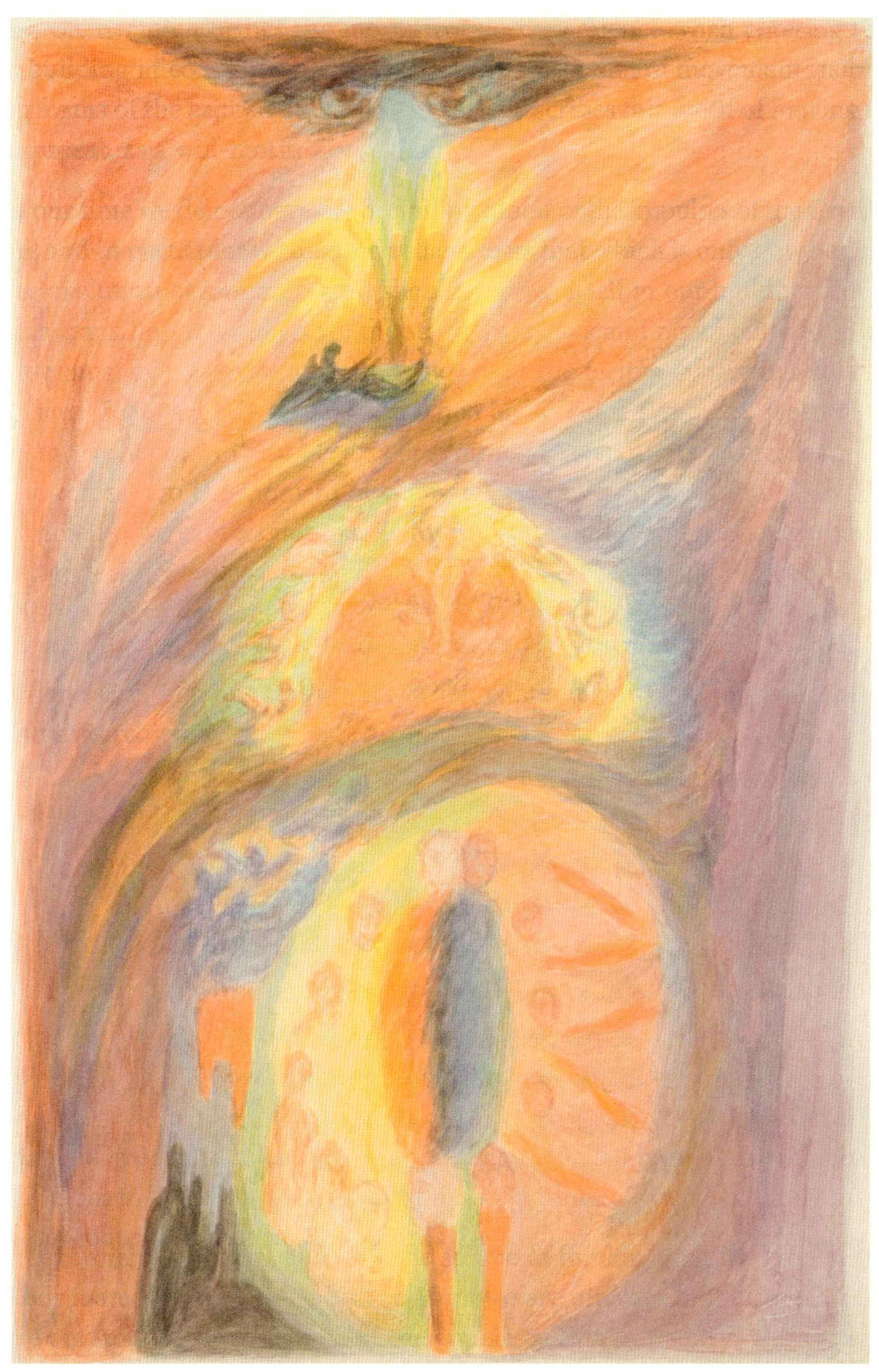

Plate 87: *I–A–O*, Top: *The Wrath of God and the Yearning Grief of God/ 'I'*
Middle: *The Round of Seven/ 'A'*
Bottom: *The Circle of Twelve/ 'O'*

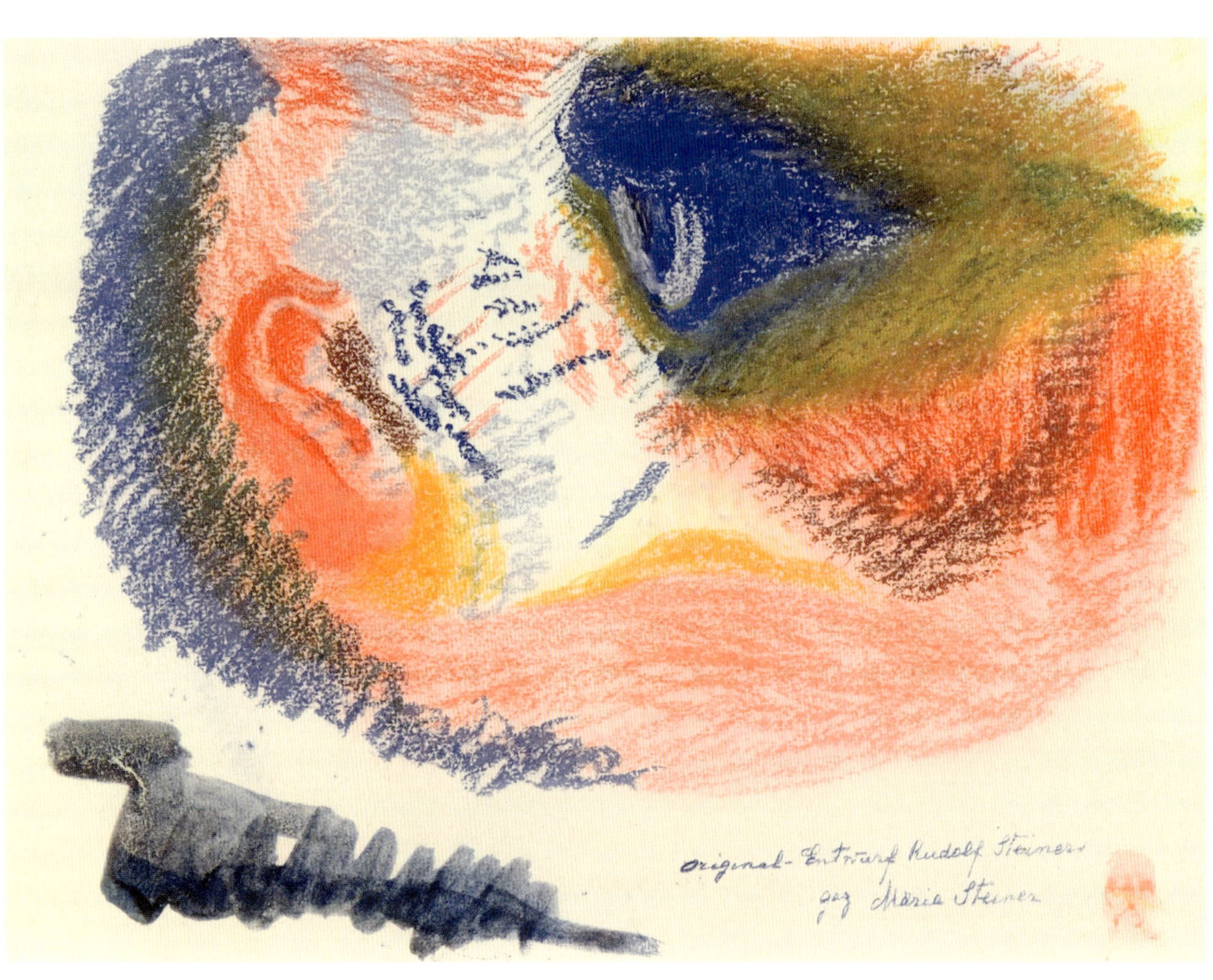

Plate 88: *Eye and Ear* motif, pastel drawing by Rudolf Steiner

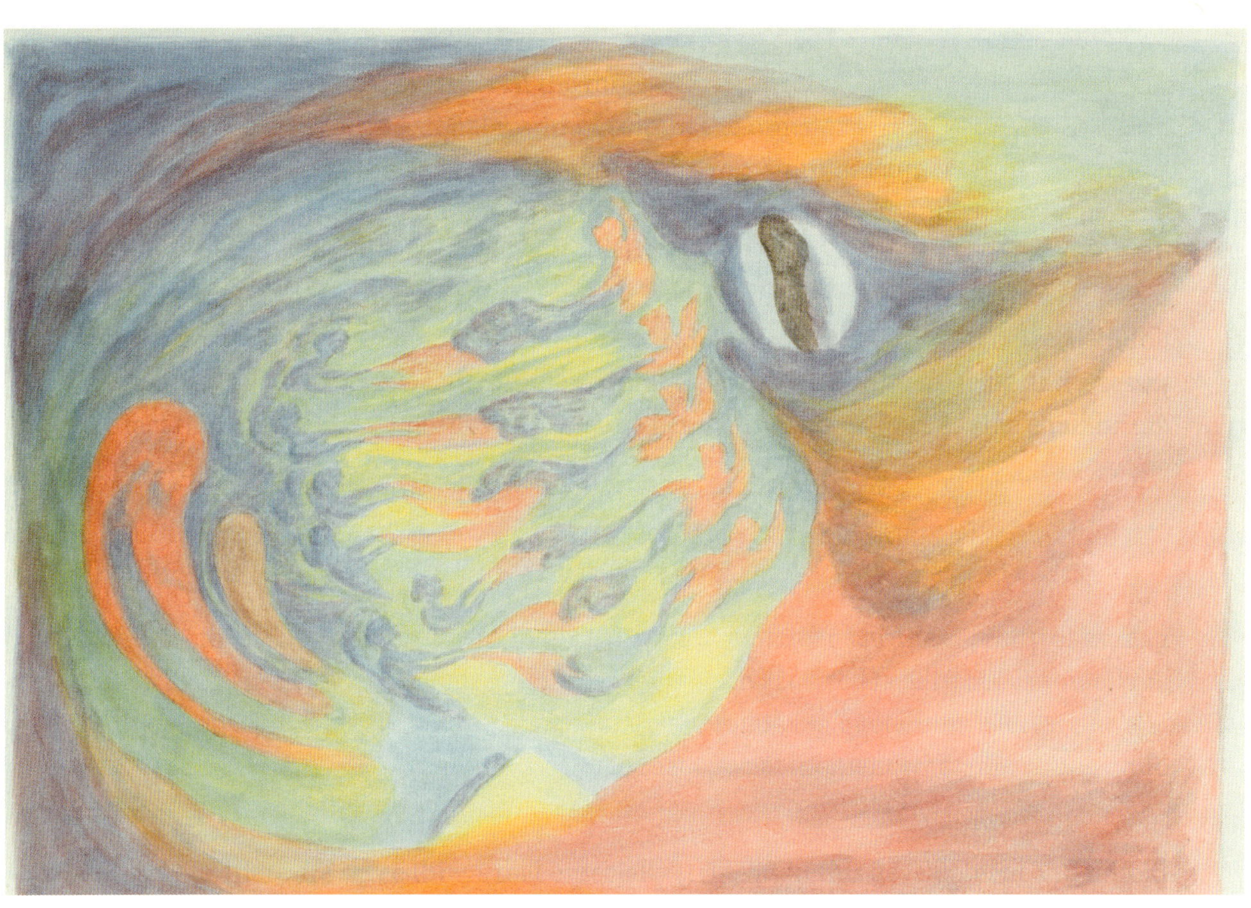

Plate 89: *Eye and Ear* motif

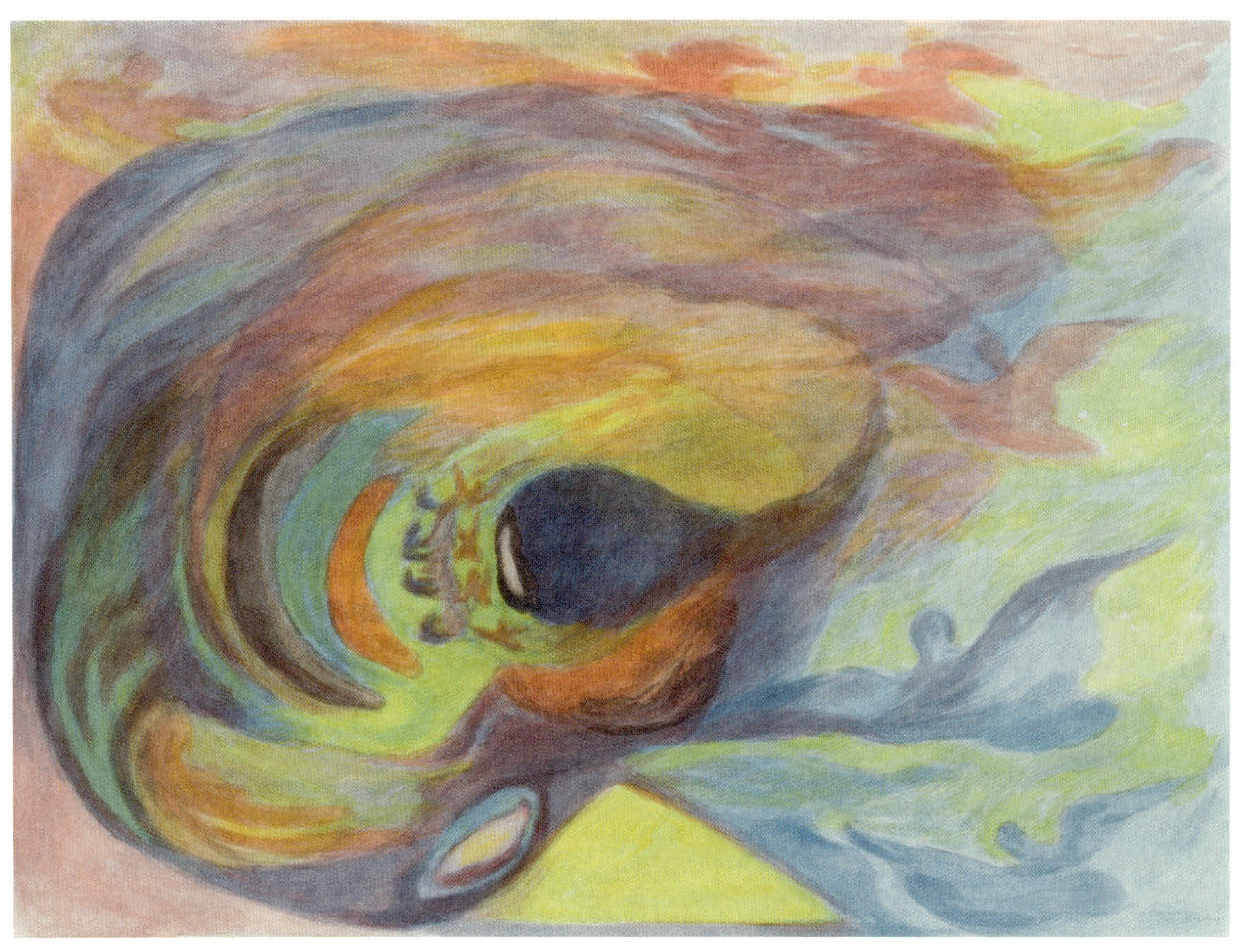

1

Plate 90: Metamorphosis of the *Eye and Ear* motif

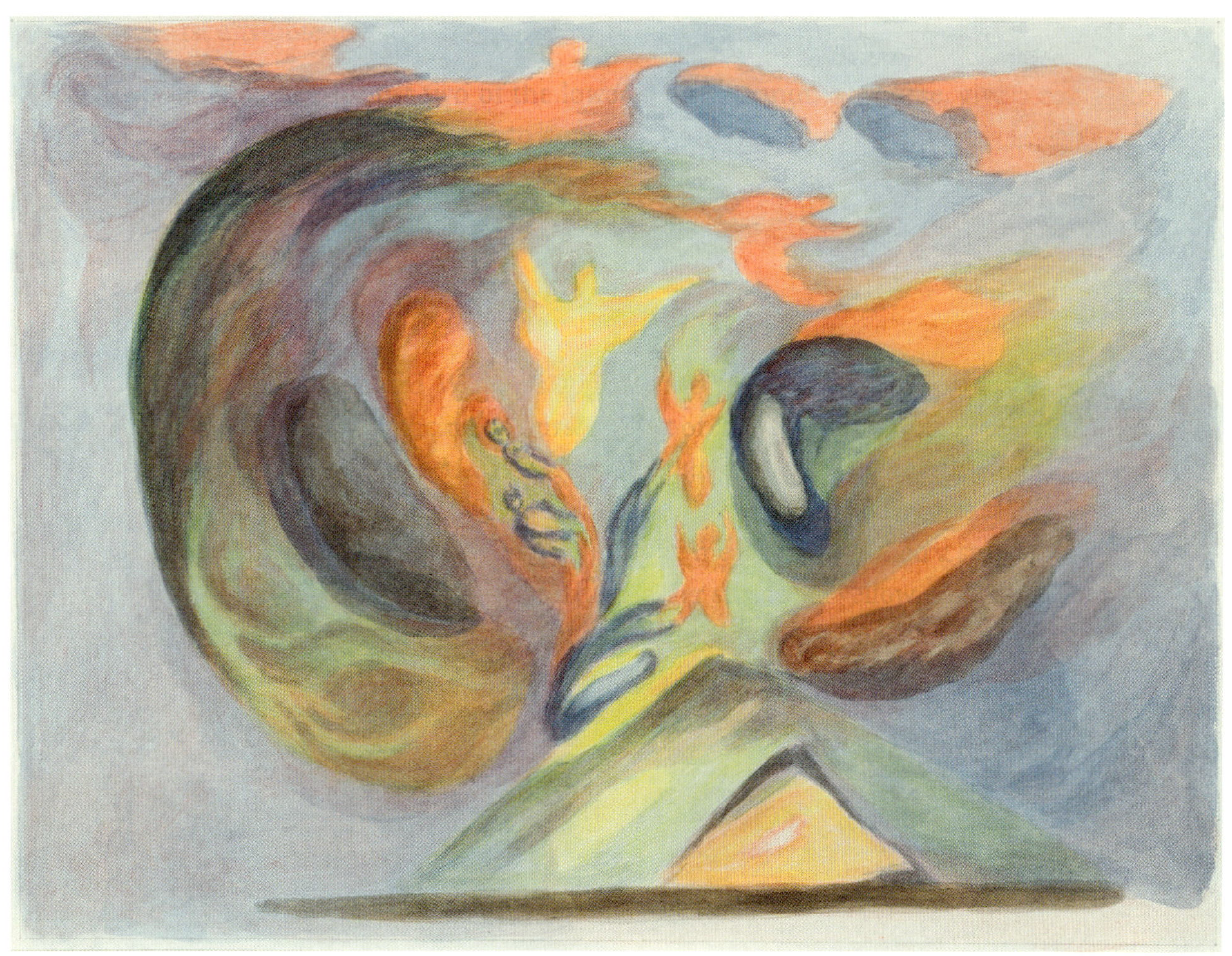

2

Plate 91: Metamorphosis of the *Eye and Ear* motif

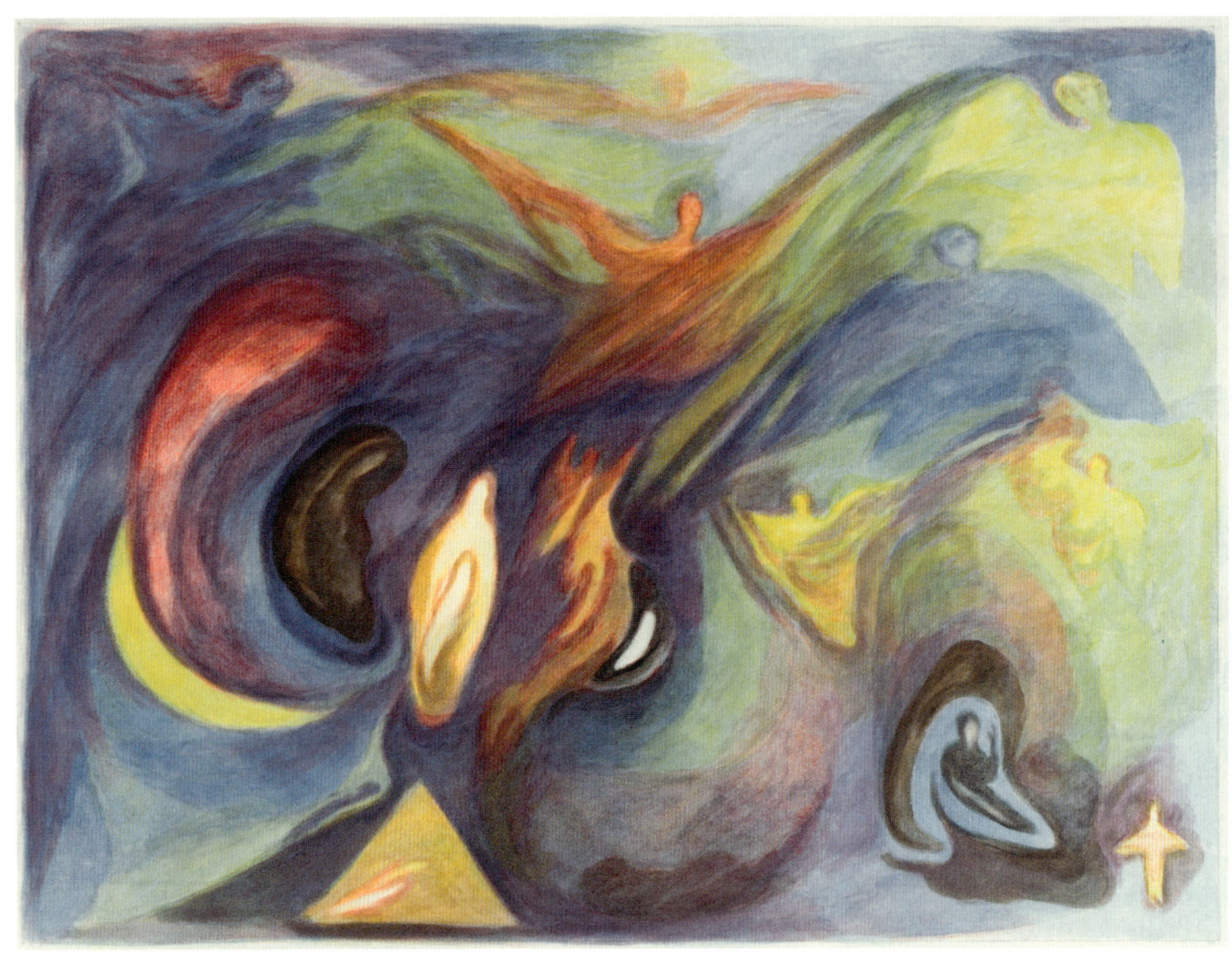

3

Plate 92: Metamorphosis of the *Eye and Ear* motif

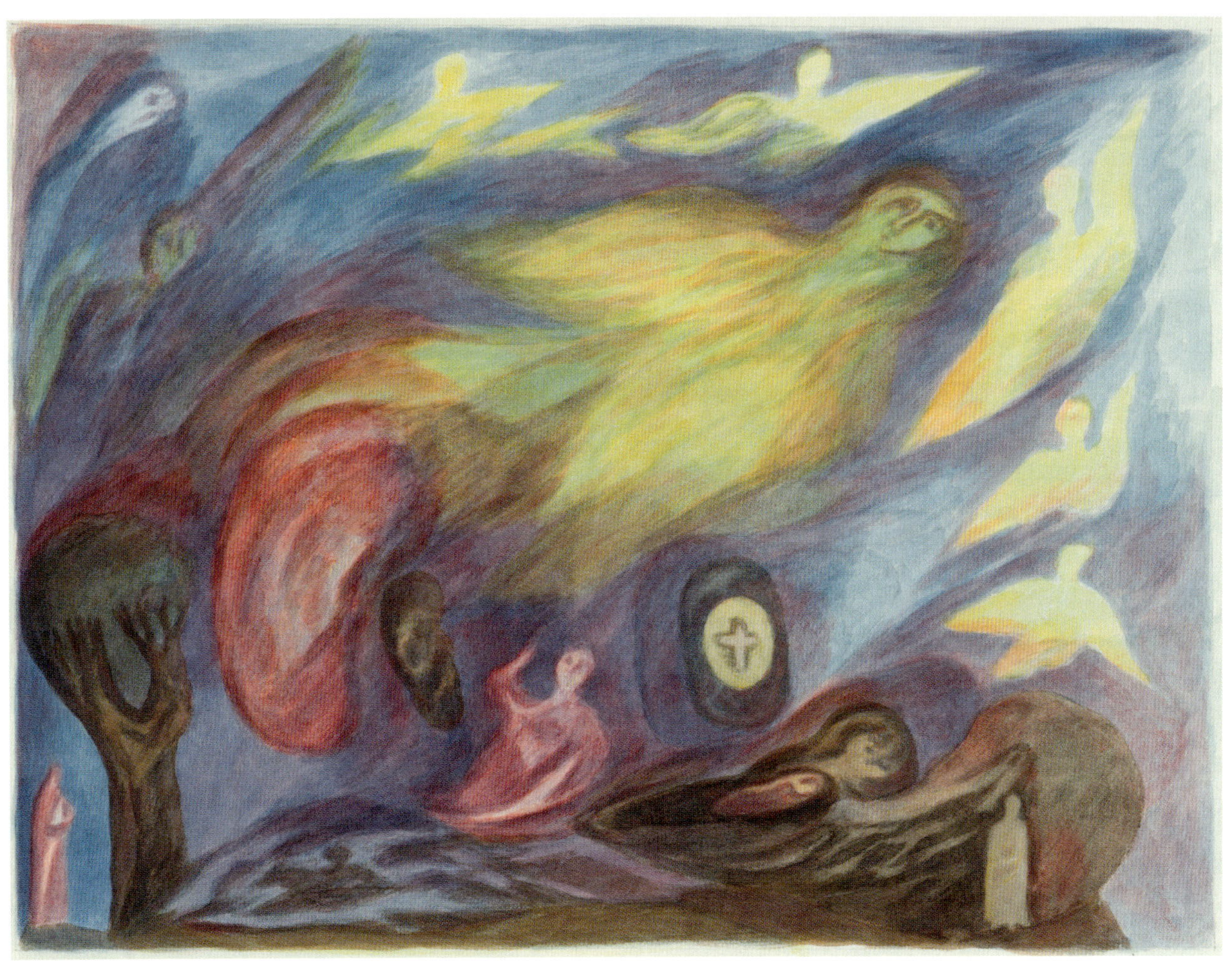

4

Plate 93: Metamorphosis of the *Eye and Ear* motif

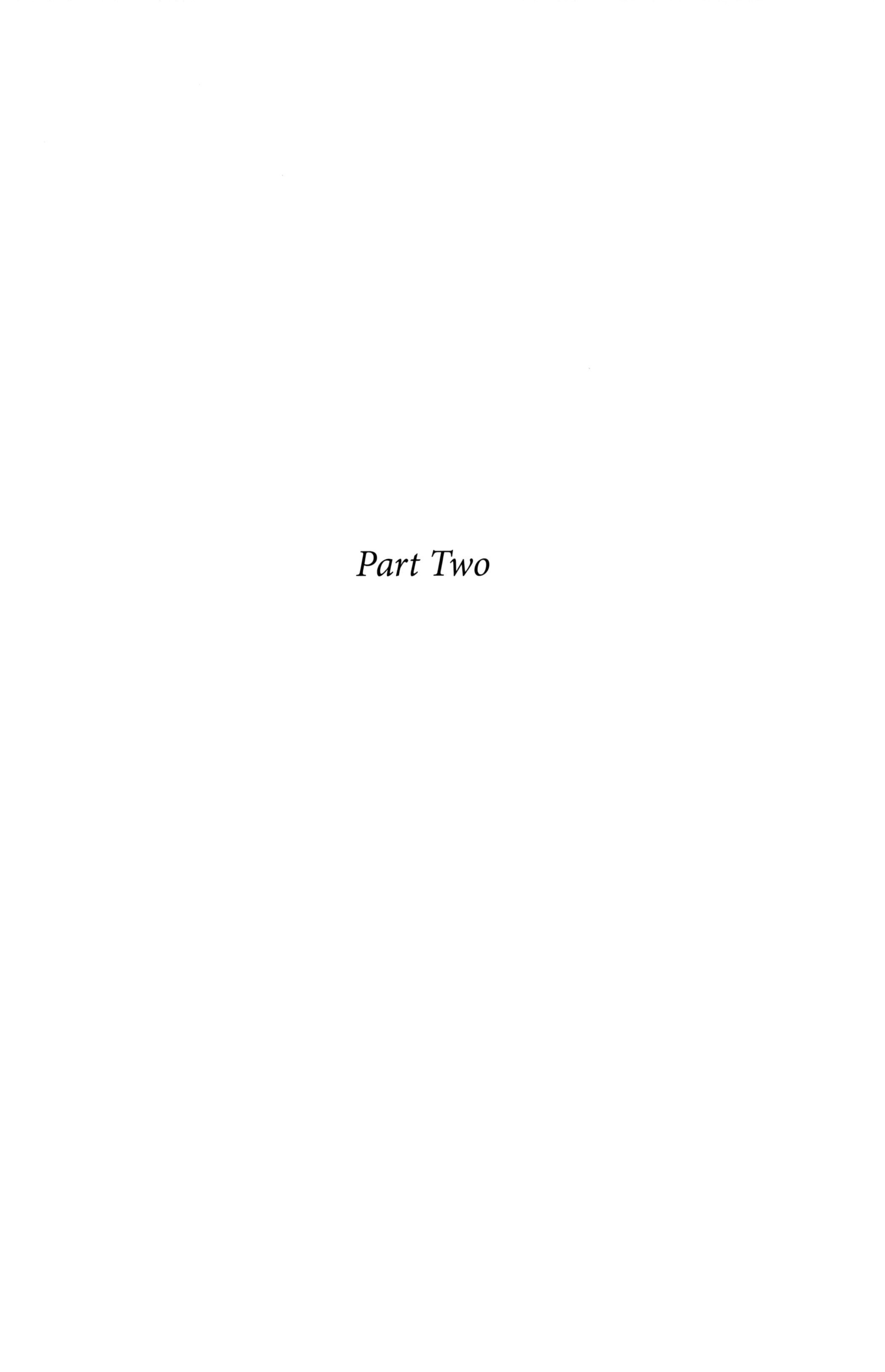

Part Two

GERARD WAGNER'S APPROACH TO BALANCE IN PAINTING

Balance has always been an essential aspect of painting. In earlier times rules of classical composition guided the artists in their ordering and harmonizing of the picture space. Centuries later painters abandoned traditional ways and developed their own individual approaches to colour and form. The creating of balance in a painting became more instinctive and was guided to a greater extent by the painter's feelings. One could say the 'inner' aspect became as important or more important than the 'outer'.

Gerard Wagner developed inwardness to a high degree in the way he painted. He practised making himself conscious of the feelings that were arising in his soul as he applied the colours. This is difficult to do. It is like looking with one part of yourself at another, less conscious part of yourself. Something we do when, say, we are thinking about our feelings. It is an ego activity during which the 'I' surveys from 'above', so to speak, what is happening 'below' in the soul (astral body). The concentration needed to bring such experiences to consciousness, to call to mind what takes place normally in the dreamy or half-conscious realm of feeling, is a will activity and can be likened to meditation. Through such activity the soul life is strengthened, and slumbering powers are awakened.

We can get an idea of the inner process Gerard Wagner went through by way of a letter he wrote to a colleague who had asked him to describe the first and last steps of painting a picture. In Wagner's detailed answer we become aware that his aim is to achieve a state of balance in the painting by creating a colour wholeness – a unity of colour which is reflected as a feeling of wholeness in the painter. This feeling of wholeness he describes as an 'experience of the awakened I-consciousness of the entire threefold human being'.

He gives an example of his approach by describing the interaction of the colours black, green and red.

He begins by 'measuring himself 'into the white picture space and then paints black. For him this is not simply an aesthetic question for he is noticing how the balance of colour is affecting his feelings, or, as he writes, his 'state of consciousness'. He explains that he is looking for a harmonious balance between the black and the white, and to achieve this he is comparing inwardly the dynamic polarities of qualities such as: life and lifelessness, weight and counterweight, closedness and openness. Too much black in relation to the white makes him feel oppressed, cramped or even ill. The right amount makes him feel awake in a healthy way.

When a harmonious balance between the black and white has been reached, green is added to the painting. Green enlivens the black and at the same time enlivens the painter who feels more complete than before. But, he says, if left at that, the colours would leave him, relatively speaking, in a dull state of mind. Then red joins the other colours and the whole situation changes dramatically. As the red is painted to the green and black a whole new world of life and joy opens up. Again, Wagner describes how the first two colours are being affected by the red but also how he himself is being affected. He feels animated, more alive in his whole being. He notices, compared with the first two colours, that he experiences the red 'much more inwardly' and that the red colour is related to 'quite another member(part) of the human being'.

Let us take a look at what Gerard Wagner wrote in the letter. As already mentioned, he begins the painting with black after having first connected himself inwardly with the white colour of the paper:

> 'The first step [when painting a picture] is to measure oneself into the white (or coloured) surface. The last step is the experience of the finished painting that gives one an experience of the awakened I-consciousness of the entire threefold human being.
>
> The fact that only little consciousness is present in the first step is shown by the second step when one measures black, for example, into the white surface. The qualitative experience of the black unites with an inner experience comparable to 'black', and allows one to place the black – on a horizontal format – below. In so doing one becomes conscious of the lightness of the white, perhaps now for the first time, and its quite different quality. This 'becoming conscious of white' begins with the first brushstroke of black, as it is applied to the bottom of the paper. Following step-by-step the feeling of becoming awake, caused by the addition of black, one reaches the point where one says to oneself: I can tolerate only so much, if I bring more black it will oppress me, stifle me, meaning my consciousness will be diminished again (if I take it too far it will rigidify me and make me ill). So I can say: so much black can be held in balance by so much remaining white, and I can pursue this state of balance and notice: so much lifelessness to so much life; so much weight to so much counter-weight; so much closedness to so much openness, and so on. My consciousness is a stage more awake when it experiences the balanced relationship between black and white than it was when it experienced the white surface only. But it is far away from a state of complete human consciousness, which is immediately apparent when one begins to introduce a third colour, e.g. green. One experiences right away, when beginning to measure in the green to the black

and white, that its place [in the painting] is determined by it being lighter than black and denser than white, that the 'spreading out' [of the green], in relation to black, is caused by it being less concentrated [than the black], so the green surface will be larger than the black one. Again the lighter value of the green causes an upward direction away from the black. One experiences 'enlivening' through the green, and the black getting lighter through the green. The remaining white changes in quality, and appears pushed back and empty. One experiences also the green as more active than black. In particular one feels more alive in oneself through the green, and in one's consciousness a good bit more satisfied than before.

Nonetheless, if one were to ask oneself how it feels in the world which has so far arisen, one must affirm: if nothing more would come to enhance one's consciousness, if I were able to experience only what the three present colours give me, I would be in a very dull, lifeless condition compared to my awakened I-consciousness; and one becomes conscious of this once more as one begins to measure the fourth colour, red, into the first three. A much stronger living quality than was possible through the green arises, a liveliness and energy which is experienced much more inwardly, which connects to a quite different member of the human being, which is lighter still, which is much more capable of overcoming the deadness of the black, which is much more concentrated (and therefore smaller

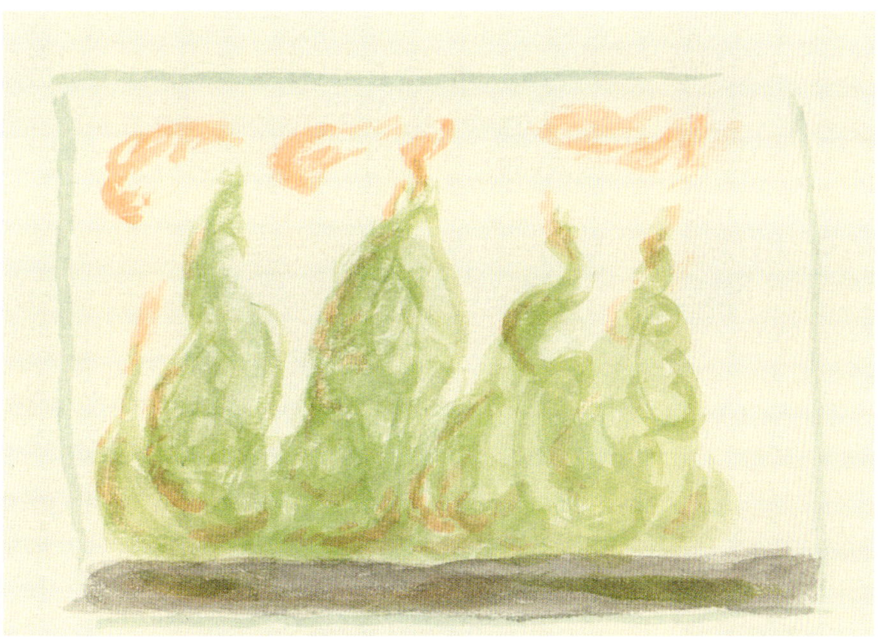

An example of the colour build-up: black, green red, by Gerard Wagner

amounts are enough compared with the amount of green); which enlivens the green (that otherwise, as we now notice, left us feeling thoroughly phlegmatic or at least in a vegetative state), and makes us feel awake, cheerful, with heightened sensibility – and one could say a thousand things more. [...]'

Although Gerard Wagner's description of the process does not continue to the final stage of the painting, it can show in what way an inner experience of balance guided him when he painted.

Readers may be baffled by the expression 'measuring oneself into the picture space'. An explanation will be attempted. Measuring oneself into the picture space can best be experienced by standing before a painting and taking a moment or two to live into the inner feeling of your upright posture. While doing this, you try to identify consciously with your whole bodily form, moving inwardly from your feet to your head and vice versa. You then transfer this upright feeling of your body to the picture in front of you. In so doing, the upper part of the picture becomes your 'upper part' (the head area); the lower part becomes your lower part (the feet area). Between this polarity a middle position, a centre, can be clearly felt. This is where you identify most strongly with your own feeling of self – your 'I' (your heart area). This inward feeling of threefoldness, reflected in the top, bottom and centre of the picture becomes a guide for experiencing the picture space.

If a painting is begun with brown, for example, it would feel right, if the aim is for an inner feeling of balance, to paint this earthy colour at the bottom of the picture. Inwardly you can 'stand' on it. This feeling of standing on something, of being supported, strengthens of your feeling of self. I feel more in balance, in a more inwardly confident state when I have ground under my feet. A comparatively weightless colour, say yellow, painted at the bottom of the picture would give me a totally different feeling. Yellow painted in the middle of the picture would correspond more naturally to my feeling of self as a radiant, spirit-filled being. The shining light-filled yellow (the colour of the spirit) and my 'I' are one. In this way colours can be experienced in relation to a feeling of inner balance. (The position of the colours in the picture space changes according to *when* in the process of creation, a certain colour is painted. The examples given here aim to show just two basic principles, not a hard and fast rule for every painting.)

Goetheanum Form-Motifs and Inner Balance

During lectures held for his co-workers during the building of the first Goetheanum Rudolf Steiner was at pains to stress the importance of *experiencing* works of art. In the lecture of 24 October 1914[36] he takes his audience through various inner experiences of the

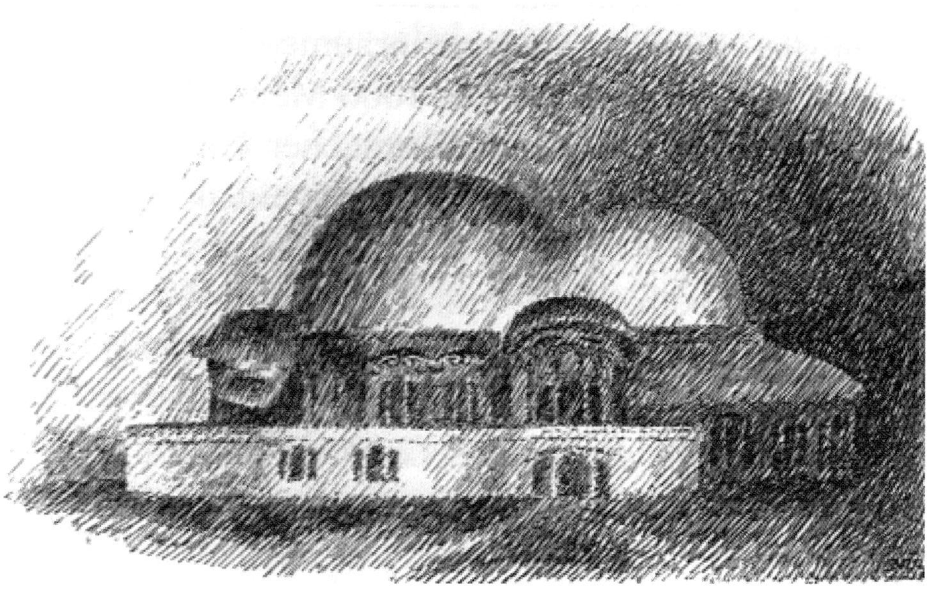

The first Goetheanum from the south

building's architectural and sculptural form-motifs. He begins by drawing a cupola resting on four columns and asks how one can live into the forces of such a motif. He explains that this form is part of a dynamic configuration between the earth and the forces of the universe, and by living into such a form-motif one can come to experience what feeling is.

> '[...] It would be short sighted to assume that such a form stands there for itself. Nothing in the world stands there closed off and for itself – no flower, no animal, no human being, and no such motif.
>
> For it is essential to realise that as part of such a motif, forces are present beyond the form's geometrical context. In geometrical terms this form consists of four columns covered by a cupola. But this is only part of it. What belongs to it is the configuration of forces inherent in the structure of the universe which make it possible for the columns to carry the cupola. The cupola rests on the columns, the columns stand on the earth: hence gravity comes into play.
>
> [...] Now, it is a question of experiencing such a motif, of trying to feel into the form artistically so that one can feel what it expresses – of course one has to really deepen one's experience of the character of the form to know what it reveals – then one can reach the point of being able to say: this motif which is lifted up from the earth, and at least in its top part is symmetrical in every direction; this motif exerts the kind of impulse on us, as if we go into ourselves and experience our feeling inwardly.'

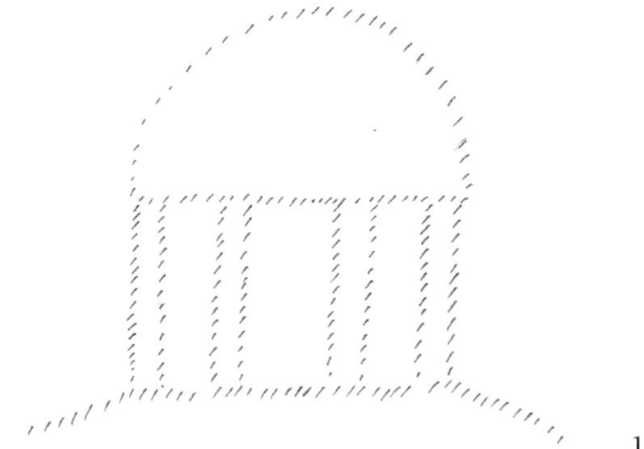
1

As help for experiencing such a form-motif, Rudolf Steiner describes the everyday experience of getting up in the morning, of lifting oneself into the upright position:

> '[...] How can one experience such a form and feel what it is expressing? You can do so in the following way: you can make clear to yourself the experience of getting out of bed in the morning and beginning your daily work: you come out of a lying position into one of standing, and of walking. This is an experience that is normally not brought to consciousness but it is an experience to change from a position of lying down to one of standing up. It is an experience. The experience consists of the fact that when you lie down gravity affects you as it affects a sack, a sack of flour, for example. Gravity works also in a deeper sense, for when you lie down, some surface or other of your body always presses down on the support you are lying on. You do not usually feel this pressure but it is there; it is an impulse that hangs together with the whole feeling experience of gravity [...].
>
> Now, in that you stand up you leave the sphere of this pressure; you place yourself over and against gravity. You place the axis of your body into the sphere of gravity. You are no longer subject to the force of gravity like a sack; you step actively into the sphere of gravity. That is an experience, yet an experience one cannot have intellectually by way of an abstract-thinking brain.
>
> Hence, one stands up and makes this experience of standing up clear to oneself: then one has an experience of 'sensing' the world, – of feeling the world; then one knows actually for the first time what feeling is. [...] What comes to expression in such an architectural motif is contained within the sphere of feeling.'

It is interesting how Rudolf Steiner brings the upright position of the human body in relation to *feeling*. Does this suggest that the upright posture is indeed a feeling instrument when we measure colour into the picture space?

Rudolf Steiner then brings the movement you experience when entering the Goetheanum building in connection with the continuous stream of movement visible in the changing forms of the capitals and architrave. He describes this motif of moving forward, of development, as a will-motif:

> 'In our time we do not have the prevailing mood of the impulses of the Greeks' inner life and in particular we do not yet have in us that which is only now beginning in the evolution of humanity, and should express itself in our building. There must be a transition not only from the state of rest to standing up but also to walking. One must get to know artistically not only the feeling-sphere but also the will-sphere. That can only be achieved when an all-sided symmetry [seen in the first form] is changed to a single axis of symmetry [seen in the second form]. So that one can say: in the moment of changing the building motif into a single axis of symmetry, we express not merely the human being's experience of moving from rest to feeling, but of passing over from feeling to willing, to walking. A motif of will is a continuous motif, a progression.
>
> Therefore for those who enter the building it must be an inner experience of progression, of being 'moved on', when contemplating the forms of the capitals and the architrave.'

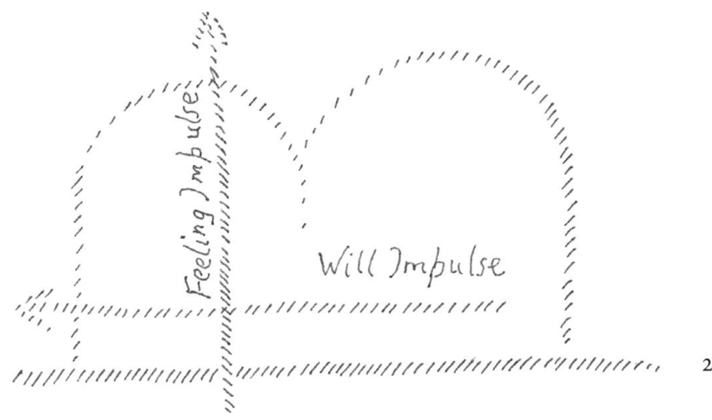

2

The third experience is connected with the sphere of thinking, but the kind of thinking that is illuminated by something higher. Here we are directed to the cupola as a motif of closure and to what is contained in the cupola paintings, namely: 'the secrets of the spiritual development of the whole of humanity'.

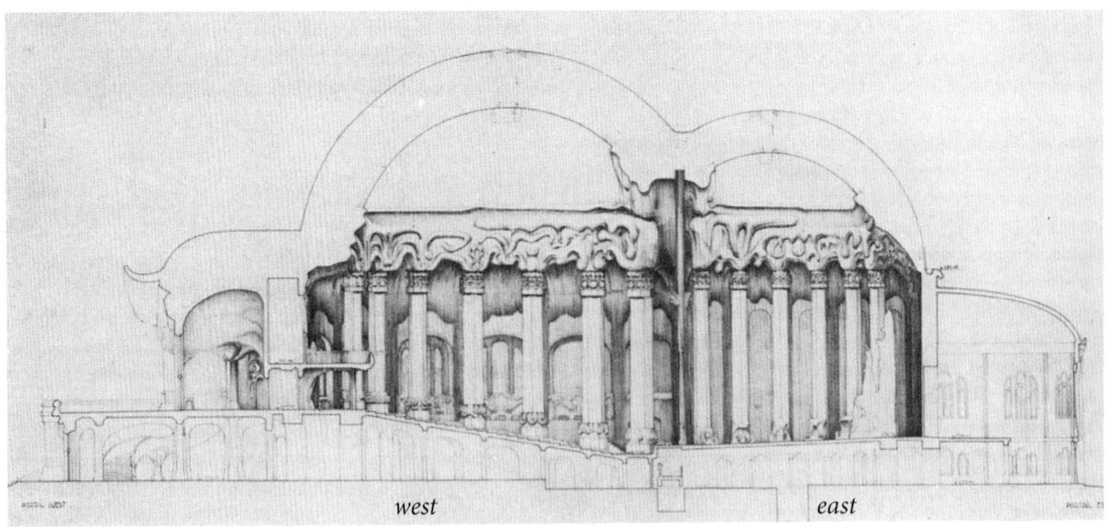

Interior of the first Goetheanum showing the west-east movement of the capitals and architraves of the large and small cupolas

In these examples we have been led through inner artistic experiences to the thinking, feeling and willing human being. Willing as experienced in the dynamic sequences of form transformation in the capitals and the architraves; feeling in the gesture of uprightness and thinking in the closing gesture of the cupola above. Rudolf Steiner sums up this threefoldness as follows:

> 'In this way our building expresses [...] willing, feeling and thinking, but in their evolution which should evolve within humanity, which strives after a certain development – towards itself.
>
> [...] We have built willing, feeling and thinking with our building –and as it is, willing, feeling and thinking are connected with each other in a mysterious way. If I go from west to east in our building, then I move as the will-sphere in the human being moves; when I look from below upwards to the forms of the columns and architrave I deepen myself in the mysteries of the feeling sphere of the human being. If I study what arches above the building and what we experience inside the building in the painting of the cupola, we study the mysteries of the sphere of human thinking.'

The nurturing of a more conscious awareness of inner artistic experiences in the way Rudolf Steiner describes them here can help the artist go beyond the usual aesthetic considerations to a deeper experience of art.

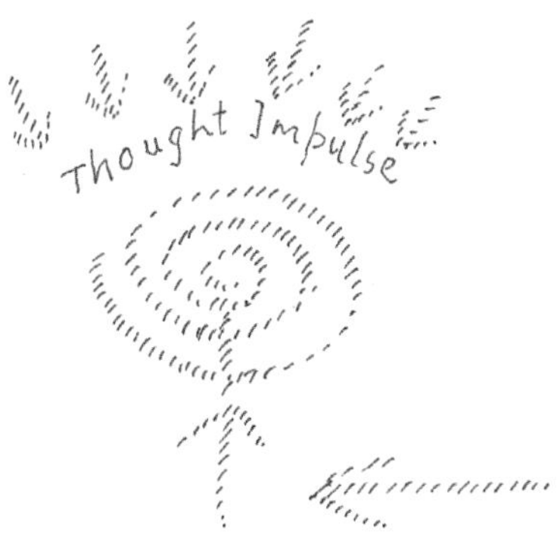

Despite obvious differences between the three-dimensional world of sculpture and architecture and the two-dimensional world of colour, the inner experiences of threefoldness described here by Rudolf Steiner also play a part in painting. Painters create out of an awareness of the different directions of space: up and down, left and right, centre and periphery and in so doing connect with invisible realms of being.

For an idea of how body, soul and spirit are united in the experience of inner balance, we will turn briefly to two senses, the *sense of balance* and the *sense of life*. Here Rudolf Steiner reiterates the significance of the upright posture of the human being and stresses the fact that in the upright position the human being is in interaction with the equilibrium of the whole universe.

The Sense of Balance and the Sense of Life

Contrary to the opinion prevalent in his time, Rudolf Steiner saw the capacity of human beings to orientate themselves in space not simply as an acquired faculty, but as something achieved through an inborn *sense of balance*. In the following quote from a lecture held at Penmaenmawr in Wales[37], Steiner describes that special moment when the young child stands upright and begins to walk:

> '[...] There are three things that especially strike us in this development and unfoldment of the young child. In ordinary life we say; a child learns to walk. That indeed is a wonderful thing, these words convey a great sense of movement. The child uses all its limbs to raise itself from a position in which the spine is parallel with the earth's surface, to an upright position. The simple words: 'The child learns to walk', in which we express this most obvious and self-evident occurrence, also imply that when this takes place the child learns to direct all its forces into different directions on earth. It learns to take its place in the cosmos through its own inner balance and the symmetry of its forces.

> […] the difference between man and animal can be discovered by studying the moment when the child, early in its life, raises itself from what makes it like the animal and balances itself in harmony with the equilibrium of the whole universe. […]'

He introduced the *sense of balance* (one of the twelve senses[38] considered from the viewpoint of anthroposophy) in this way:[39]

> 'We become aware of a third sense when we consider that a human being differentiates between above and below. If this is no longer perceived, it can be dangerous for one cannot hold oneself any longer and can fall. We can indicate the organ that has a great deal to do with this sense: the three semicircular canals in the ear. If this organ is injured, one's sense of orientation is lost.'

In his book *Sinnesentwicklung und Leiberfahrung* (Development of the Senses and Body Experience)[40] Karl König explains how the processes taking place within this organ of balance are intimately connected with experiences of gravity and levity, and with the pulse and breathing rhythm. One can have the impression that in this organ the human being and the universe meet in a cosmic-human-interaction of breathing, perception and orientation. Rudolf Steiner describes the inner experience of the sense of balance as a feeling of unity with the spirit:[41]

> '[…] Just think how little we can really directly experience that we are placed in the world in balance. How do we then experience the sense of balance as it shines into the soul? […] We experience it as inner repose which results in the fact that when I walk from here to there, I don't leave behind what is incorporated in my body, I take it with me; what is there remains the same even if I were to fly through the air. That is what makes us seem to appear independent of time. I don't leave myself behind; tomorrow I will be the same as I am today. This 'being independent from the body' is the shining-in of the sense of balance in the soul. It is 'feeling oneself as spirit'.'

Another sense intimately connected with such bodily experiences is the *sense of life*. This sense gives an inner feeling of certainty that my body and myself are one. The sense of life, as Rudolf Steiner describes below, gives human beings their first perception of themselves as a bodily unity:[42]

> '[…] What is the sense of life? It is something which when everything is in order one doesn't actually feel. It is felt only when something is out of order. When you are tired you have an inner experience of this tiredness, as you would experience a colour. And

> that which comes to expression in a feeling of hunger or thirst, or what one can call a particular feeling of energy, that must be inwardly perceived as one perceives a colour or sound. [...] The first human perception of self is given through the sense of life, through which human beings become conscious of their corporeality as an entirety. [...] That I can call the body "my" body, that I identify with this same body through "my", is the result of the sense of life. The assumption that my body is mine is given through the sense of life. "I and my body are one" is the experience that we must first attribute to the sense of life.'

This brief reference to just two of the lower senses cannot, of course, give a complete picture. For this, you would have to consider all 12 senses, and much more besides. It can only touch on a spiritual physiology that can give a foundation for inner artistic experiences.

Colour Measuring

An essential part of Gerard Wagner's approach to painting was his practice of 'colour measuring' – a way of balancing colours. The art of 'colour measuring' was presented by Rudolf Steiner in the lecture *Measure, Number and Weight – Weightless Colour Essential for a new Direction in Painting.*[43] Here Rudolf Steiner says it is possible to measure colours not physically but qualitatively. To show what he meant, he sketched a small surface of red on the blackboard and encircled it with a larger surface of yellow. He then compared the yellow with its lighter expansive quality to the red with its more concentrated intense quality and gave the exact measurement of the yellow to the red as 5:1.

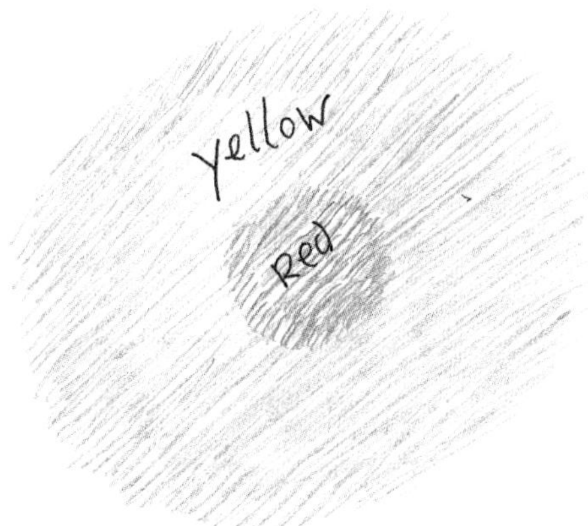

Gerard Wagner followed up this one example by exploring the comparative qualities and weights of all the colours. He refers to this aspect of his work briefly in the monograph *The Art of Colour*:[44]

> 'A particular help in shutting out subjective arbitrariness is the exercise of 'qualitative measuring', indicated by Rudolf Steiner. This measuring of colour qualities is so important because it allows the painter to develop awareness and direction at the same time as letting his colour experience connect completely with the 'sleeping' activity of creating. One strives during the act of painting to 'doing', to hold nothing back of one's own feelings, which may not remain focused on oneself, on one's 'feeling of self' but rather, become pure, controllable will activity.'

By practicing and understanding the qualitative measuring of colour Gerard Wagner entered a new sphere of painting. In the continuation of the quote above, he writes how balancing and measuring the colours helped him to find form out of colour. He also speaks of a path of painting that begins with 'the forces of sun and moon' (the Nature Mood Sketches) and ends his description with some illuminating words about the archetypal images Rudolf Steiner has created in his sketches and paintings. Gerard Wagner refers to himself here as the 'painter':

> 'By way of a chosen order of colours, and out of the measuring and balancing of the colours, forms came into being. The painter followed up their justification by searching for the cause of their appearance. Numerous attempts at plant and animal forms arose, and he sought access to the human form as well.
>
> Rudolf Steiner gave many indications which lead to these different realms. They start with the forces of sun and moon in the life-organism of nature and the human being, and lead step by step to the four large watercolour paintings: New Life, Easter, Archetypal Plant, Archetypal Human Being/Archetypal Animal. Also the motif of The Threefold Human Being gave rise to a long preoccupation with the colour archetype of the human form. For these pictures of Rudolf Steiner's belong to the sphere of archetypes, and between where they came into being, and here, where we as human beings exist on the earth, lie all the realms of nature. We are invited to discover these newly, from within, out of the colour.'

A NEW ART

When considering Gerard Wagner's lifetime of colour research, it can come as a surprise to learn that he wrote down next to nothing about his work. In keeping with his conviction that the path of painting inaugurated by Rudolf Steiner is closely connected with an inner path of soul-spirit development, he did not record the results of his experiments intellectually.

In 1998 however, a year before his death, he wrote some notes in which he gives a brief sketch of his approach to painting, his view of what makes a painting artistic, and reiterates the value of Rudolf Steiner's training sketches for painters:[45]

> 'A painting, if it is at the same time a work of art, will convey a complete human experience purely through the medium of colour and form. The whole human being = the threefold human being (Rudolf Steiner's motif sketch). The wholeness of our being lives in the *experience* of the colour circle, in its polarity and intensification: yellow to warm red, blue to cool red, and in incarnadine – black, white, red. In the balancing of the polarities: in and out breathing, concentrating-expanding, tightening-loosening, warming-cooling, enlivening-deadening, and so on.
>
> The various colours, even singly, lead into the different regions of nature, the human being, and the cosmos. E.g. yellow, red, blue, cool red to the four ethers: light, warmth, chemical and life ether. Brown and black lead into regions lying far outside the purely human. Incarnadine (black, white, red) = the incarnated 'I' in the physical body.
>
> The painter schools himself through the experience of his own colour wholeness. He wants to convey this complete colour experience through the picture. If he takes up a colour on a white or coloured paper, this colour is a single part taken from the inner colour totality of the painter, or of nature. He experiences the need to complement this one colour with a second one – an intensification or a polarity, and then again through a third, fourth etc. colour, until an experience of what has appeared outwardly, together with the inwardly experienced colour totality of his own being has arisen.
>
> How the path – the process – develops from the single colour through to the harmonious totality, how it forms itself to motif, depends largely on the choice of the first colour, or on the relation of the first two colours to one another. The aim lies always in the attainment of a harmonious totality. – The choice of the

first colour determines the way one reaches the goal. If one takes brown or black as first colour, one has deadness as a beginning, and what follows will need to accommodate this within the human 'wholeness'. This can happen in different ways.

[...] One sees in the sketches of Dr Steiner how the astral colour forms the etheric body. With physical eyes one sees the imprint of a pure, supersensible reality. Hence the value of these 'sketches' and the importance of a schooling path based on them.

[...] The (long) path of the painter would be to school an objective colour feeling which, at the same time, is the entry to the objective etheric world of formative forces; to follow the process of creating as the picture unfolds, and to bring it to one's consciousness. [...]'

A noteworthy feature of Gerard Wagner's work was his gesture of wanting to shine a light on his path for others who may be looking for a new painting impulse and needing guidance. He understood Rudolf Steiner's indications as a step towards a universal art which could have meaning for everyone.

Quite often the question is raised as to whether Rudolf Steiner's indications for art are still relevant. After all, it has been at least a hundred years since he gave them and since then the development of art on the world stage has seen to it that painting has more or less disappeared and given way to other mediums. But precisely because of these changes and the challenges human facing human beings in our time, a way of painting that enlivens the senses and helps to develop more human feelings is more needed than ever.

In the lecture *Technology and Art* Rudolf Steiner sheds light on the relevance of a new art which is valid for our present cultural epoch. (Each cultural epoch lasts 2160 years. Our present epoch began in 1413 and will end in 3573.) He concludes the lecture by saying that this new impulse has only just begun and as such can only be imperfect. I personally feel that this statement is still relevant today, more than 100 years later:[46]

'Art obviously had to speak differently to the souls that were less exposed to the influences of Ahriman than we are today. Art has to speak in a new way to souls today, and our Goetheanum building [this includes the painting impulse] is meant to be the very first step, really and truly the very first step towards art of this kind, and not anything perfect. It is an attempt actually to create the kind of art that calls on the soul to be active, on the lines of the whole conception of modern life, yet a spiritual conception of modern life.

[...] These are things which are not created arbitrarily by the human soul, but have to do with the innermost impulses we have to go through, because we are in the first third of the fifth post-Atlantean epoch. It has been, as it were, ordained by the spiritual beings that guide this evolution.

[...] The important thing is not the perfection we achieve in what we must will to happen, but that a start is made on what must come to life here, however imperfect it has to be. For everything new that comes into the world is imperfect compared with the old that has stood the test of time. The old has reached its highest level, whereas the new is still in its infancy. That is self evident.'

SUPPLEMENTARY IMAGES

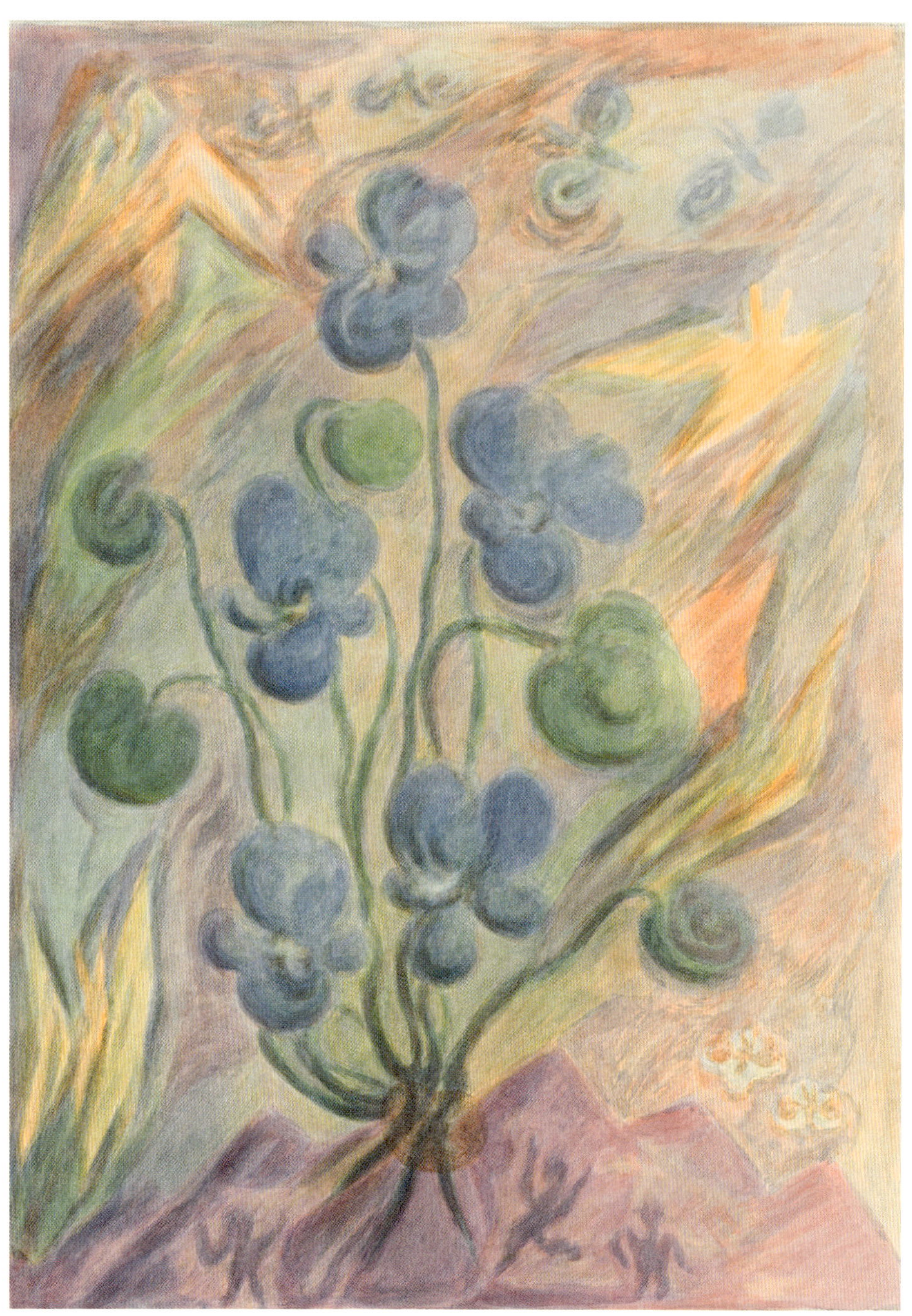

Plate 94: Plant with blue blossoms

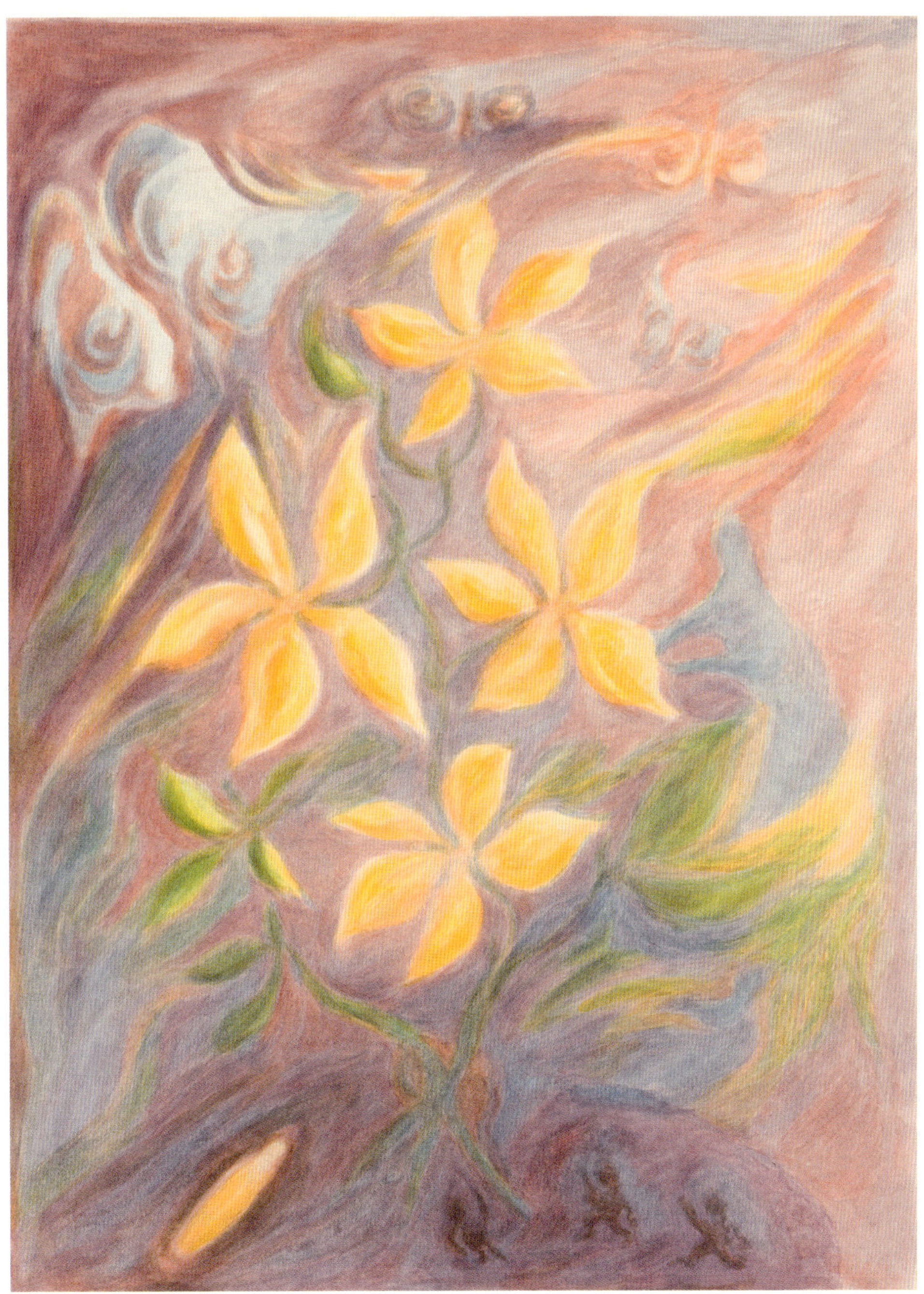

Plate 95: Plant with yellow blossoms

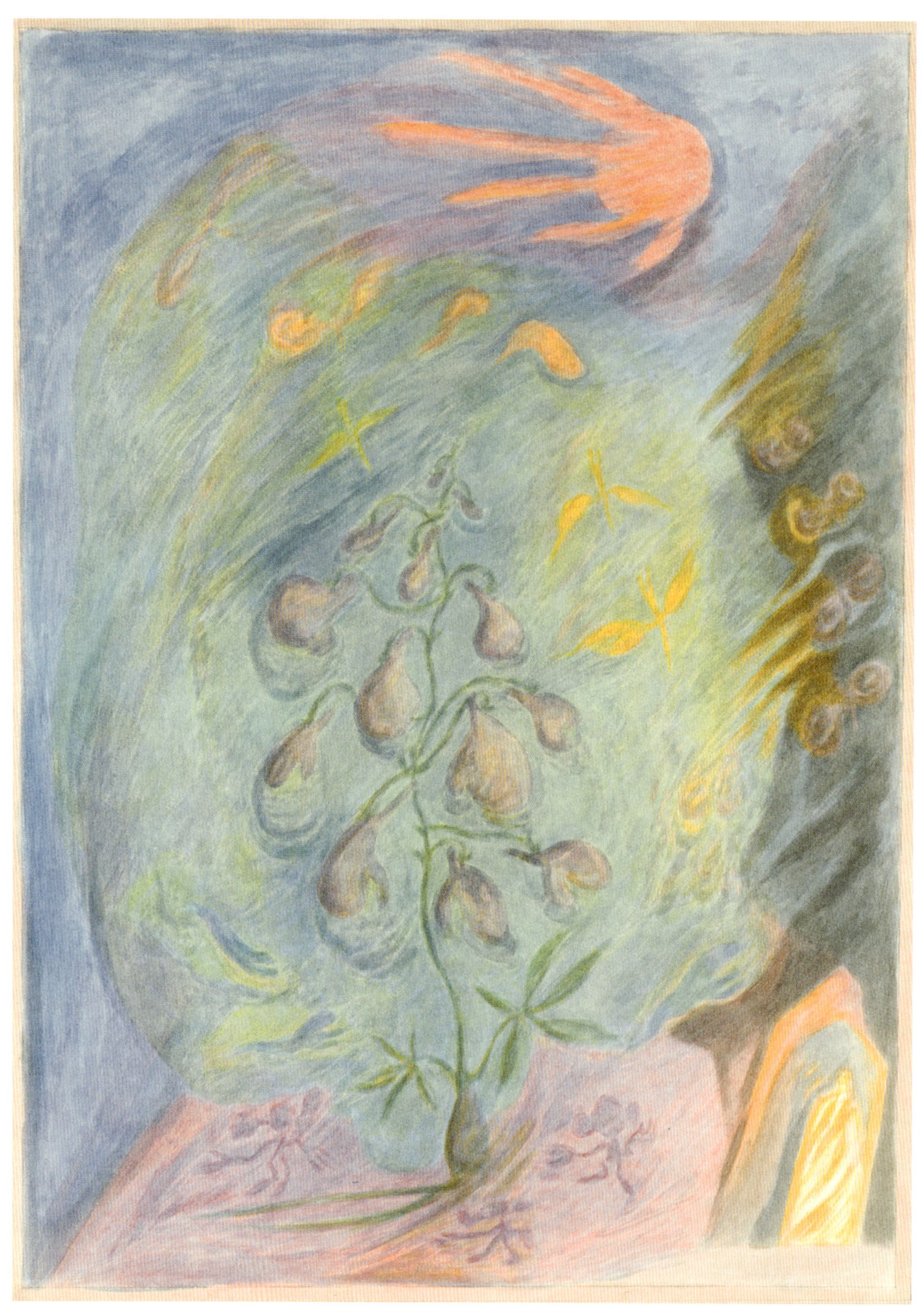

Plate 96: Plant with violet blossoms

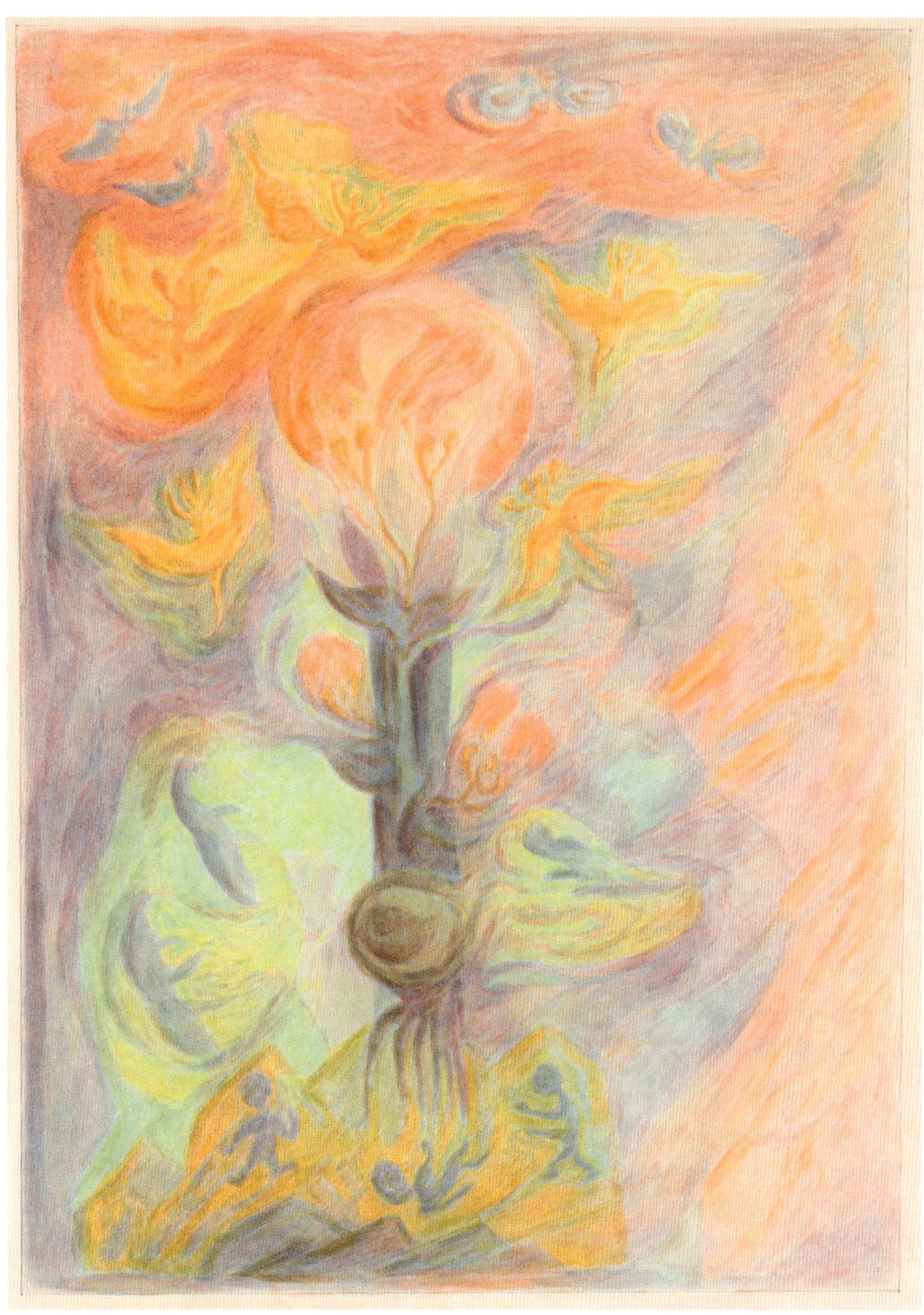

Plate 97: Archetypal Plant with Elemental Beings

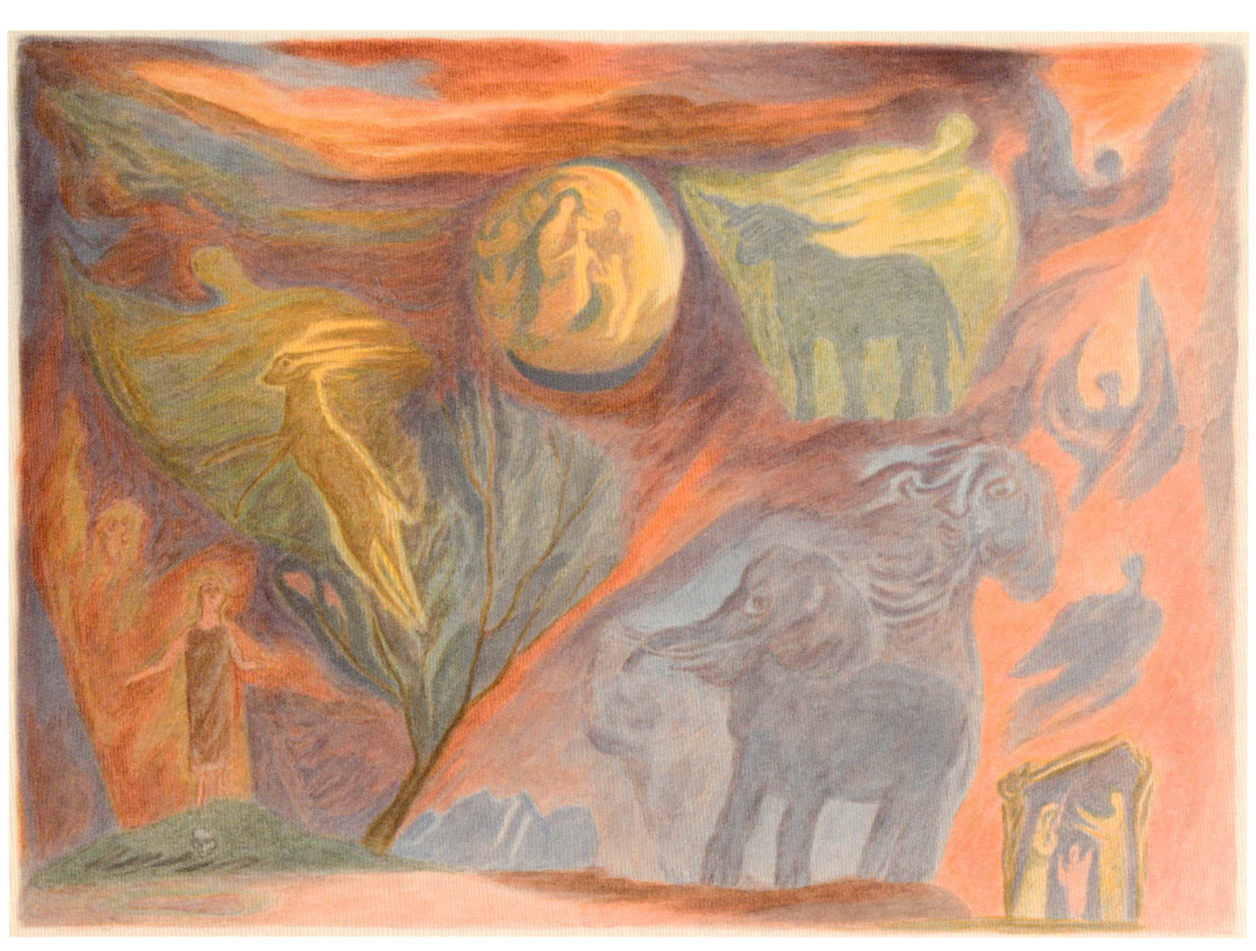

Plate 98: Animal World

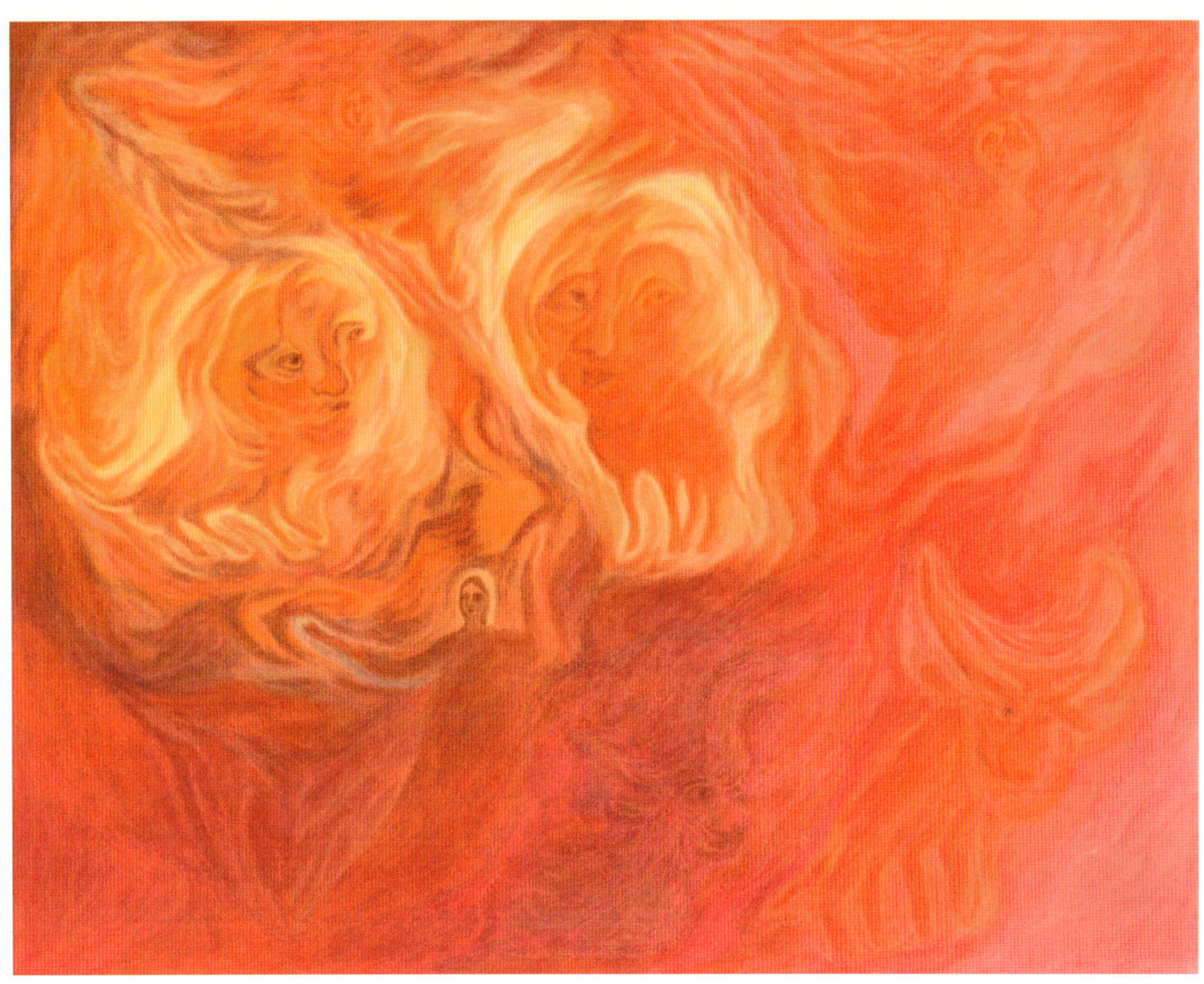

Plate 99: Lions

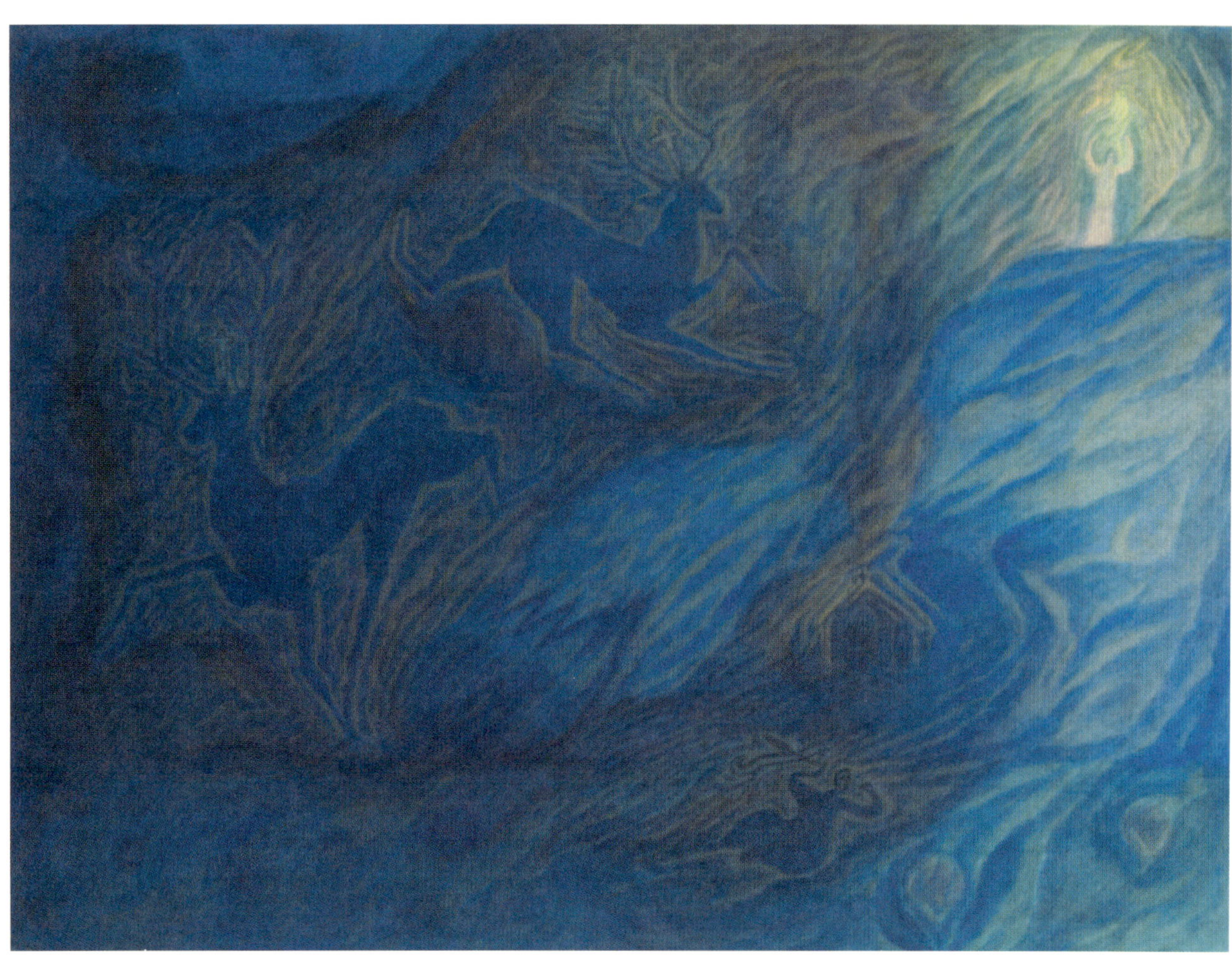

Plate 100: Hubertus Motif (Deer)

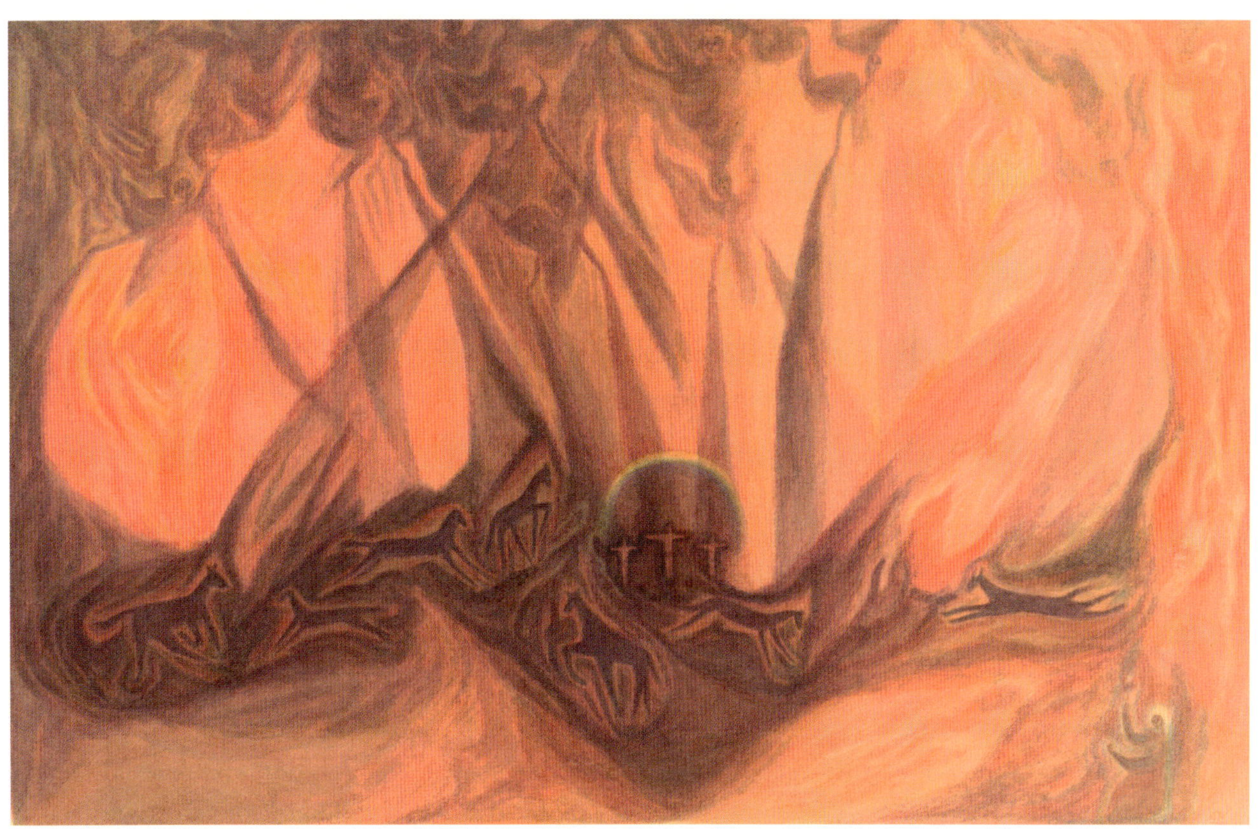

Plate 101: Golgotha (Horses)

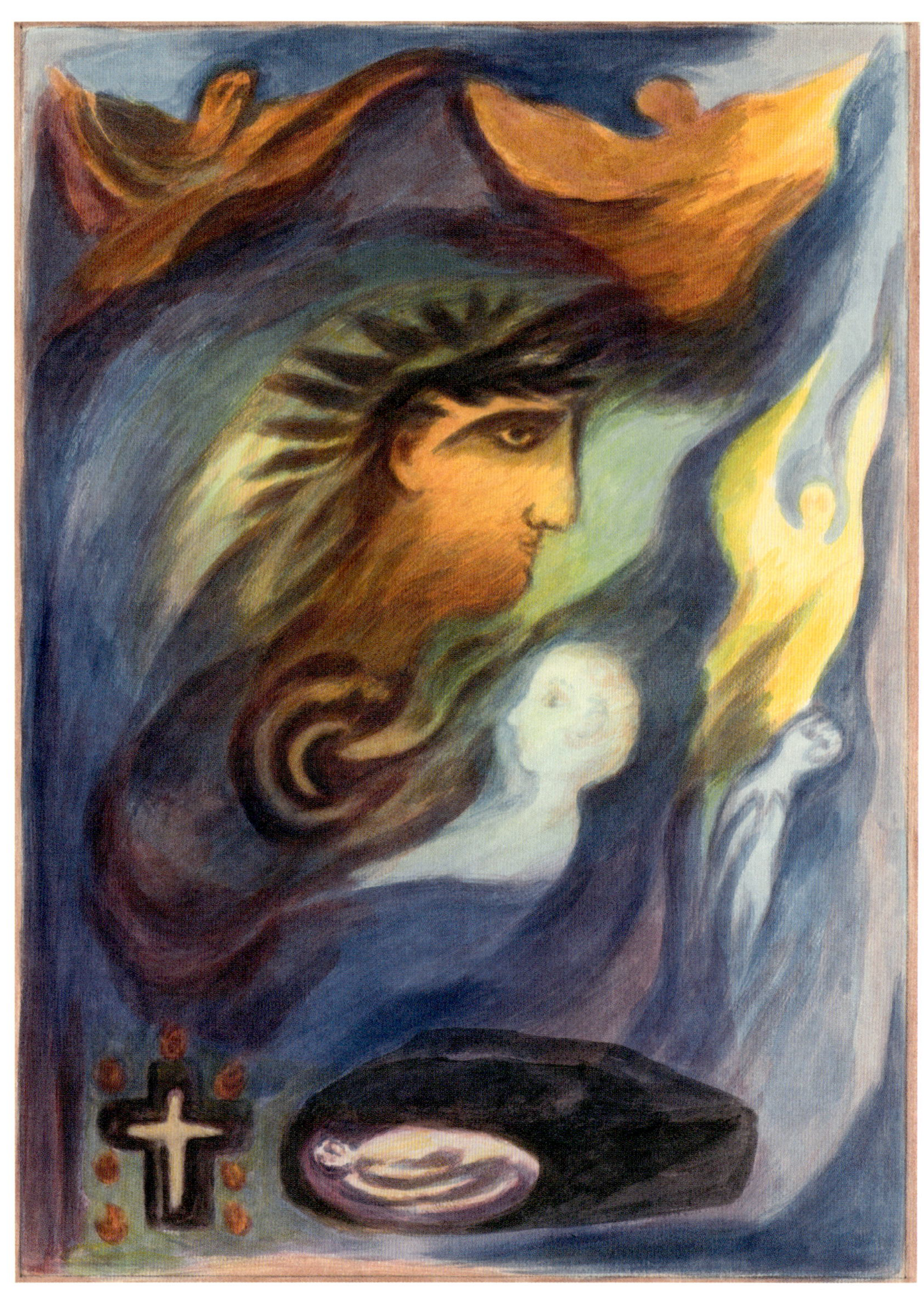

Plate 102: Quo Vadis

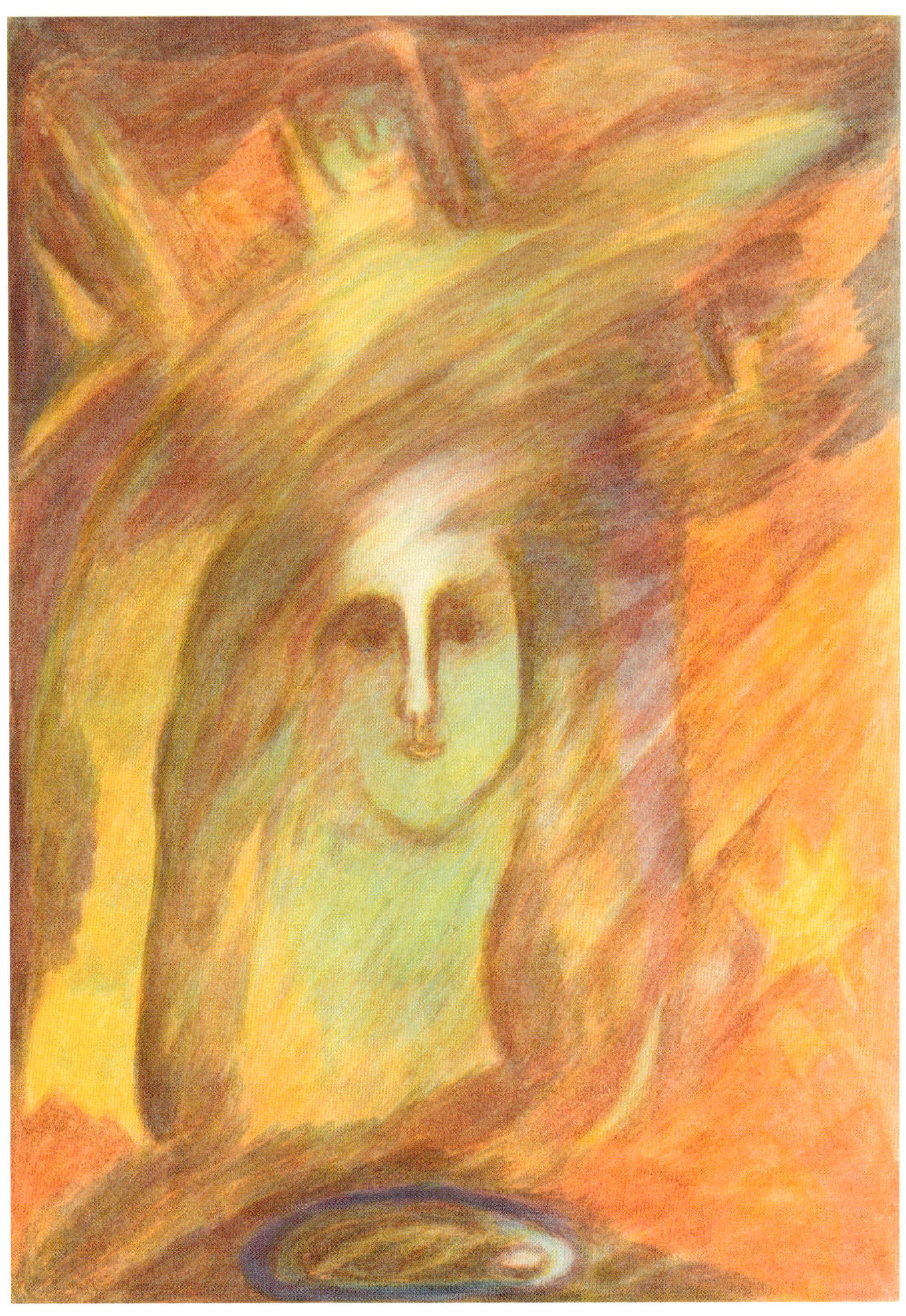

Plate 103: The Novice

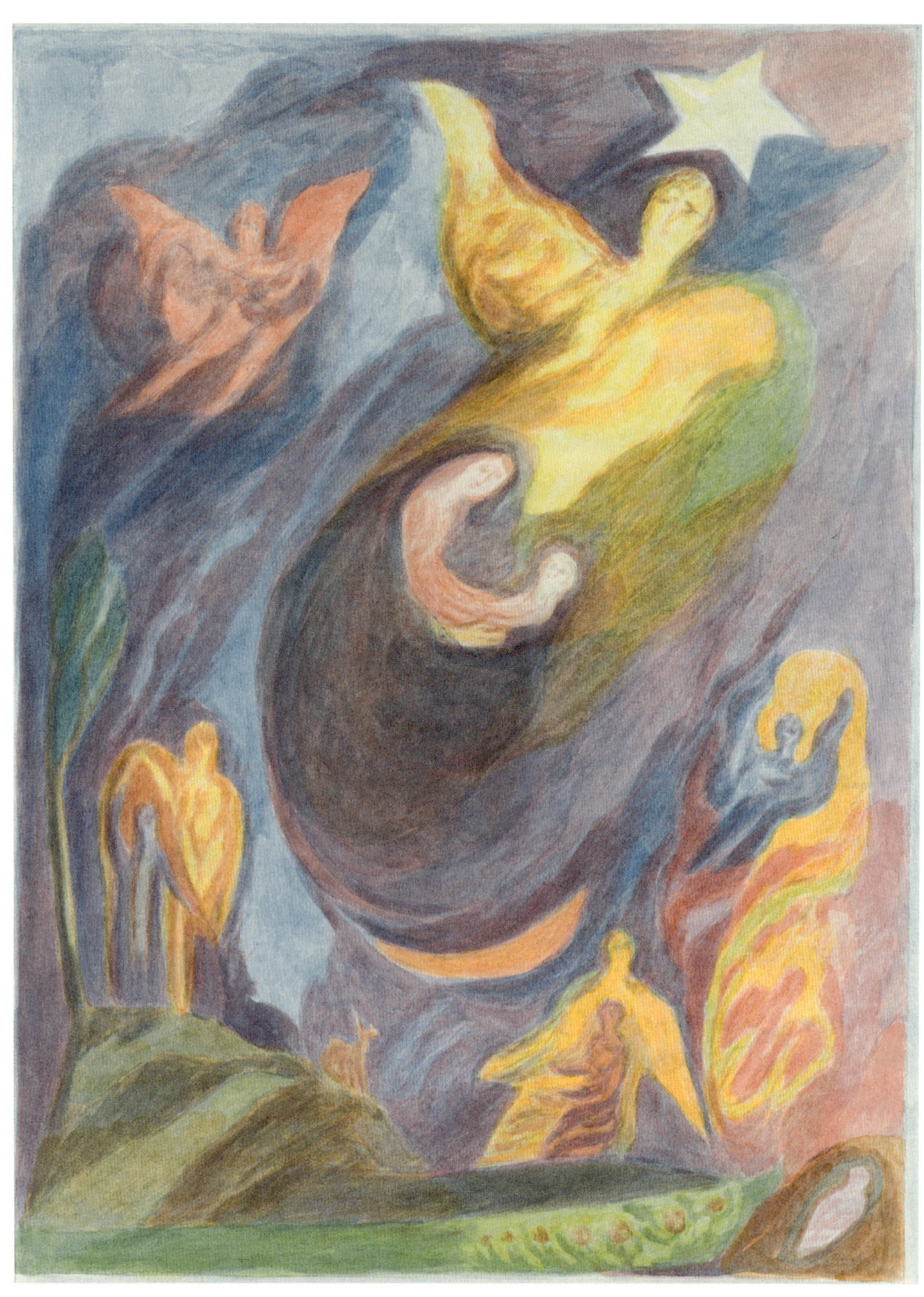

Plate 104: Madonna Motif

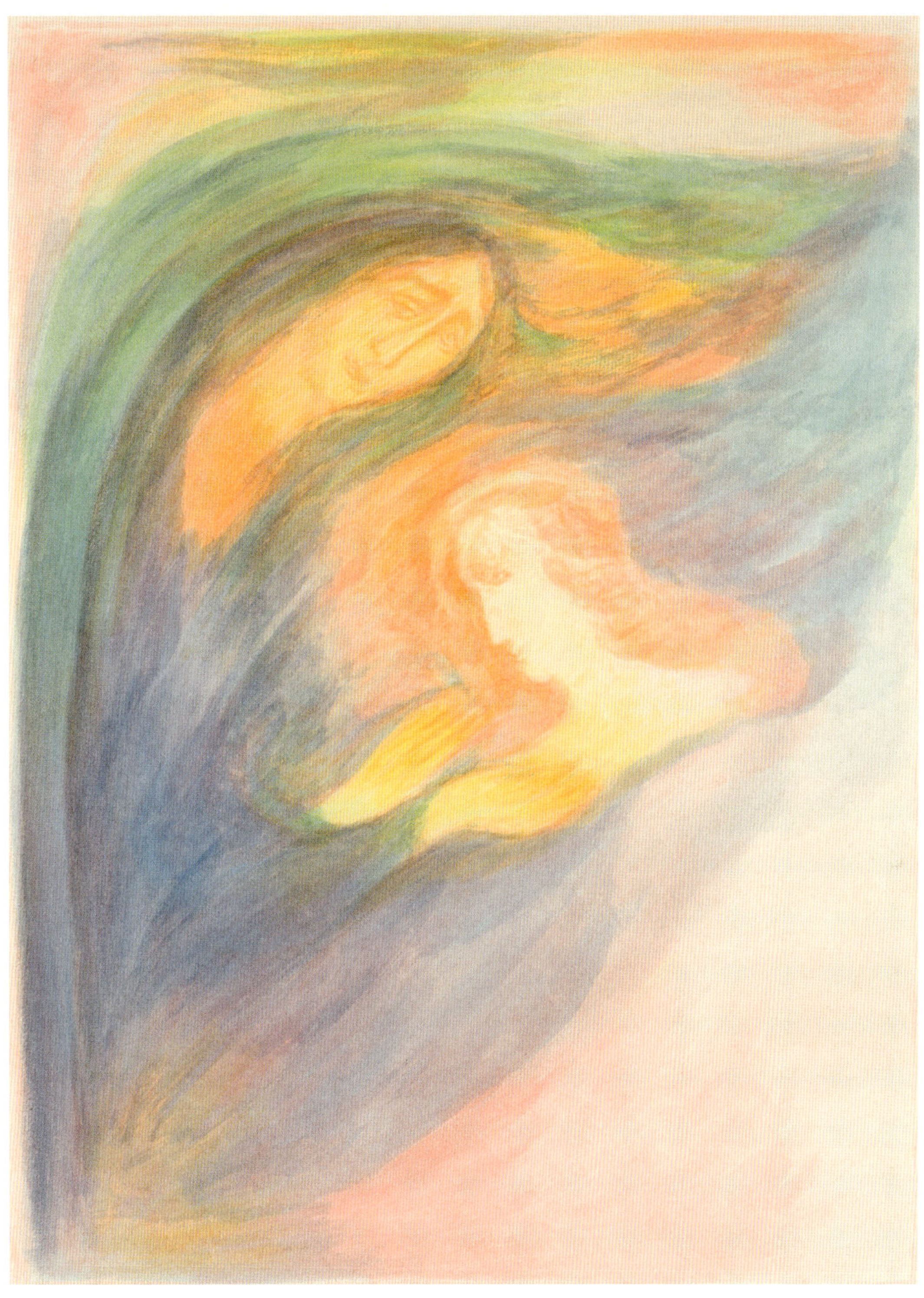

Plate 105: Madonna Motif

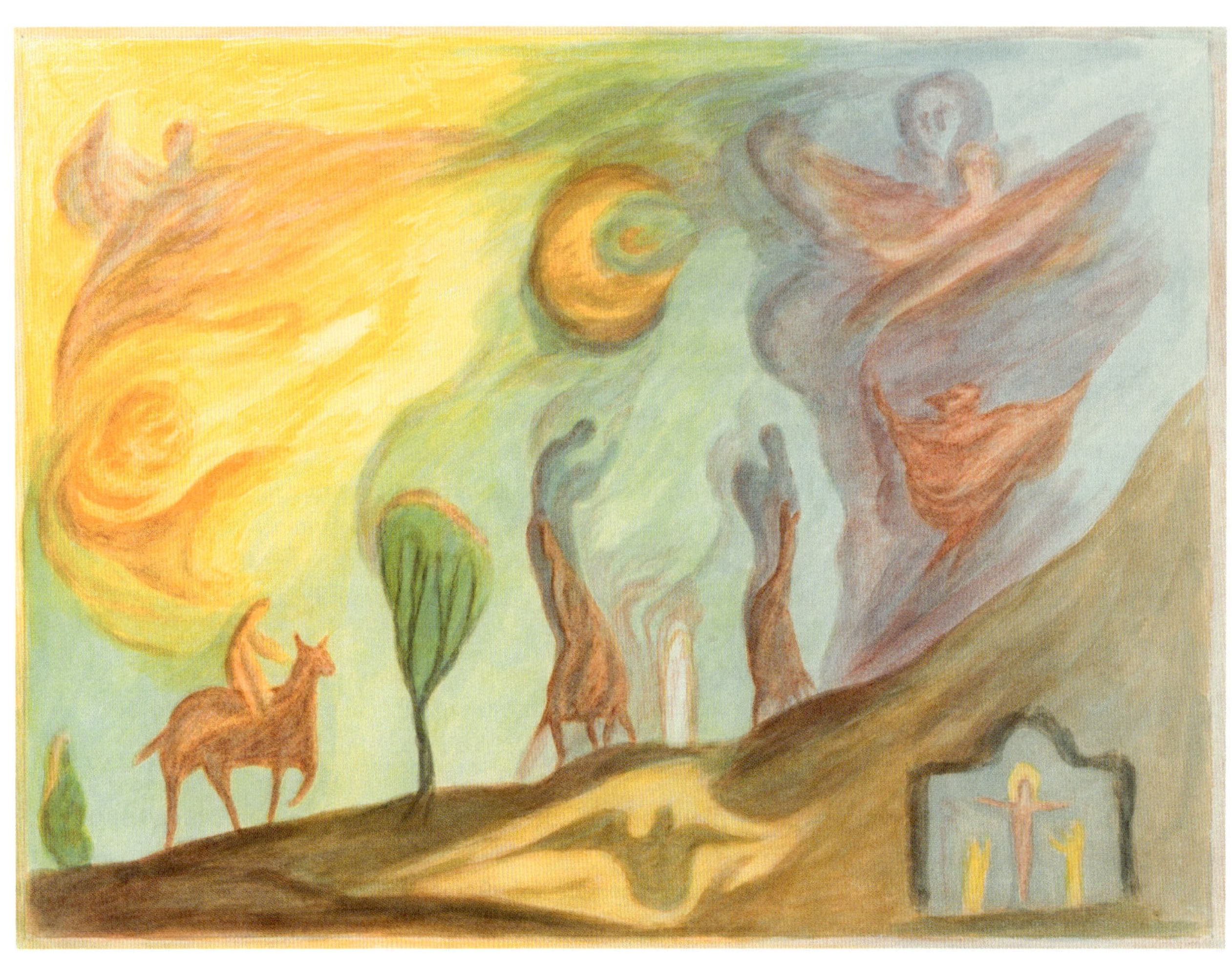

Plate 106: Moonlit Night

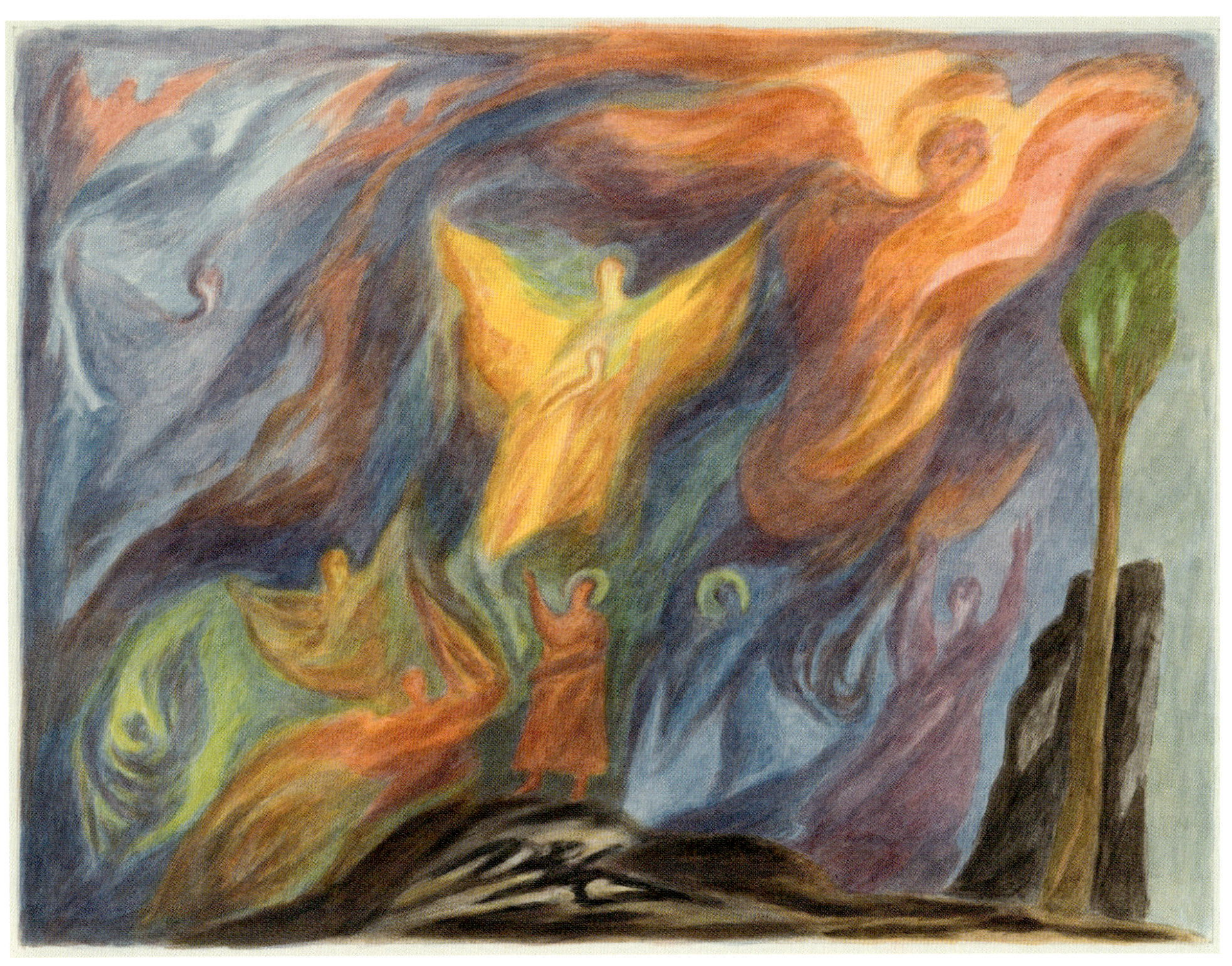

Plate 107: Colour Beings

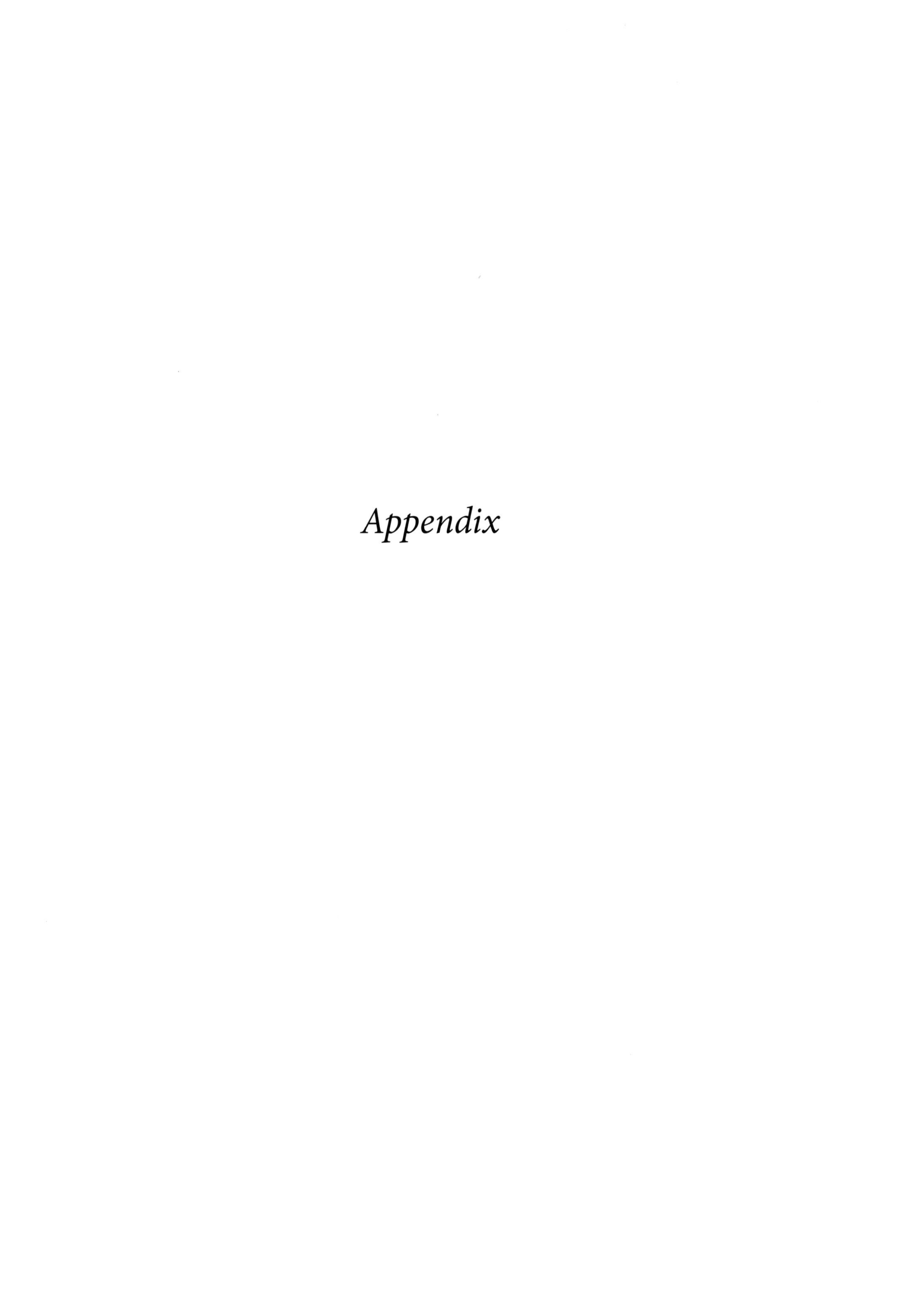

Appendix

SUMMARIES OF THREE LECTURES BY RUDOLF STEINER ABOUT COLOUR

by Albert Steffen[47]

Lecture 1

The physicist, the psychologist and the artist occupy themselves with colour. The psychologist, these days, would acknowledge having something to say about subjective colour experience, but would fall short of an objective knowledge of colour. This is ascribed to the physicist alone. To a still lesser degree is an artist considered able to understand colour from an objective standpoint. In our present time art is by no means what it was for Goethe: '... the worthiest interpreter of nature's open secrets'.

In the course of the nineteenth century it became customary to say that colour, appearing either on the surface of things or as fluctuating colour (as in the case of the well-known prismatic experiments), exists only as a reality for our senses whilst outside in the world the existence of colour is considered nothing more than undulations of the finest matter of so-called physical ether. This ether-vibration theory can tell us nothing whatsoever about the essential nature of colour.

If one wants to come to an understanding of colour in an objective way, one should not depart from colour itself, especially not by means of such intellectual manoeuvres. For this purpose Dr. Steiner lifted the whole subject into the sphere of exact experimentation in relation to inner experience. He took certain colours from the many faceted realm of colour and questioned our feeling responses to them. Let us imagine, he said, a surface of green (he drew it in the blackboard), and let the green work on our feelings. We would have the same feeling when experiencing the green plant-covered earth whilst shutting out all other colours from our sight.

After that he drew onto this green surface, which he separated into three parts, the colours red, peach-blossom and blue. Thereby a different feeling content arose in each case.

Abstract definitions were not possible so other ways had to be found. For this purpose Dr Steiner let figures arise out of the red, the peach-blossom (which corresponds to incarnadine) and the blue. He did this not to imitate nature but to make clearer the feeling content which arose in the soul. He let these three different coloured figures walk over the green meadow.

The first example produced the following result: the red people enliven the green. Through them the meadow appears greener, more saturated and lively. But the red figures cannot rest. They excite simply through their redness. They bring movement on the meadow. To be true to their nature one must draw them in a ring. They could even resemble lightening. This is not the case with the peach-blossom people. They can stand quietly for hours. They don't bother us. They are neutral to the meadow which remains as it is. Its green does not change.

The blue figures damp down the green, they dull it. The meadow stops being green and becomes somewhat blueish. One cannot imagine that these blue beings who wander over the green meadow can hold themselves there. They disappear and take the meadow away with them. One is tempted to think that there must be an abyss somewhere and they pull the green surface towards it.

This is colour experience. This is how one can immerse oneself in colour.

Green is the colour that belongs to the plant. The plant which is green can only be green. We never feel the same necessity as regards animals. If they are green we always have the feeling they could just as well be some other colour. Green belongs to the plant world. Let us try to gain entry into the objective nature of green by way of the plant.

The plant *lives.* Its physical body is penetrated by a life-body. Here lies its essential being. Without it, it would be a mineral. Minerals have no life. The being of the animal is soul. The essence of the human being is spirit. The being of the plant is life as such. What makes the plant green however lies in its physical body. So one would have to say: green belongs to the plant but it is not its archetypal being. That is its life-body, or as Dr. Steiner expresses it in his books, the etheric body. In the green we have simply an image of the life of the plant and not the life itself. So we can say quite objectively: *Green represents the dead or lifeless image of life.*

Peach blossom colour, or incarnadine, is visible from the outside through the colour of the skin. [Incarnadine is made up essentially of different proportions of black and red – so all human skin colours are included.] But this colour also lets itself be experienced inwardly. If one tries to imagine that one is an ensouled being, and this feeling of being ensouled goes over into the physical bodily form, one finds its expression in incarnadine. People become pale when their soul shuts down. When the soul withdraws one perceives a peculiar greenish complexion. A red complexion shows the soul is present again. In incarnadine we have the image of the soul which lives. It is not dead, like the green which we have learnt to know as the dead image of life. Only when the human soul withdraws from the incarnadine, does the skin colour become green. Then the person moves towards death.

Once more something objective has been gained if we say: *In incarnadine (which is more or less peach blossom colour) we have the living image of the soul.*

The colour blue has no connection to a particular being as is the case with green or peach blossom. We are not able to build up a conception about this colour in the same way. Dr. Steiner put off dealing with this colour until later. He moved on to white.

When we have white, illuminated before us, we get the feeling: white is related to light. The source of the light, the sun, appears as white. But this white of the sun, which represents light to us, does not appear as other colours do directly on the surface of things. There is an essential difference between the other colours and the light. One cannot say that one perceives the light as one perceives the colours. Colours are invisible. Light makes them perceptible. Light illuminates space, but we do not see it as we see red, yellow or blue and so on. It must be retained or reflected in order to become visible. The colours adhere to the surface of things, but not light. Light is something altogether fluctuating.

But we ourselves when we wake in the morning and are radiated upon by the light, feel the essence of our true being. We find an inner relationship to the light. At night, in darkness, starting up from sleep, we are not in our element. The light is necessary for us to come to ourselves, to our 'I'. (This does not contradict the fact that blind people do not see yet have an 'I'. They are organized to see in spite of blindness and it is the organization that counts here.) Naturally there is a difference between the light and that which lives as spirit in the 'I'. The light gives us something of our own spirit. The 'I' awakens itself inwardly on account of the light.

To summarize, Dr. Steiner said: The 'I' is spiritual but it must be experienced on a soul level. It experiences itself in the soul in that it feels itself illuminated.

White or light represents the psychical image of the spirit.

The counter image of white is black. We may in a certain sense equate black with darkness (as white with light). In nature carbon represents the essence of black. Life is driven out of the plant in that it becomes carbon. Blackness is essentially opposed to life; it is an enemy to life. The soul too withers in the darkness. But the spirit blossoms. It can penetrate the darkness. It can shine in the darkness. Here we get the formula:

Black represents the spiritual image of death.

At this point Dr. Steiner spoke guiding words about the possibilities of chiaroscuro, about the task of black and white art, about drawing as such.

After consideration of green, peach blossom, white and black in their objective nature we arrive at the following characterization:

the four colours are images:
of life (green),
of the soul (peach blossom),
of the spirit (white or light),
of death (black).

The previous noun leads on to the later adjective of the image. (Life to living, soul to psychical and so on.) A meaningful cycle reveals itself thereby. Black, green, peach blossom, white (or light) show an ascent from death to life, to soul, to spirit.

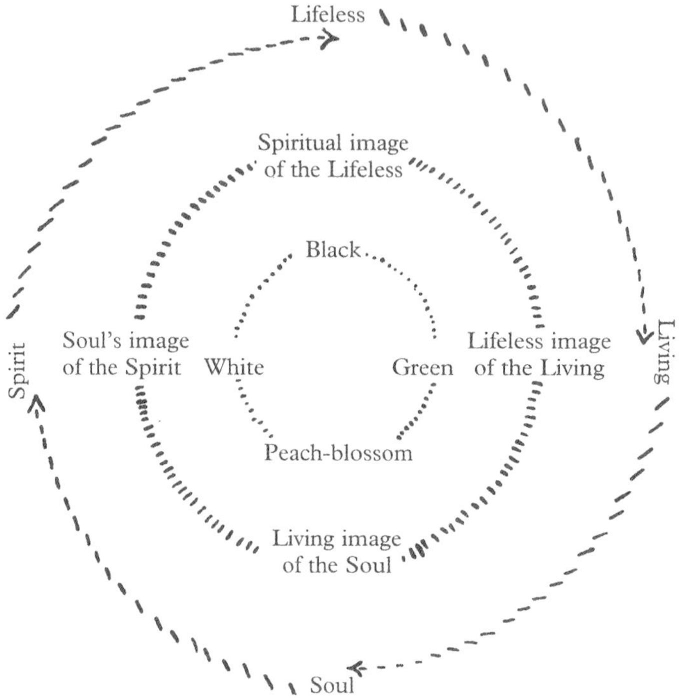

For the coming into being of each colour there is always a receiver and a giver. That means something in which the image forms itself and the impulse for the image. We call the first the *shadow-thrower* and the second the *illuminant.*

When the spirit, as the shadow-thrower, receives that which death, as the illuminant, throws towards it (in this case, a negative illuminant so to speak), then black forms itself.

If the shadow-thrower is death and the illuminant, as with the plant, is the living, then green forms itself. When the shadow-thrower is the living and the illuminant the soul, then peach blossom forms itself. When the shadow-thrower is the psychical, the illuminant the spirit, then white forms itself.

Shadow-thrower	*Illuminant*	*Image*
Spirit	Death	Black
Death	Living	Green
Living	Soul/Psychical	Peach Blossom
Soul/Psychical	Spirit	White

Lecture 2

Dr. Steiner began the lecture by describing two specific visual experiences so as to bring the being of colour closer to his audience. Imagine, he said, a still white surface with blue shining in from one side and yellow from the other. Green arises. Then imagine black and white weaving into one another, not still as in the previous example but in constant movement. When this is shone through with red, peach blossom arises.

Green is to be found in the realm of plants; peach blossom in healthy ensouled human beings.

The process by which the colour incarnadine (peach blossom) comes about (black and white playing into each other and illuminated by red) actually takes place within the human organism. Because constant movement is required it cannot be depicted in a complete way. Most portraits remain masks.

Green allows itself – in keeping with its character – to be painted with borders. This limitation lies in the feeling that goes out from this colour. One can well imagine green card tables because card playing is a somewhat narrow minded pedantic activity. But playing cards at lilac covered tables would be something unbearable. On the other hand it would fit well to have lilac carpets in a room where mystical conversation, in the best and worse sense, takes place. Lilac may really only be painted as a mood without taking borders into account. In contrast to green, its nature causes it to want to dissolve away from something definite.

Each colour has its character, which demands a more or less definite form.

Let us immerse ourselves in the inner being of yellow. The soul cannot stand a yellow surface with a border. One feels tempted to laugh at it. It does not express the yellow but rather the restriction. One sees always the person in it, the confined, restricted person. An unspoilt artistic feeling cannot stand such a thing. For the opposite feeling to being restricted lies in this colour. Yellow must radiate, it must shine. It must get weaker towards its borders. In the middle it must be more intense. That is the secret of yellow.

One experiences the opposite with blue. Blue demands out of its own nature to be fuller at the edges and lighter towards the centre. It dams up on its borders and flows in, wave-like, towards its middle point. It shines from outside inwards.

It is possible to imagine a uniform surface of blue but one would have the feeling of being led away from the human element. When Fra Angelico painted his blue, he called a supersensible element into the earthly sphere. He allowed something godly to take hold. Blue, out of its own nature, would not invoke such a thing.

The soul has certain feelings when confronted with colour. And the artist fulfils the colours' wishes if he allows himself to be led by them. He paints out of the colour if he does what the colours themselves demand. When he dips his brush into the green and thinks: now you must be almost a little philistine and paint the pointed blades of grass with sharp edges; with yellow you must place yourself within the active spirit; with blue you must close yourself, build a crust around yourself. Then you live with the being of colour.

Blue can be applied when something naturally contracts, withdraws into itself.

We can accept red as a uniform surface. It is effective in its stillness. It wants neither to radiate like yellow nor dam itself up like blue. It also does not want to disperse like peach blossom. Peach blossom likes to spread itself out getting thinner and thinner, to disperse into the indefinable. Peach blossom instantly dissolves any attempt to solidify it: just imagine this colour with lumps in it (a hideous sight). Peach blossom strives to dissolve itself. In order for it not to disappear completely, it must be constantly formed anew. It cannot assert itself. Red asserts itself. Red is movement come to rest. But the confined tendency of green is remote from it. Red gives the effect of being boundless. Red holds the middle position between raying out and damming up, between dissolving and consolidating.

There is an essential difference between black, white, green and peach blossom, colours with image character, and red, blue and yellow, which are lustre colours. The first depict something. The latter shine; they are themselves the shine. That is why Dr Steiner called them lustre colours.

White, black, green and peach blossom, have shadow character. They are in the broadest sense shadow-colours. The shadow of the spirit in the being of soul is white. The shadow of death in the spirit is black. The shadow of life in death or lifelessness is green. The shadow of the soul in the living is peach blossom.

Shadows and images are related.

On the other hand, blue, yellow and red radiate, they shine. Blue shines inwards, yellow shines outwards, red shines in repose. These colours are themselves modifications of the shining element. They have to do with essential being, they are not merely reflections of it.

Contemporary physics takes no account of differences based on the inner nature of colour. Colours are simply written down as follows:

Red Orange Yellow Green Blue Indigo Violet

If we follow the sequence starting with red, lustre character stops at green. Green does not shine. It has image character. Green, as we saw, is the shadow of life in the element of death, and is essentially different from red, orange, yellow, which shine. After green we come to blue, which again is a lustre colour. Going on to indigo and violet we are led out of the physical to something that basically only lets itself be grasped in movement. Here the colour of human incarnadine finds its place: when white and black in movement are shone through with red, peach blossom, the shadow of the soul in the element of the living, appears.

If one bends the band of colours at each end to make a closed circle, one may say that peach blossom, the colour of human incarnadine, is the transition from the physical world to a higher world.

Peach blossom

Red *Violet*

Orange *Indigo*

Yellow *Blue*

Green

Peach blossom, the shadow of the soul in the living, and green, the shadow of the living in lifelessness, stand opposite to one another: Peach blossom with its tendency to disperse; green with its tendency to form borders.

The band of spectrum colours, which leads right and left into infinity, unites in spirit and soul. In peach blossom, the image of the soul within the living, we move away from the physical-material of our bodies towards the soul-spiritual. We gaze into a supersensible world.

Yellow, blue and red are shining colours, lustre colours. What shines in them?

Whoever can grasp the essential being of yellow with feeling, without the bias of abstract intellect, must say: when I make myself receptive to yellow so that it lives on within me, it makes me joyful. To be joyful means to be filled inwardly with great vitality.

Through the yellow colour I become tuned to my 'I'. I become filled with spirit. Yellow in its archetypal being is the lustre (the shine) of the spirit.

Blue, which in its true nature wants to dam up, draw itself together, is the lustre (the shine) of the soul element.

Red, as a uniform filled-out space, is the lustre (the shine) of the living.

Yellow, blue and red tint the other colours. White becomes green through the raying in of yellow and blue. Red that shimmers into black and white, which battle against each other, gives rise to peach blossom.

Red is the lustre of life. Green is the image of life. If we look at red on a white surface and then look away from it, green appears as an after-image. Red shines into us leaving behind its image, the dead green, within us.

Such experiments show that yellow, blue and red as lustre colours have an active nature; they have inner movement that gives them a certain character, whereas black, white, green and peach blossom are essentially motionless.

If one considers the contrast between the planets, which differentiate the cosmos with their radiating quality, and the signs of the zodiac which have their place as quiet symbols in the heavens, it is justified to say: in yellow, blue and red, the lustre colours in their shine have a planetary quality whereas black, white, green and peach blossom have attributes of the fixed stars.

A colour-cosmos opens up before our eyes. The painter is guided by the universal cosmic soul. His art unites human beings with the heavens.

Dr Steiner ended his lecture with a description of the colour gold. This was like a sunset which illuminated once more the theme of lustre and shadow colours.

If one wants to consolidate yellow, despite its intolerance to being confined, one must give it weight. This can be done by letting the yellow become golden. In so doing one holds the radiating nature of yellow together.

When painting a gold background, one may make the surface uniform. Old Masters like Cimabue, who felt yellow to be the lustre of the spirit, looked up to the godly and wanted to give it a dwelling on earth. For this reason they gave their paintings a gold background and let figures appear as the creation of the Gods. In gold the godly was given an earthly presence.

From above, colour sinks down to the earth's surface. From below, it leads the soul upwards to the cosmos.

Lecture 3

One perceives colour on the rainbow, as spectrum colour, and on material objects as fixed colour. The painter who must make use of the material components of colour is confronted immediately with the question: how does colour, as we have come to know it as image colour (black, green peach blossom, white) or as lustre colour (yellow, blue, red), relate to matter? How does it appear to us coloured? For art this is a highly relevant question for the artist carries out this phenomena visibly in that he fixes the colour on the paper when he paints.

How does a physical object become coloured? Optics gives the answer: an object is red, for example, because it has absorbed all the other colours and reflects only the red. A definition which when applied to everyday life would lead to absurdity. One might just as well say: a person is stupid because he has absorbed all cleverness and radiates only stupidity. Goethe in his honest striving for knowledge knew that his means of research were not adequate to answer this question. We do not find it referred to in his colour theory.

Green is the fixed colour of the plant world, it is the image of life, only the *image,* not life itself, as we have shown. It has image character.

So as to establish the essential being of the colour green we must refer to the evolution of the earth. For this purpose we are directed to the cosmology presented by Rudolf Steiner in his comprehensive work 'Esoteric Science'. There Dr Steiner describes the different metamorphoses of the earth which preceded our present stage of evolution. He describes how the solid stage arose out of a fluid stage of development which in turn evolved from an airy stage. It was in the fluid stage that the plant was incorporated; it did not originally have the solid form it has today.

In this fluid state flowing colour existed. It did not need to fix itself. Gradually as the mineral element was incorporated it became the fixed green of vegetation.

Now during the metamorphosis of the plant, green changes into a variety of bright colours – blossom colours of yellow, blue, red, and colours of fruits that ripen. This colourfulness points to another facet of the world of colour. A merely superficial observation tells us that the sun is active here. When it sinks, the plant curls up its blossoms and hides them. Light seizes the green and transforms it. When looking for the connection between the bright colours of the blossoms and a heavenly body we would have to search for some other cosmic influence.

We are led initially to the moon which is the counter image of the sun. The sun shines. The moon reflects its light. It has no light of its own. When we look at the very different characteristics of moonlight and sunlight we can understand the connection between the green of the plant which has image character, and the colours of the blossoms which have lustre character. In the plant we actually see the working together of moon and sun qualities. And we have the explanation as to why green has shadow character and blossoms light. Blossoms shine out towards us whereas green remains fixed. Moonlight reflects the sunlight. In the plant we have the shining colours (lustre) through the sun and the reflected colours, mere images, through the moon.

If we could comprehend the plant in such way as to feel in the configuration of colour the cosmos playing in through the working together of the forces of sun and moon (this is of course only possible with spiritualized feeling not with the crass concepts of physics), it would be possible to understand how flowing colour can fix itself onto an object, how the material body of the plant becomes coloured.

During the stage of development when the earth which is now solid was still in a fluid state, our planetary system had not yet reached the degree of differentiation it has today. Moon and earth were still united. In the separation of the moon from the earth we find the actual origin of the green of the plant world.

Our feelings know well this cosmic interrelation of sun and moon which lives within the plant world, but the intellect which has become mechanistic must first free itself from prejudice. Only an artistic understanding of green can bring us further.

Painters of earlier epochs portrayed mostly human beings and human situations but hardly nature, at least not in relation to the plant world. Why was this? The trivial explanation is that it wasn't usual at that time to observe the world with sharpened senses. The real answer however lies deeper. Landscape painting only really began when materialism and intellectualism grasped the soul. It is a product of the last three hundred years.

Those paintings of older times show no difference between image character (black, green, peach blossom, white) and lustre character (yellow, blue, red). Masters of that time also understood lustre colours as image colours. They did not take into consideration the inner will-nature of lustre colours, be it a radiating gesture (as with yellow) or a damming up (as with blue). They only considered this when portraying the spiritual not when portraying nature. But if one gives lustre character image character no true representation of vegetation can arise. In order to invoke the impression of life, the plants in their image colour of green must be painted somewhat darker than they are in reality, also the red and yellow, to give them image character. Then one has to 'pour' over the whole a yellow-whitish mood in order to give image the shine (lustre) of illuminated air. One does not create a feeling of life by simply copying what one sees. Without the shine (lustre) radiating down from the cosmos one grasps only one part of the plant world, its dead shadowy image. This is the secret of portraying the plant.

We must learn to grasp colour with feeling especially in regard to lifeless objects. When painting the inorganic it would be appropriate to give image a lustre quality. The actual image colours (black, green, peach blossom, white) must be given a shining quality. Then one can combine them with the lustre colours (yellow, blue, red). The painter who portrays the lifeless must continually have in mind that a light source lies in the things themselves. He must think of the canvas or paper as something luminous. He needs the appearance of light in the surface. This should be as if transparent for him. If the colour does not have the character of luminosity, we do not paint but only draw. A painted wall that does not shine is, from the perspective of painting, not a wall but only an image of it.

By making the colours shine inwardly, we give them mineral character. The minerals have, albeit in varying degrees, such a shine. If we want to understand their essential being we need to understand their light-origin. Where does this lie?

When considering this question, we have to say: the colour of minerals does not depend on the sun as much as plants do. The sunlight conjures up the colourfulness of the blossoms. In this case of the minerals the light only makes the colours visible. But the reason for their colouration lies deeper.

Again, in order to solve this question we must consider the evolution of the earth. Those stars which circle the sun as planets were once united with the earth, and during the course of mighty epochs have separated themselves. The colours of the minerals have come about because the planets separated from the earth. Those solid parts of the earth became coloured because the forces of the planets with which they were previously united, are now working from without, from the cosmos. An ancient past shines as a memory in the minerals. And it is quite justified for poets like Novalis to make a connection between stones and stars.

The subject of colouration will always remain a riddle until the decision is made to think of the earth and the cosmos as a unity. If one wants to understand what shines towards us from within mineral substances and what has been transformed from a fluctuating colour into a fixed colour, we must remember that the planets shining from the cosmos (Mars, Mercury, Venus and so on) were once united with the earth and radiated from within it. We must look beyond the earth for the cause of what conceals itself 'under' the surface of the minerals.

When we paint lifelessness, the mineral, it must be totally *lustre*. When we paint the living, the plant, lustre colours (a yellow-white shine) must be painted over the image colours (the darkened green and its metamorphosis). In this way we paint *lustre-image*. When we paint ensouled beings, animals, and place them in a landscape, we must paint their bodies lighter than they are in reality, and paint a soft blue light over them, and then bring this in harmony with the yellow-white of the vegetation. By simply remaining within the realm of natural representation one gives the impression of image character but not of the real essence of being. Through an understanding of the essential being of the animal we paint it in an opposite way to the plant. The green of the plant we paint darker, as its shadow nature demands, and let it be illuminated with light. In regard to the animal which has soul fire we let its body appear lighter but we dull down the pure transparency of the atmosphere over it. In this way we paint *image-lustre.* And when we paint human beings, who have spirit, we must make them *image* as such. This means giving lustre colour (yellow, blue, red) image character. That is the main requirement of the true art of portraiture. Image character is nearer to thought. If we want to portray a person we can only really paint our thoughts about them. We must see them spiritually, as imagination, as image.

So we may summarize by saying: when we paint the lifeless mineral as lustre, the living plant as lustre-image, the ensouled animal as image-lustre, the spiritualized human being as image, we follow the being of the colour itself and not a contrived theory. It is a matter of conversing with the colours themselves to find out what lives in them. I must be able to be active and happy with yellow, noble and serious with red, gentle and sad with blue. I must develop an inner faculty when relating to each and every colour. Without this spiritually active understanding which continually lifts and enhances my love for colour, I am no artist.

Sunrise

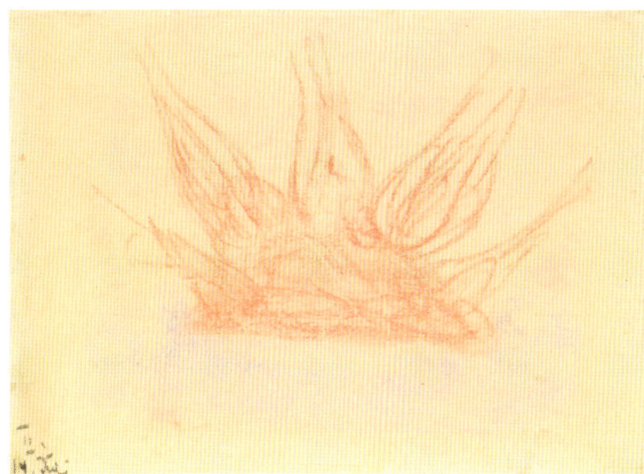

Sunset

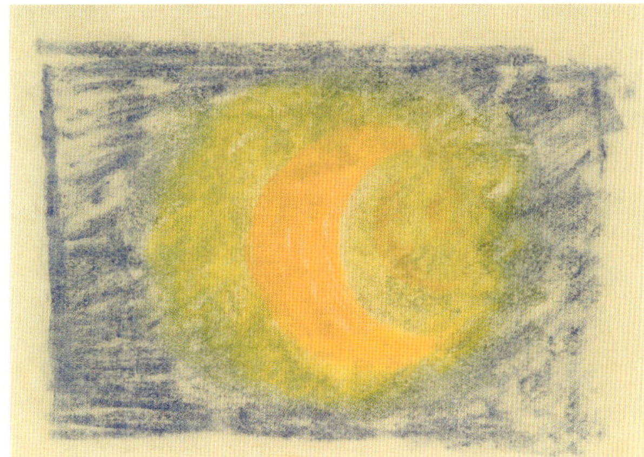

Shining Moon

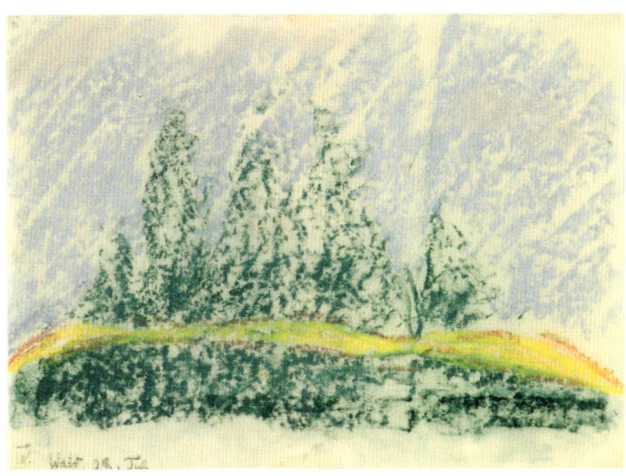

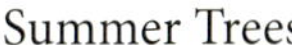

Summer Trees

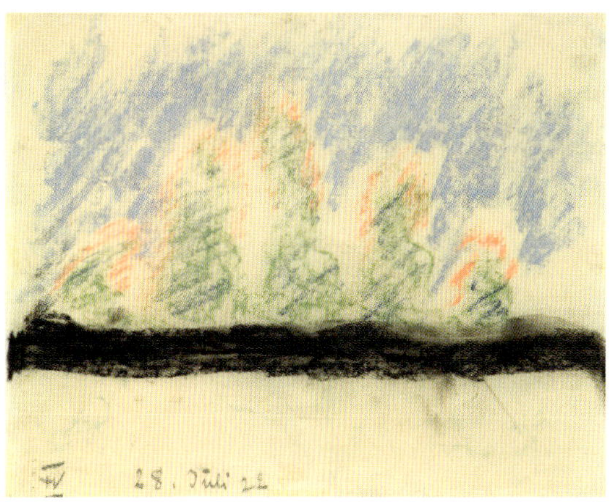

Fruiting and Blossoming Trees

Plate 108: The Nature Moods

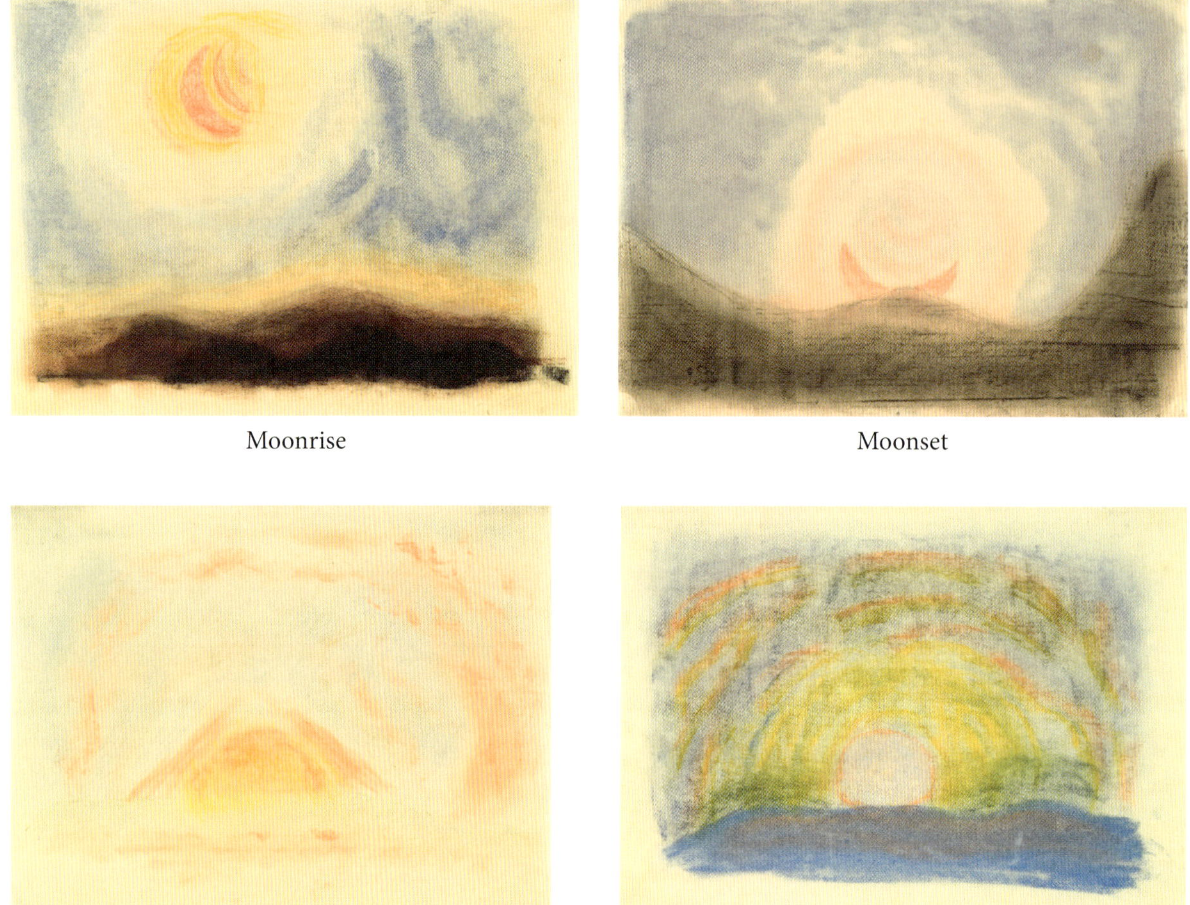

Moonrise

Moonset

Sunrise

Sunset

Plate 109: The Nature Moods

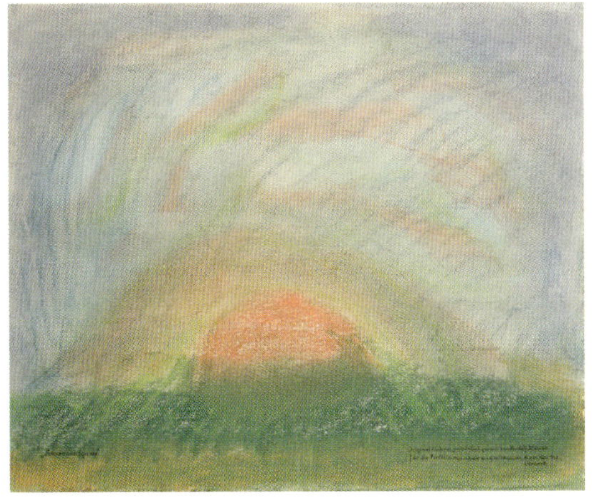

Sunrise

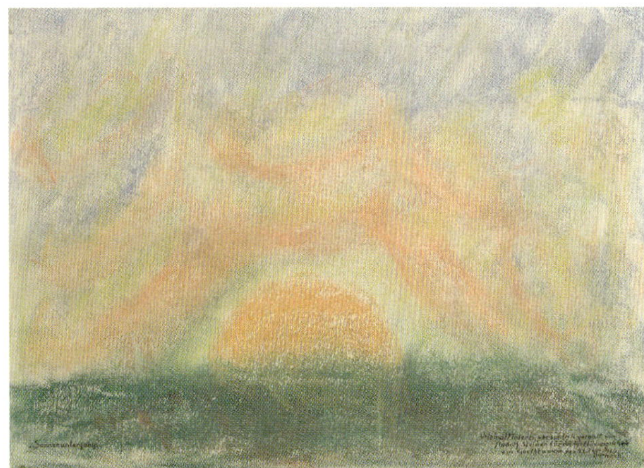

Sunset

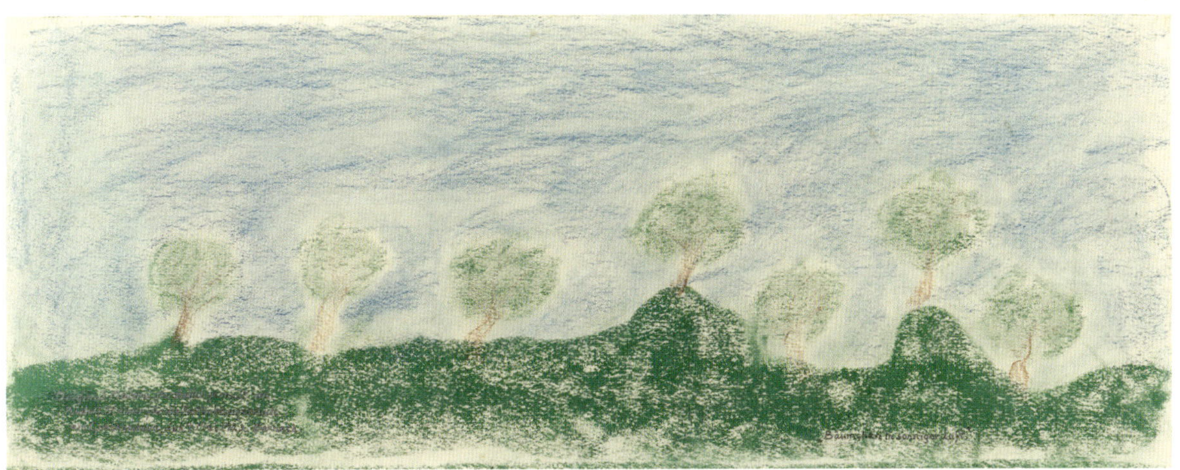

Trees in Sunny Air

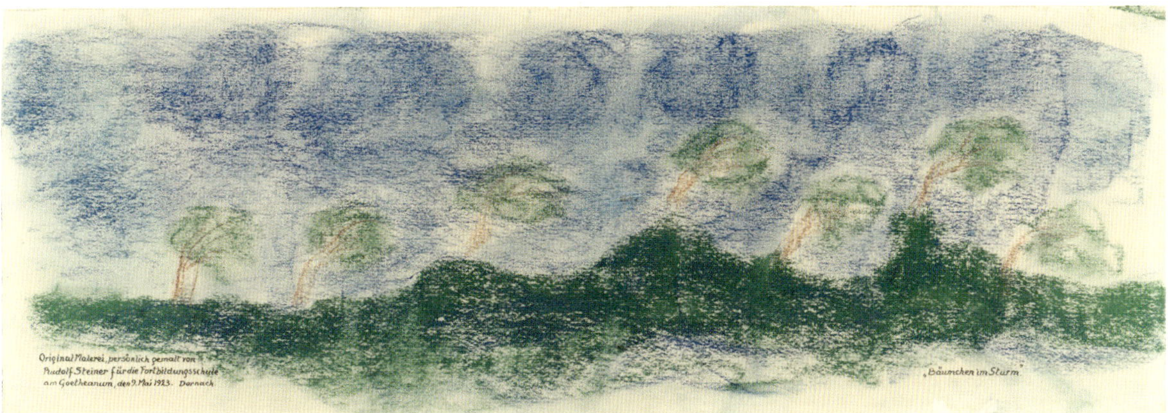

Trees in Storm

Plate 110: The Friedwart Sketches

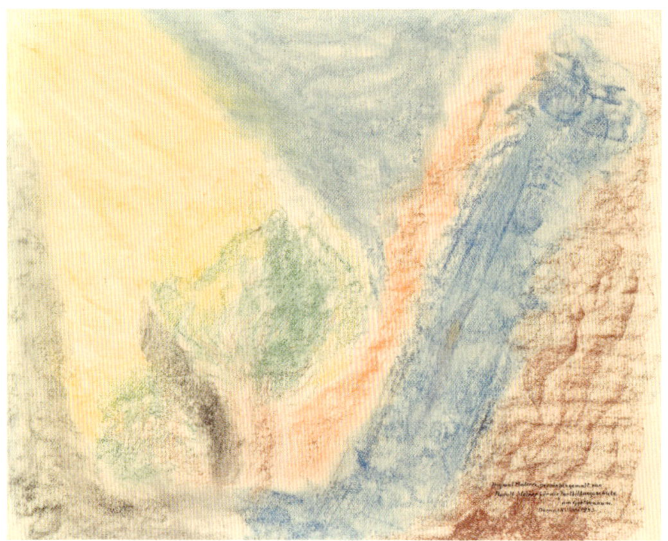

Sunlit Tree by a Waterfall

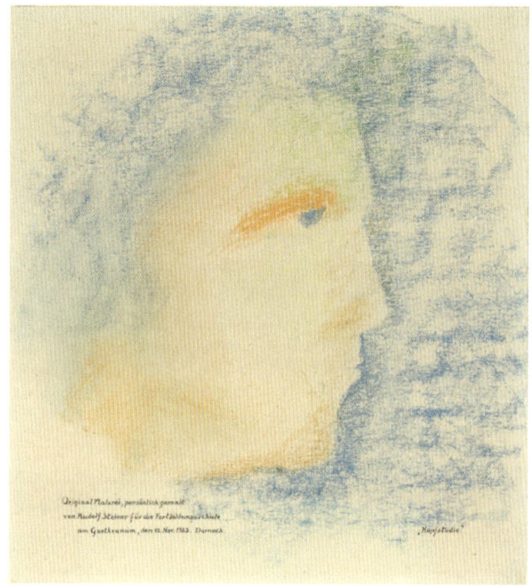

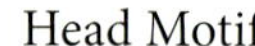

Head Motif

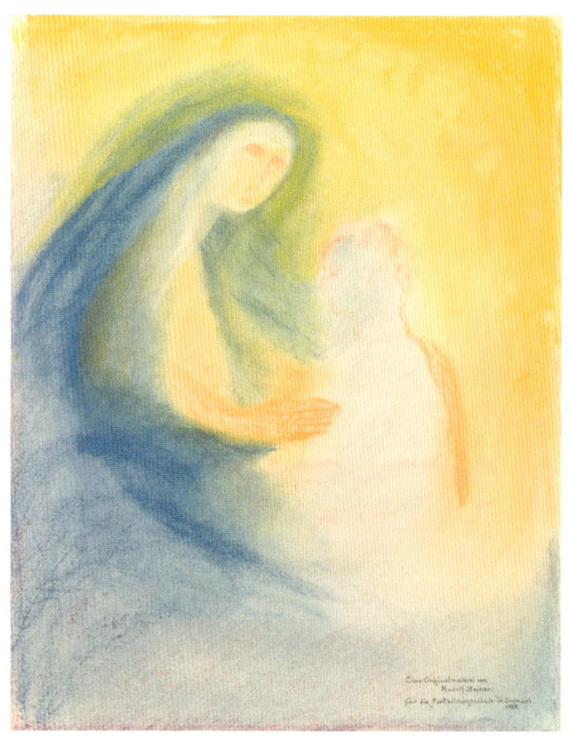

Mother and Child

Plate 111: The Friedwart Sketches

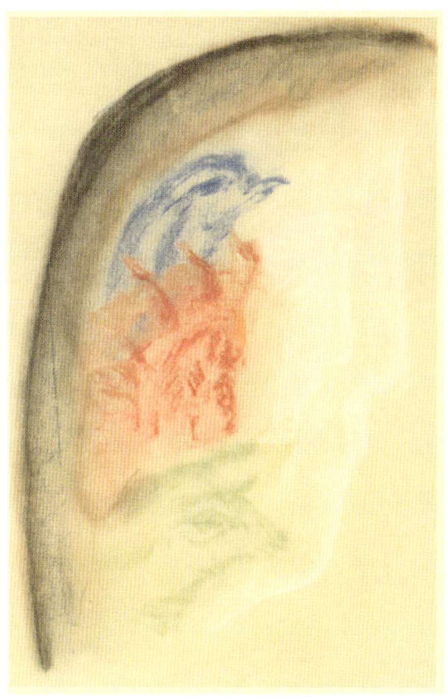

Group Souls – The Human Being

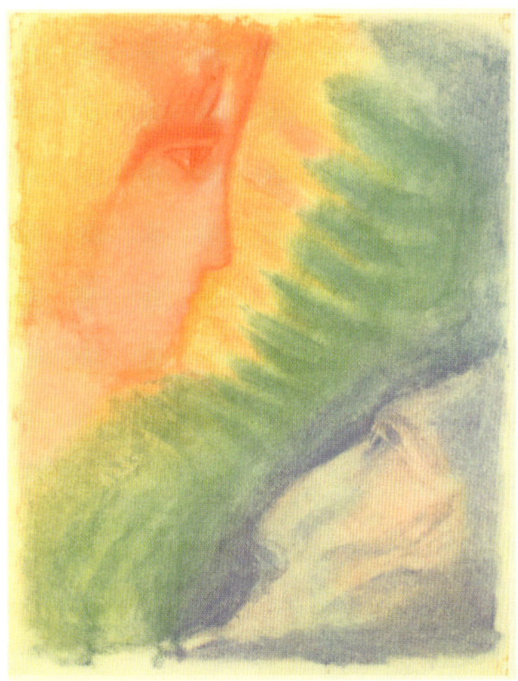

Light and Darkness (Lucifer and Ahriman)

Plate 112: The Motif Sketches

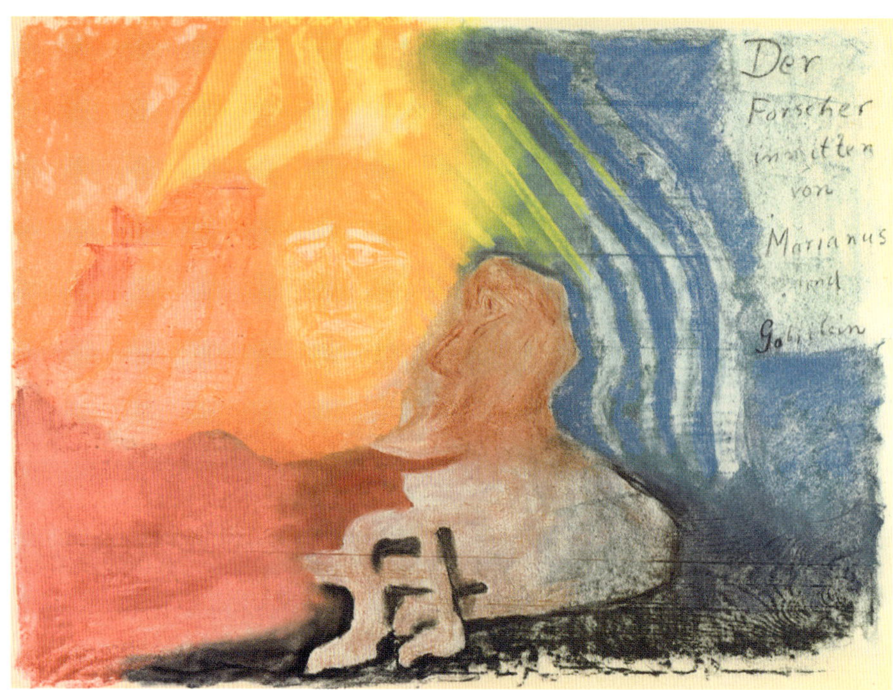

The Researcher between Marianus and Gabrilein

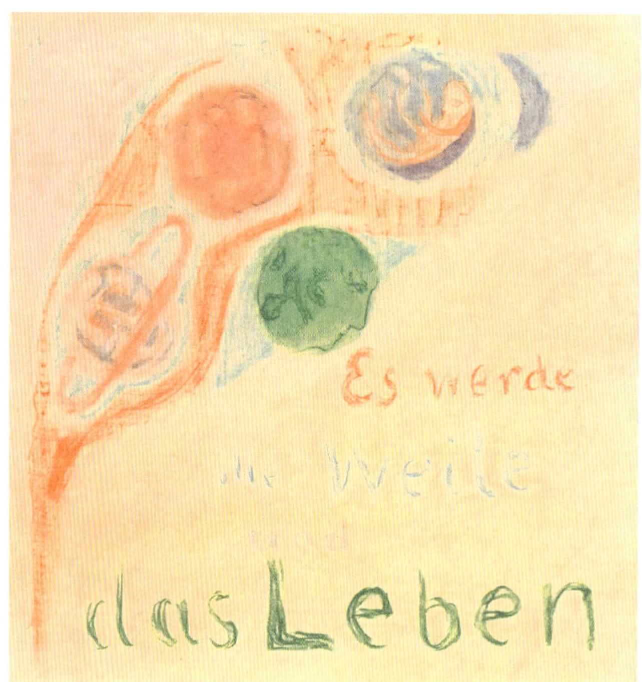

Distance and Space arise

Plate 113: The Motif Sketches

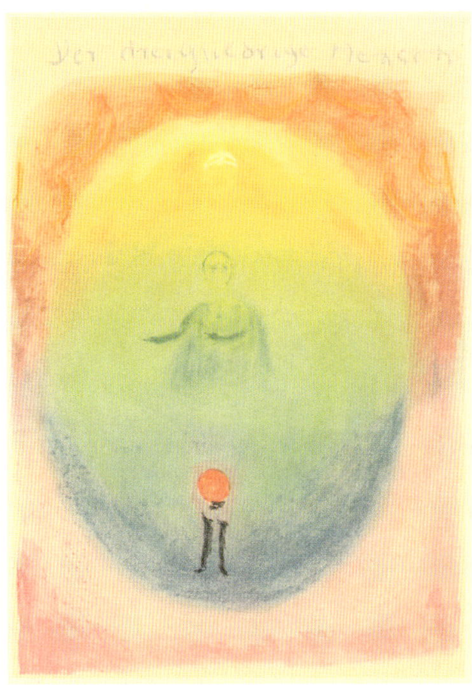

The Threefold Human Being

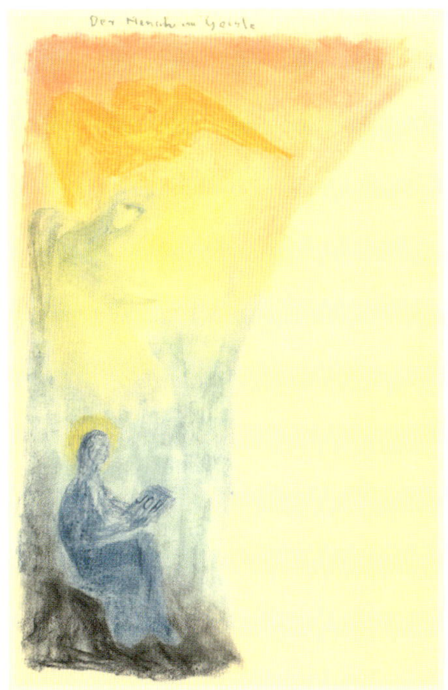

The Human Being in the Spirit

Plate 114: The Motif Sketches

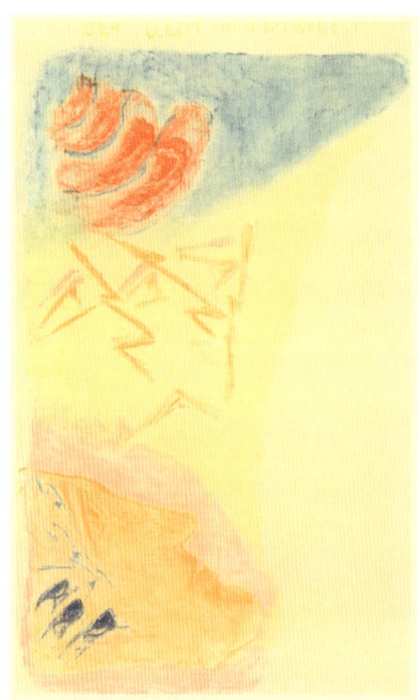

The Spirit in the Human Being

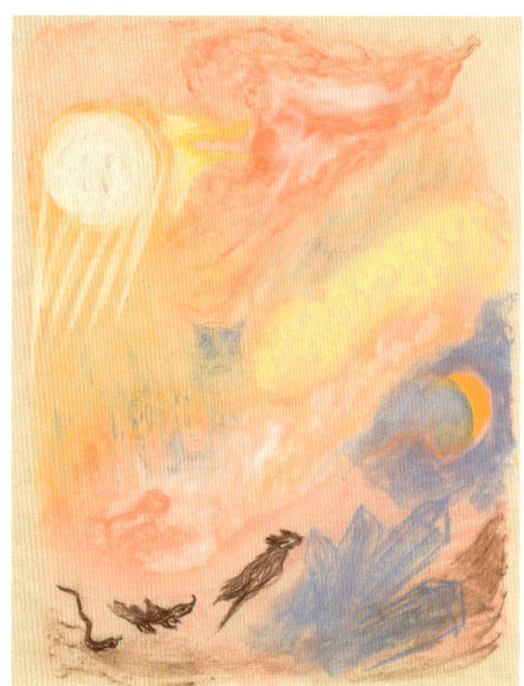

St John's Tide Imagination

Plate 115: The Motif Sketches

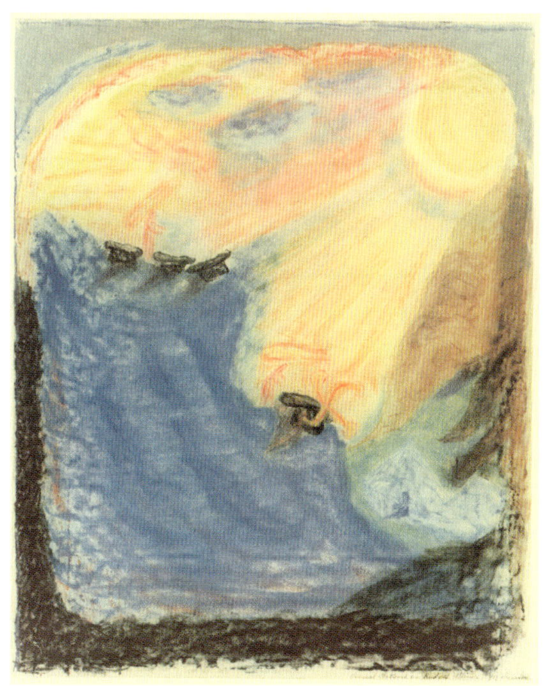

Druid Motif

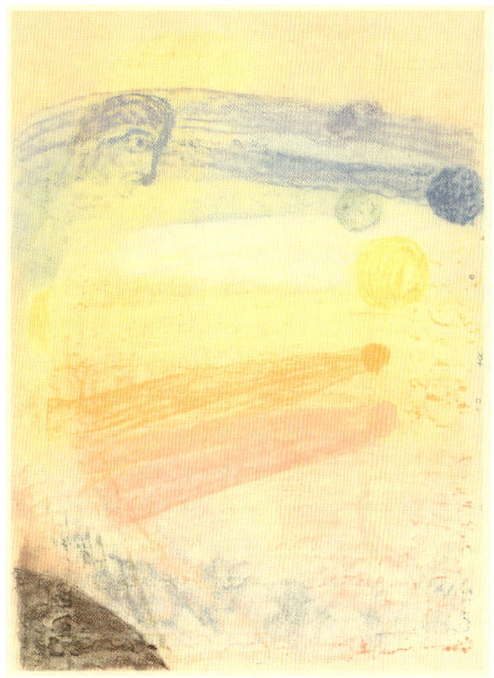

The Human Being in Relation to the Planets

Plate 116: The Motif Sketches

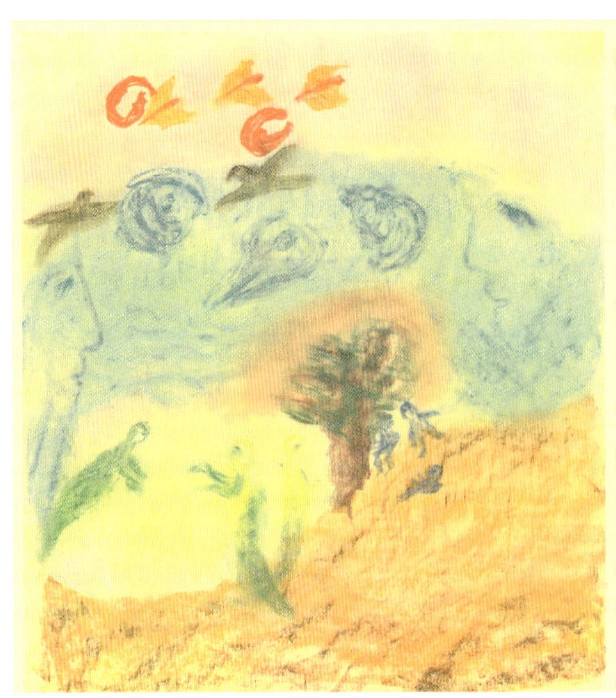

Elemental Beings

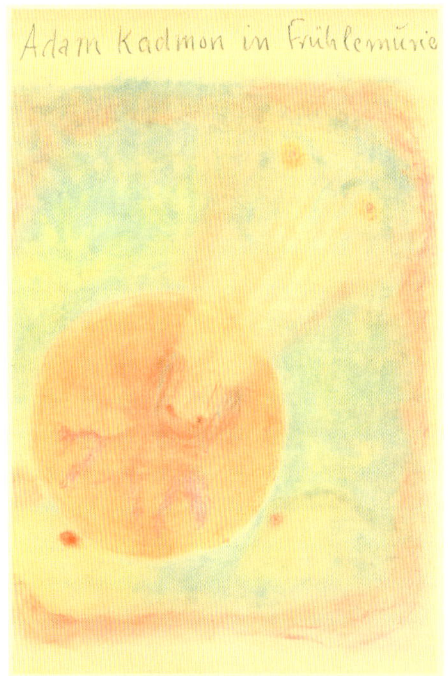

Adam Kadmon in Early Lemuria

Plate 117: The Motif Sketches

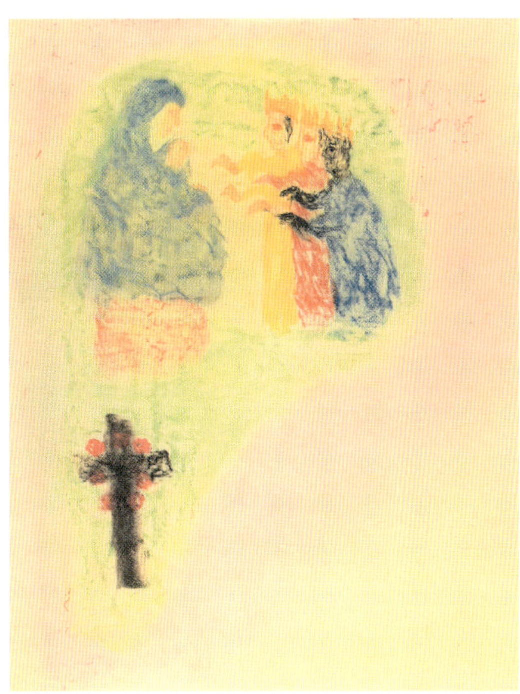

Three Kings Motif

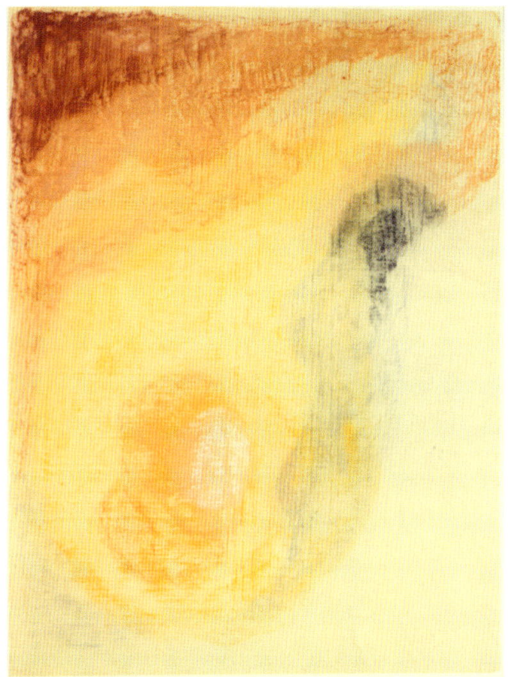

Colour Sketch for the 'Moonrider'

Plate 118: The Motif Sketches

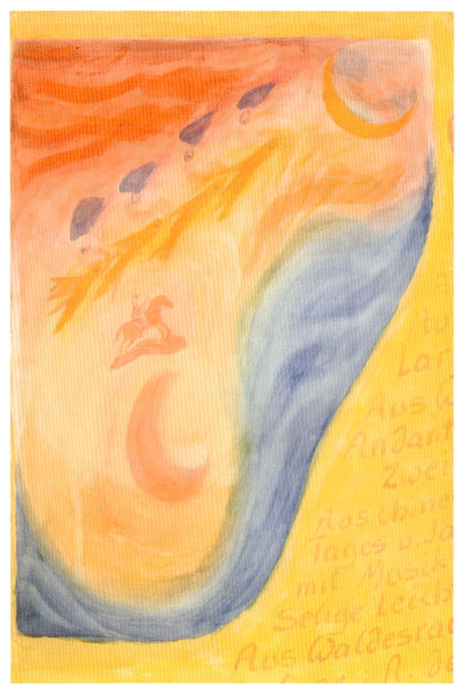

The Moonrider

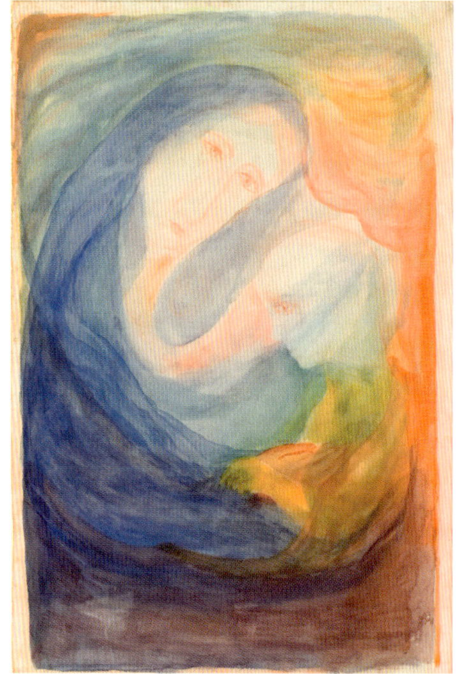

New Life, Mother and Child

Plate 119: The Motif Sketches

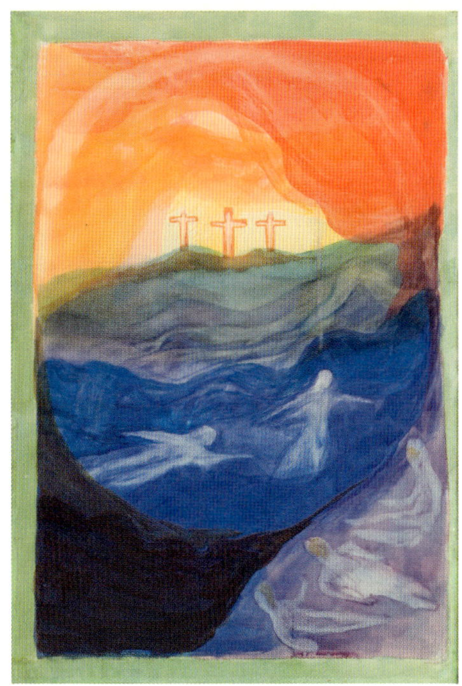

Easter / Three Crosses

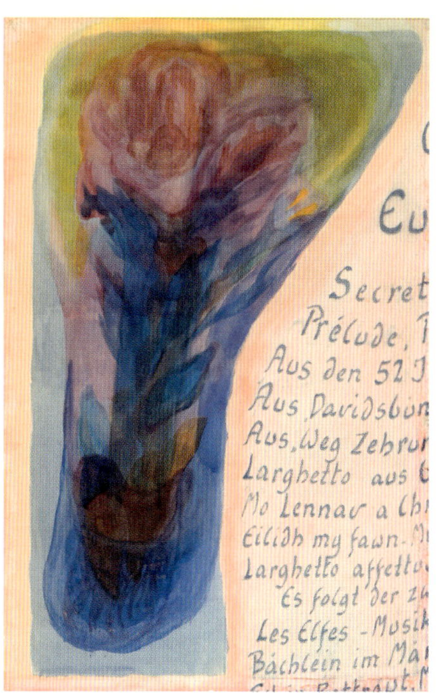

Archetypal Plant

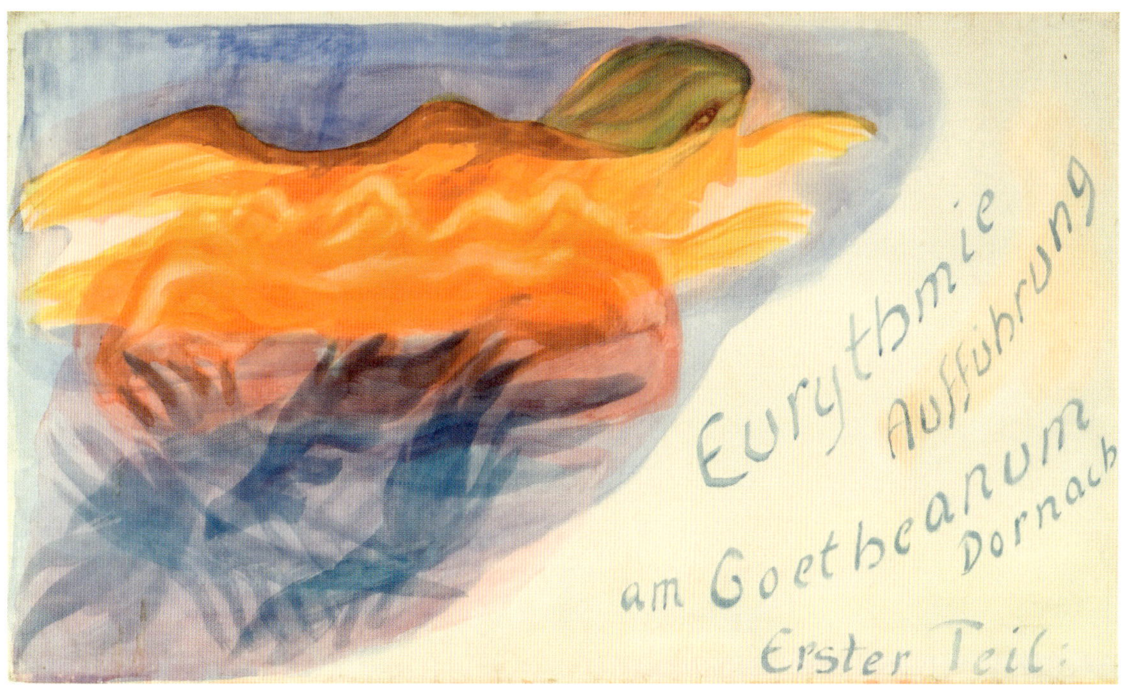

Archetypal Animal/Archetypal Human Being

Plate 120: The Motif Sketches

REFERENCES

1 Rudolf Steiner was born in Kraljevec (then Austria, now in Croatia) in 1861, and died in Dornach, Switzerland in 1925. He studied science and philosophy in Vienna and soon became a respected thinker, editing Goethe's scientific works and publishing his philosophical treatise *The Philosophy of Freedom* in 1894. As a philosopher, scientist and social reformer, he extended scientific research beyond existing parameters of natural science to investigate the non-physical, spiritual realities of life. Using clear and accessible means for attaining spiritual knowledge, he offered insights that have inspired new approaches in many fields of contemporary practical life.

During the course of his life, Steiner collaborated with doctors, therapists, farmers, business people, teachers, scientists and artists. These collaborations brought about Waldorf schools, biodynamic agriculture, new economic and social models, the Camphill movement, anthroposophic medicine, artists, architects and many other initiatives that exist today across the world.

In 1913 the foundation stone was laid for the first Goetheanum at Dornach in Switzerland. This extraordinary building in wood, with its vast interlocking cupolas, gradually took shape during the years of the First World War, when an international group of volunteers collaborated with local builders and craftsmen to shape the unique carved forms and structures which Steiner designed. The building stimulated much innovation in the use of form and colour and is now increasingly recognised as a landmark in twentieth century architecture. Yet Steiner was not concerned to build an impressive monument. He regarded architecture as the servant of human life, and designed the Goetheanum to support the developing work of anthroposophy (spiritual science), and particularly the work in drama and eurythmy.

An arsonist caused this building to burn to the ground during the night of December 31, 1922. There survived only the great sculpture of the 'Representative of Humanity' on which Steiner had been working in a neighbourhood workshop with the English sculptress Edith Maryon. Steiner soon designed another building which was completed after his death and now serves as a centre for the worldwide Anthroposophical Society and its School of Spiritual Science.

This text has been composed of excerpts from a biographical sketch written by John Davy (1927–1984), and from the website of the Anthroposophical Society of Great Britain. It has been slightly edited in places by the author.

For further reference see: Peter Selg, *Rudolf Steiner – Life and Work,* 7 volumes, SteinerBooks, 2014–2019. Translated by Margot M. Saar.

2 Dornach lectures:

Rudolf Steiner: *Architecture, Sculpture, and Painting of the First Goetheanum,* CW 288, SteinerBooks, 2017.

Rudolf Steiner: *Architecture as a Synthesis of the Arts,* CW 288, Rudolf Steiner Press, CW 286, 1999. Editor Christian Thal-Jantzen.

Rudolf Steiner: *Architecture as Peacework, The First Goetheanum,* Dornach, 1914, CW 287, SteinerBooks, 2017.

3 Munich lectures: Rudolf Steiner: *Art and Theory of Art,* CW 271, SteinerBooks, 2021.
4 Rudolf Steiner: *The Four Mystery Plays,* CW14, Rudolf Steiner Press, 1982.
5 Gerard Wagner, Elisabeth Koch, K. Theodor Willmann: *Gerard Wagner – Die Kunst der Farbe* (The Art of Colour), p. 26, Freies Geistesleben, 1980.
6 Marie Steiner-von Sivers (1867–1948) was an actress. The collaboration between her and Rudolf Steiner in the field of the art of speech, dramatic performance and the art of eurythmy was an essential element in the development of anthroposophy. She was a member of the executive council of the Anthroposophical Society at the Goetheanum. See Bodo von Plato: *Anthroposophie in 20. Jahrhundert – Ein Kulturimpuls in biografischen Porträts* (Anthroposophy in the 20th Century – A Cultural Impulse in biographical Portraits), Verlag am Goetheanum, 2003, p. 794.
7 Albert Steffen (1884–1963) was a poet, painter, dramatist, essayist, novelist. He was a member of the executive council of the Anthroposophical Society at the Goetheanum and from 1925 its chairman.
8 Elisabeth Wagner Koch: *Gerard Wagner – Katalog zur Ausstellung in der Ermitage Sankt Petersburg* (Catalogue of an Exhibition at the Hermitage, St Petersburg), Novikoff Verlag, 1997.
9 Elisabeth Wagner Koch, Gerard Wagner: *The Individuality of Colour,* Rudolf Steiner Press, 1980. Second edition 2009.
10 Gerard Wagner: *Animal Metamorphosis.* Philosophisch-Anthroposophischer Verlag, Dornach, 1972.
Gerard Wagner: *A Glance into Nature's Workshop. An artistic and scientific study,* Philosophisch-Anthroposophischer Verlag, 1974.
Gerard Wagner, Elisabeth Koch, K. Theodor Willmann: *Gerard Wagner – Die Kunst der Farbe* (The Art of Colour), Freies Geistesleben, 1980.
Caroline Chanter: *A Life with Colour – Gerard Wagner 1906–1999,* Rudolf Steiner Press, 2021.
11 Austin Wormleighton: *Morning Tide. John Anthony Park and the Painters of Light,* Stockbridge Books, 1998.
12 Henni Geck (1884–1951) was a German painter who had an academic art training in Berlin, Düsseldorf and Munich. In 1914 she moved to Dornach to help with the artistic work of the first Goetheanum building. See: Peter Stebbing: *Conversations about Painting with Rudolf Steiner,* SteinerBooks, 2008.
13 Gerard Wagner: *Animal Metamorphosis.* Philosophisch-Anthroposophischer Verlag, Dornach, 1972.
14 Rudolf Steiner: *Colour,* CW 291, Rudolf Steiner Press, 2012.
15 The reviews by Albert Steffen were published in Goetheanum periodicals ('Das Goetheanum') in 1922 and can be found in the book *Geist-Erwachen im Farben-Erleben* (Spirit Awakening through Colour Experience) by Albert Steffen, Verlag für Schöne Wissenschaft, Dornach, 1968.
16 *Motif Sketches:*
Group Souls – The Human Being
Light and Darkness (Lucifer and Ahriman)
The Researcher between Marianus and Gabrilein
Distance and Space arise
The Threefold Human Being

The Human Being in the Spirit
The Spirit in the Human Being
St John's Tide Imagination
Druid Motif
The Human Being in Relation to the Planets
Elemental Beings
Adam Kadmon in Early Lemuria
Three Kings Motif
Colour Sketch for the 'Moonrider'
Watercolours
The Moonrider by Henni Geck & Rudolf Steiner
New Life, Mother and Child
Easter / Three Crosses
Archetypal Plant
Archetypal Animal/Archetypal Human Being
For further reference: *Das Malerische Werk* (The Paintings of Rudolf Steiner), CW K 13–16/52–56, Rudolf Steiner Verlag, 2007.

17 Rudolf Steiner: *Architecture, Sculpture, and Painting of the First Goetheanum,* CW 288, lecture of 25.1.1920, p. 71, SteinerBooks, 2017.

18 Rudolf Steiner: *Architecture, Sculpture, and Painting of the First Goetheanum,* CW 288, lecture of 25.1.1920, p. 71, SteinerBooks, 2017

19 Gerard Wagner, Elisabeth Koch, K. Theodor Willmann: *Gerard Wagner –Die Kunst der Farbe* (The Art of Colour), p. 24, Freies Geistesleben, 1980.

20 Rudolf Steiner: *Colour,* GA 291, Rudolf Steiner Press, 2012. Lecture of 1.1.1915, p. 82–87.

21 Gerard Wagner, Elisabeth Koch, K. Theodor Willmann: *Gerard Wagner – Die Kunst der Farbe* (The Art of Colour), p. 22, Freies Geistesleben, 1980.

22 Gerard Wagner, Elisabeth Koch, K. Theodor Willmann: *Gerard Wagner –Die Kunst der Farbe* (The Art of Colour), p. 24, Freies Geistesleben, 1980.

23 Interview with Gerard Wagner, filmed by Witali Kovalenko, 1995. See Caroline Chanter: *A Life with Colour – Gerard Wagner 1906–1999,* p. 230, Rudolf Steiner Press, 2021.

24 Gerard Wagner, Elisabeth Koch, K. Theodor Willmann: *Gerard Wagner – Die Kunst der Farbe* (The Art of Colour), p. 26, Freies Geistesleben, 1980.

25 Rudolf Steiner: *Colour,* CW 291, Rudolf Steiner Press, 2012. Lecture of 26.7.1914, p. 70–73.

26 Gerard Wagner: *A Glance into Nature's Workshop. An artistic and scientific study,* Philosophisch-Anthroposophischer Verlag, 1974.

27 Rudolf Steiner: *Man as Symphony of the Creative Word,* CW 230, Rudolf Steiner Press, 1970. Lecture of 2.11.1923, p. 120–131.

28 Rudolf Steiner: *Universe, Earth and Man,* CW 105, Rudolf Steiner Publishing Co., 1955, lecture of 6.8.1908, p. 38/39. Up to date book title: *Universe, Earth, Human Being,* Rudolf Steiner Press, 2022.

29 Gerard Wagner, Elisabeth Koch, K. Theodor Willmann: *Gerard Wagner –Die Kunst der Farbe* (The Art of Colour), p. 32, Freies Geistesleben, 1980.

30 Rudolf Steiner: *Architecture as Peacework, The First Goetheanum, 1914,* CW 287, lecture of 25.10.1914, p. 80, SteinerBooks 2017.

31 Rudolf Steiner: *Occult Reading and Occult Hearing,* CW 156, Rudolf Steiner Press, 1975. Now published as *Inner Reading and Inner Hearing,* 2009, SteinerBooks.

32 Rudolf Steiner: *Colour,* CW 291. Lecture of 7.5.1922, p. 33.

33 Rudolf Steiner: *Isis Maria Sophia,* CW 57, SteinerBooks, 2004. Lecture of 29.4.1909, p. 101 / p. 98.

34 See Hilde Raske: *The Language of Colour of the First Goetheanum,* Walter Keller Verlag, Dornach, 1987. Peter Stebbing: *The Goetheanum Cupola Motifs of Rudolf Steiner, Paintings by Gerard Wagner,* SteinerBooks, 2011.

35 Gerard Wagner, Elisabeth Koch, K. Theodor Willmann: *Gerard Wagner –Die Kunst der Farbe* (The Art of Colour), p. 31, Freies Geistesleben, 1980.

36 Rudolf Steiner: *Architecture as Peacework, The First Goetheanum,* Dornach, 1914, CW 287. SteinerBooks, 2017. Lecture of 24.10.1914, p. 63–73.

37 Rudolf Steiner: *The Evolution of the World and of Humanity,* CW 227, Anthroposophical Publishing Co., 1936. Lecture of 30.8.1923, p. 209.
New title: Rudolf Steiner: *The Evolution of Consciousness,* CW 227, Rudolf Steiner Press, 2006.

38 The 12 Senses are:
The Lower Senses: Life, Balance, Touch, Own Movement
The Middle Senses: Sight, Smell, Taste, Warmth
The Upper Senses: Hearing, Word/Speech, Thought, Sense for the 'I' of oneself and for others.
See Rudolf Steiner: *A Psychology of Body, Soul, and Spirit,* CW 115, SteinerBooks, 1999. Lecture of 23.10.1909, *The Human Being and the Senses.*
See also Albert Soesman: *Our Twelve Senses,* Hawthorn Press, 1998.

39 Karl König: *Sinnesentwicklung und Leiberfahrung* (Development of the Senses and Body Experience), Verlag Freies Geistesleben, 1978, p. 70. See Rudolf Steiner: *A Psychology of Body, Soul, and Spirit.* Lecture of 23.10.1909, *The Human Being and the Senses,* SteinerBooks, 1999.

40 Karl König: *Sinnesentwicklung und Leiberfahrung* (Development of the Senses and Body Experience). Chapter: *Die Erfahrungen des Gleichgewichtsinns* (Experiences of the Sense of Balance), Verlag Freies Geistesleben, 1978.

41 Karl König: *Sinnesentwicklung und Leiberfahrung* (Development of the Senses and Body Experience), Verlag Freies Geistesleben,1978, p. 82. See Rudolf Steiner: *Spiritual Science as a Foundation for Social Forms,* CW 199, SteinerBooks, 1986.

42 Karl König: *Sinnesentwicklung und Leiberfahrung* (Development of the Senses and Body Experience), Verlag Freies Geistesleben, 1978, p. 31. See Rudolf Steiner: *Psychology of Body, Soul, and Spirit.* CW 115, lecture of 23.10.1909, *The Human Being and the Senses,* SteinerBooks, 1999.

43 Rudolf Steiner: *Colour,* CW291. Rudolf Steiner Press, 2012. Lecture of 29.7.1923, p. 178.

44 Gerard Wagner, Elisabeth Koch, K. Theodor Willmann: *Gerard Wagner – Die Kunst der Farbe* (The Art of Colour), p. 25, Freies Geistesleben, 1980.

45 Caroline Chanter: *A Life with Colour – Gerard Wagner 1906–1999,* p. 296–298, Rudolf Steiner Press, 2021.

46 Rudolf Steiner: *Art as seen in the Light of Mystery Wisdom,* CW 275, lecture of 28.12.1914, p. 27–29, Rudolf Steiner Press, 1984.

47 Translated by Caroline Chanter with kind permission from the Albert Steffen-Stiftung, Dornach, Switzerland. The original German text is published in *Geist-Erwachen im Farben-Erleben* by Albert Steffen, Verlag für Schöne Wissenschaften, Dornach 1968.

LIST OF PLATES

All paintings unless otherwise indicated are by Gerard Wagner and have been painted in watercolour – plant-based pigments (Günter Meier Colours)

* Watercolour (Windsor and Newton Colours)

Cover images: Head Motif, 1992, 57 × 39 cm / Animal Motif, 1994, 12 × 18 cm / Experiment with Green, 1960s, 51 × 69 cm

Photos back of book: Gerard Wagner, 1983 / Gerard Wagner painting a mural, 1986

The drawings on pages 33, 88, 144, 145, 147, 149 have been copied by the author from those sketched by Rudolf Steiner during the relevant lectures.

Colour experiments

Plate 1–5: Experiments with Brown, Violet and Green (Trees), ca. 1955, 69 × 51 cm*

Plate 6–10: Experiments with Black and Green (Plants), 1975, 70 × 52 cm*

Colours and their Gestures

Plate 11: Colour Exercise, 1960s, 52 × 70 cm

Plate 12: Colours and their Gestures, 1950s, 52 × 70 cm*

Plate 13: Colours and their Gestures, 1950s, 52 × 70 cm*

Plate 14 & 15: Colours and their Gestures, 1950s, 52 × 70 cm*

Plate 16: Colours and their Gestures, 1950s, 59 × 80 cm*

Plate 17: Colours and their Gestures, 1950s, 77 × 53 cm

Nature Motifs

Plate 18: Nature Motifs, 1994, 77 × 53 cm

Plate 19: Nature Motifs, 1989, 53 × 77 cm

Plate 20: Nature Motifs, 1993, 77 × 53 cm

Plate 21a: Tree motifs, 1994, 53 × 77 cm

Plate 21b: Motif-Transformation, 1980s, 40 × 57 cm

Plate 22–24: Sunrise to Fruiting and Blossoming Trees, 1988, 53 × 77 cm

Moon Motifs

Plate 25: Explorations of the Moon Motifs of the Nature Mood sketches, 1966, 39 × 56 cm

Plate 26–29: Explorations of the Moon Motifs of the Nature Mood sketches, 1966, 51 × 69 cm*

Plate 30: Transformation from *Moonrise* to *Moonset,* 1984, 77 × 53 cm

Plate 31: *Moonrise,* painted on a blue background, 1989, 53 × 77 cm

Plate 32: *Moonrise* and *Moonset,* 1992, 77 × 53 cm

Plate 33: *Fruiting and Blossoming Trees,* 1992, 77 × 53 cm

Plant Motifs

Plate 34: New Life, 1997, 77 × 53 cm

Plate 35: Archetypal Plant Metamorphosis, 1966, 48.5 × 66.5 cm*

Plate 36: *Archetypal Plant,* ca. 1966, 77 × 57 cm*

Plate 37–38: Plant Forms, 1965, 68 × 50 cm*

Plate 39: Black and Brown Seeds, 1980s, 50 × 70 cm

Plate 40: Black – Green – Red on coloured backgrounds, 1980s, 70 × 50 cm

Plate 41: Experimental painting on yellow and blue backgrounds, 1981, 70 × 102 cm

Plate 42: Experimental painting on yellow and blue backgrounds, 1992, 53 × 77 cm

Plate 43: Plant Metamorphosis, 1985, 53 × 77 cm

Plate 44: Plant Metamorphosis, 1986, 53 × 77 cm

Plate 45: Plant Transformation – the colour of the blossoms change from yellow to warm red, 1987, 53 × 77 cm

Plate 46: Plant Transformation – the colour of the blossoms change from cool red to blue, 1987, 53 × 77 cm

Plate 47–53: Plant and Elemental Beings Metamorphosis 1993, 77 × 53 cm

Animals

Plate 54: Animals in Moonlight, 1993, 53 × 77 cm

Plate 55: Animals (Group Soul), 1947, 68 × 50 cm*

Plate 56: Motif-Transformation, early 1990s, 53 × 77 cm

Plate 57: Motif-Transformation, 1994, 53 × 77 cm

Plate 58: Motif-Transformation, 1994, 53 × 77 cm

Plate 59: *Archetypal Animal / Archetypal Human Being,* 1996, 53 × 77 cm

Plate 60: Metamorphosis of the *Archetypal Animal / Archetypal Human Being* motif, 1969, 70 × 50 cm*

Plate 61: Metamorphosis of the *Archetypal Animal / Archetypal Human Being* motif, 1969, 70 × 50 cm*

Plate 62: Metamorphosis of the *Archetypal Animal / Archetypal Human Being* motif, 1969, 70 × 50 cm*

Plate 63–66: Examples of experiments with different animal colours, 1966, 63 × 48 cm*

The Human Being

Plate 67: *The Threefold Human Being,* 1990, 77 × 53 cm

Plate 68: *Group Souls – The Human Being,* 1991, 77 × 53 cm

Plate 69: *Light and Darkness / Lucifer and Ahriman,* 1988, 77 × 53 cm

Plate 70: Birth, 1975, 77 × 53 cm

Plate 71: Head motifs: research of the *Head Study,* profile and enface, 1970s, 78 × 56 cm*

Plate 72: *Head Study* of the Friedwart Sketches, ca. 1960s, 16 × 13 cm*

Plate 73: Meeting, 1994, 77 × 53 cm

Plate 74: Conversation, 1978, 49 × 67 cm

Plate 75: Laddie, 1996, 77 × 53 cm

Plate 76: Flower Child, 1998, 77 × 53 cm

Plate 77: *Mother and Child* (Friedwart Sketch) 1987, 77 × 53 cm

Plate 78: *Mother and Child,* 1987, 77 × 53 cm*

Plate 79: *Mother and Child,* (number 4 from a metamorphic sequence of 14 paintings), 1975, 77 × 53 cm

Plate 80: *Mother and Child,* (number 6 from a metamorphic sequence of 14 paintings), 1975, 77 × 53 cm

Plate 81: Incarnadine on different colour backgrounds, 1988, 50 × 70 cm

Plate 82: Incarnadine on different colour backgrounds, 1988, 50 × 70 cm

Plate 83: Youth, 1997, 77 × 53 cm

Plate 84: Age, 1997, 77 × 53 cm

Goetheanum Cupola Motifs

Plate 85:

a) A sketch of the coloured background of the ceiling of the second Goetheanum, 1980s, 50 × 70 cm

b) *The Elohim work creatively into the Earth; Light-Beings radiate into it,* 1976, 53 × 77 cm

c) *The Senses are Born (Eye and Ear),* 1995, 53 × 77 cm

d) *Jehovah and the Luciferic Temptation / Paradise,* 1995, 53 × 77 cm

Plate 86:

a) *The Ancient Indian,* 1995, 53 × 77 cm

b) *The Ancient Persian,* 1995, 53 × 77 cm

c) *The Ancient Egyptian,* 1995, 53 × 77 cm

d) *Greece and the Oedipus Motif,* 1995, 53 × 77 cm

Plate 87: «I–A–O» (Painted by Elisabeth Wagner), 1995, 100 × 68 cm

Top: *The Wrath of God and the Yearning Grief of God / 'I'*

Middle: *The Round of Seven / 'A'*

Bottom: *The Circle of Twelve / 'O'*

Plate 88: *Eye and Ear* Motif, pastel drawing by Rudolf Steiner, 1914, 20 × 35 cm

Plate 89: *Eye and Ear* Motif, 1989, 53 × 77 cm

Plate 90–93: Metamorphosis of the *Eye and Ear* Motif, 1994, 53 × 77 cm

Supplementary Images

Plate 94: Plant with blue blossoms, 1994, 77 × 53 cm

Plate 95: Plant with yellow blossoms, 1994, 77 × 53 cm

Plate 96: Plant with violet blossoms, 1989, 77 × 53 cm

Plate 97: Archetypal Plant with Elemental Beings, 1989, 77 × 53 cm

Plate 98: Animal World, 1978, 49 × 67 cm

Plate 99: Lions, 1946, 43 × 56 cm*

Plate 100: Hubertus Motif (Deer), 1946, 52 × 70 cm*

Plate 101: Golgotha (Horses), 1946, 33 × 55 cm*

Plate 102: Quo Vadis, 1993, 77 × 53 cm

Plate 103: The Novice, 1993, 77 × 53 cm

Plate 104: Madonna Motif, 1994, 77 × 53 cm

Plate 105: Madonna Motif, 1987, 77 × 53 cm

Plate 106: Moonlit Night, 1993, 53 × 77 cm

Plate 107: Colour Beings, 1994, 53 × 77 cm

The 'Training Motifs' – Pastel Sketches and Watercolours by Rudolf Steiner (Some colours have changed since the 1920s partly through fading.)

Plate 108–109: The Nature Mood Sketches by Rudolf Steiner, 1922, © Kunstsammlung am Goetheanum

Plate 110–111: The Friedwart Sketches Sketches by Rudolf Steiner, 1923–1924, © Rudolf Steiner Archiv, Dornach

Plate 112–120: The Motif Sketches by Rudolf Steiner, 1922–1924, © Kunstsammlung am Goetheanum

Images of the first Goetheanum

The first Goetheanum, from the south, drawing by Bettina Müller

The inside of the first Goetheanum showing the movement from west to east of the capitals and the architraves, drawing by L. Witta.